TOPICAL ISSUES
IN
NIGERIA'S POLITICAL
DEVELOPMENT

J. ISAWA ELAIGWU

Published by

Adonis & Abbey Publishers Ltd
P.O. Box 43418
London
SE11 4XZ
Tel: + 44 845 388 7248
Website: http://www.adonis-abbey.com
Email: editor@adonis-abbey.com

Nigeria
Adonis & Abbey Publishing Company
P.O. Box 10546 Abuja,
Nigeria
Tel: +234 816 5970458

First Edition, June 2012

Copyright 2012 © J. Isawa Elaigwu

British Library Cataloguing-in-Publication Data
A catalogue record for this book is available from the British Library

ISBN: 978 – 978 – 48340 – 1 – 8

The moral right of the author has been asserted

TABLE OF CONTENTS

DEDICATION

This book is dedicated to all my compatriots in our collective search for a united, stable and prosperous Nigeria, which we would be proud to hand over to our children.

Topical issues in Nigeria's political development

J. ISAWA ELAIGWU

Adonis & Abbey
Publishers Ltd

INTRODUCTION

TOPICAL ISSUES IN NIGERIA'S POLITICAL DEVELOPMENT

Nigerians love debates. Even under colonial rule, the authorities realized that Nigerians could not be repressed and that they always expressed their views on topical issues of development. This partly explains the fact that the Nigerian press was probably the most vivacious press in colonial Africa. Nigerian nationalism had witnessed forceful pressures for change and erudite contributions of nationalists to the imperial agenda for decolonization.

From the debates over the Richards Constitution in 1946 through the MacPherson and Lyttleton Constitutions of 1951 and 1954 respectively, to the constitutional conferences which led to the Independent Constitution of 1960, Nigerians demonstrated that they were concerned about their country and its future.

During various military regimes, debates among Nigerians continued over the appropriate polity – structures, institutions and processes – which Nigerians should have, after the retreat of the military to the barracks. In addition, there were debates over the pattern of civil-military relations suitable for Nigeria. In 1978-79 Nigerian Constituent Assembly resolved to adopt the Western liberal model of civil-military relations. Yet, the debate on civil-military relations continues.

Over the period of fifty years of her independence, Nigeria has debated and drafted, at least, six constitutions/wholesale constitutional reviews. These include the 1979 Constitution which was drafted between 1976/77 and debated through 1978 before it was passed by the Constituent Assembly, known as the 1979 Constitution. In 1988-1989, there was another Constitutional Review exercise which resulted in the 1989 Constitution. In 1994/95, there was a new constitution-making exercise which produced the 1995 Draft Constitution. This constitution was never promulgated because Nigeria's military leader (General Sani Abacha, who initiated the process) died in 1998.

Thereafter, his successor, General Abdulsalami Abubakar, who operated a tight transition schedule, set up a Constitutional Panel to review the old constitutions and come up with a draft for the Fourth Republic. This effort produced the 1999 Constitution, which many of the operators of the constitution never saw or read before they were elected to various offices. Yet, not satisfied, Nigerians pushed for a review of the 1999 Constitution. While some people called for a Sovereign National Conference, others demanded a National Conference to discuss what many referred to as the *National Question* – that is, the terms of association among Nigerian groups. The 1999 Constitution was massively amended in 2010.

In essence, it does seem from all the above and events on the ground, that Nigerians are more concerned about constitution-making than about constitutionalism (ie. adherence to the constitution in practice).

Among major topical issues of debates in Nigeria are:

- Democracy
- Constitution and Constitutionalism
- The National Question
- Civil-Military Relations (or the Armed Forces and Society)
- Federalism
- State-and Nation-building
- Local governance
- Leadership
- The Role of Traditional Rulers
- The Economy
- Religion

The list is interminable.

This volume comprises a selected number of my contributions to the various debates on the Nigerian nation-state and its political development. I shall refrain from explaining conceptual issues, such as 'political development' and others, because they are discussed in the relevant chapters. I have only chosen these few contributions to illustrate my thoughts on these matters and my concern about a country that has given me much, (inspite of its short-comings); a country I love and about which I am very passionate. I believe very strongly that I owe Nigeria far more than she owes me. I am concerned about future generations whose prospects for good life are getting more bleak by the day. I am worried about the waste of resources by our leaders without adequate thoughts about the future. I am anxious about Nigeria's future.

I believe that while Nigeria is potentially great, it cannot be manifestly great, unless Nigerians imbibe and exhibit certain values – self-discipline, patriotism and demonstrable sense of accommodation of one another. Nigeria is a beautiful country. She has varied and good people. Unfortunately, she is having difficulties in putting its act together.

My belief is that Nigerians can, and must, take up their destiny and pursue their goals with a sense of dedication, patriotism, discipline and maturity. In doing so, it must turn inwards to deal with her weaknesses, in order to strengthen her capacity to launch forward as an industrialized and powerful country, in the comity of nations by 2050.

Thus, my contributions to the Nigeria debates are summarized under six chapters. Chapter One discusses topical issues in Nigeria's practice of *Federalism*. Chapter Two takes on the issue of *Leadership and Governance*. In Chapter Three, we discuss the dynamics of Nation-*Building* in Nigeria, while Chapter Four, survey the subject of *Democracy, Peace and Good Governance*. The *Armed Forces* and *Society* is the subject of Chapter Five. Chapter Six looks the role of *Traditional Institutions in Nation-Building*.

The chapters in this volume are essentially my views, contributed to debates in various parts of Nigeria and beyond. In the process of exchanging views, I have learnt many things from others. It is my hope that while reading this, you will learn at least one thing from me – if nothing else, about how I feel; about my thoughts (no matter how simple) and about these topical issues in Nigeria's political development. I believe that with patience and respect for one another, we can collectively arrive at some consensual values which will serve as a basis of our society. We must endeavour to constructively appraise the *past*, positively contribute to the *present*, as we build the foundations for the *future*.

CHAPTER 1

FEDERALISM

Introduction

The end of the Twentieth Century witnessed the shrinking of the world into a global hamlet, thanks to the revolution in information technology. Not only have national borders been rendered porous, national economies have been penetrated by uncontrollable extra-national economic forces. The forces of globalization have added a new dimension to inter-state relations.

Increasingly as the world becomes a smaller place, it also becomes more complex, posing new challenges which often overwhelm the capabilities of the individual nation-state. In these contexts, there are increasing attempts to find federal-type solutions to such challenges. The European Union graduating from a Common Market is a successful example of this.

However, our concern here is the federal-type solution to the multifaceted problems of integration in multinational societies. While some societies have experimented with and dropped this solution, it is still in operation in others. Its operation also differs from one situation to another, across and within nation-states. Federal structures and processes are also fine-tuned regularly to keep pace with the multidimensional challenges of the nation-state or 'State Nation'. Perhaps, one of the most topical issues of development in Nigeria today is Federalism. The debate on federalism has been robust and interesting.

We will focus on the Nigerian experience with federalism. Certain questions arise in this regard: What are the foundations of Nigerian federalism? How has federalism evolved and what are its peculiarities or distinguishing features? What problems have arisen in the federal process? How are these being resolved? Are there lessons to be learnt from the Nigerian experience in the use of federalism as a technique of managing conflicts in the process of Nigeria's political development?

To answer these questions, we suggest that:

i) The foundations of Nigeria's federal system are to be found in the nature of administration under colonial rule and the responses of Nigerians to it;

ii) The problems of Nigeria's federal compromise are also historical and multidimensional;

iii) Nigerian federalism has come to be characterized by strong unitarist streaks as a response to almost three decades of military rule;

iv) There is an explosion of sub national identities, as Nigeria embarks on its new experiment in democratic governance in the Fourth Republic;

v) The current and future threat to the survival of the Nigerian federal system is over the distribution of scarce but allocatable resources; and

vi) Leadership is important in effecting necessary compromises in Nigeria's reconciliation system as part and parcel of the federal process.

Let us now turn to the first of our suggestions.

The Foundations of Nigerian Federalism

It was the late James Coleman who argued that the "present unity of Nigeria as well as its disunity, is in part a reflection of the form and character of colonial government - the British superstructure - and changes it had undergone since 1900"[1]. By 1900, what later came to be known as Nigeria comprised three colonial territories under the umbrella of British colonialism, but administered separately, receiving orders direct from the metropolis: London. These were the Colony of Lagos and what came to be known as the Protectorates of Southern Nigeria and Northern Nigeria. In 1906 the Colony of Lagos and the Protectorate of Southern Nigeria were unified under a single administrator. In 1914 the Colony of Lagos and Protectorates of

Northern and Southern Nigeria were brought together[2]. In 1939, Nigeria was divided into the Colony of Lagos, the Northern, Eastern and Western Groups of provinces, with each province having a Chief Commissioner who was responsible to the Governor in Lagos.

It is our contention that the period 1914 to 1946 witnessed the mere *co-existence* of Nigerian groups who hardly knew of one another nor interacted in any substantial way horizontally. Like most colonial authorities, the British administration encouraged vertical relations between the individual communities and their administrators. Close horizontal relations among Nigerian groups would have nailed the colonial coffin earlier than the British would have wished, assuming they had any intentions of leaving. It was the Richards Constitution of 1946 which formalized the division of Nigeria into three regions within a unitary colonial state. If the year 1914 marked the birth of colonial Nigeria, 1946 was the beginning of effective horizontal relations among Nigerian groups.

Thus, within this period, there was no concept of colonial Nigeria as a State. Nor had Britain consciously created Nigeria. Nigeria evolved in the context of British colonial policies in West Africa, in piecemeal fashion. As Chief Obafemi Awolowo noted:

> Nigeria is not a nation. It is a mere geographical expression. There are no "Nigerians" in the same sense as there are "English" "Welsh" or "French". The word "Nigerian" is merely a distinctive appellation to distinguish those who live within the boundaries of Nigeria from those who do not[3]

Chief Awolowo was correct. Nigerians in the Northern and Southern parts had not been exposed to one another in any political forum. They were operating as distinct entities and the only visible elements of unity were the colonial administration and its officers. It was the same frustration which has forced Sir Abubakar Tafawa Balewa (later Prime Minister), in the Legislative Council Debate of 1948, to declare that

> Since 1914 the British Government has been trying to make Nigeria into one country, but the Nigerian people themselves are historically different in their backgrounds, in their religious beliefs and do not

themselves show any sign of willingness to unite..Nigerian unity is only British creation for the country.[4]

Again, Sir Balewa was correct. What later became the Nigerian colonial state was heterogeneous. *The British were creating a union and not unity among Nigerians.* In fact, there was no legislative forum for Nigerians from all parts of the country to meet until 1947, after the Richards Constitution. It is therefore true that Nigerians suffered from parochial nationalism based on ignorance of one another in the state.

In 1947 Nigerians began to interact with one another in the Legislative Council. In response to global trends, the wave of nationalism had begun to sweep across the Southern part of the country. The aggressiveness with which the Richards Constitution was attacked illustrated the upsurge in the political awareness of the emerging Nigerian political elites. Among the serious critics was Dr. Nnamdi Azikiwe operating under the *National Council of Nigeria and the Cameroons* (NCNC). Dr. Azikiwe's NCNC had criticized the imposition of the constitution without due consultation with the Nigerian people. The NCNC also opposed the role given to the Chiefs and the number of regional units. Actually, in 1943, Dr. Azikiwe had recommended the creation of eight political units in Nigeria within the framework of federalism[5].

Chief Awolowo, bitterly criticizing the 1946 constitution, called for a federation to allow the various groups to develop at their own pace, and opposed the unitary elements in the constitution which, according to him, did not reflect Nigeria's multi-ethnicity. In 1947 Chief Awolowo suggested the division of Nigeria into ten units, along ethnic and linguistic lines.[6]

It had become evident that the colonial administration would soon go, in response to a combination of international and national events. This realization came as Nigerians had begun to establish contacts with one another. No sooner had they started to interact than they realized that they were strange bedfellows in the same polity. They had not interacted long enough with one another to work out an acceptable mechanism of conflict resolution. Given the competitive setting in which they found themselves; Nigerian politicians withdrew into their ethnic ethnoregional or geo-ethnic[7] cocoons in order to mobilize their followers effectively for competition. The new parochialism was not the old one (based on ignorance of one another) but parochialism based on the awareness of others in a competitive setting, after various group had established contacts. As Mallam Aminu Kano told this writer in an interview,

> I think regional grouping was a result of sudden awakening. I think there was a period of sudden awakening in Nigeria, but the awakening was misdirected.... The sudden realization of we can take power' resulted in ethnic grouping and therefore regionalism[8]

If the very process of decolonization had spurred regionalism, regionalism also determined the form of government Nigeria was to have - one based on the mutual fears and suspicions among Nigerian groups. Perhaps the situation was lucidly captured by Clifford Geertz when he wrote of Nigeria's terminal period of colonialism:

> Whereas in most of the other new states the final phase of the pursuit of independence saw a progressive unification of diverse elements into an intensely solidary opposition to the colonial rule, open dissidence emerging only after the waning of revolutionary comradeship in Nigeria, tension between the various primordial groups increased in the last decade of dependency.[9]

The sense of distrust among Nigerian leaders and the prevalence of centrifugal forces in the country were amply demonstrated at the constitutional conferences between 1951 and 1958. If the McPherson Constitution of 1951 had initiated the gradual political decentralization of the colonial central government, the Lyttleton Constitution of 1954 confirmed the direction of constitutional reforms in favour of federalism. Regional legislatures had not only sprung up, the central marketing boards had been decentralized. Regional governments became effectively established with Nigerianized executives and legislatures. Political parties that had followed the regional pattern had also grafted themselves in regional governments. By 1957 a central government under the leadership of Balewa as Prime Minister had emerged. Regional leaders operated a federal constitution in the context of the Westminster model of government. The 1960 Independence Constitution only ratified what had started in 1954 - Nigeria as a federation.

Our argument is that the pattern of colonial administration had encouraged the emergence of federal government in Nigeria. Even though the British (with a unitary government at home) are noted for including federalism in their political will to their new states, we argue that federalism emerged as a political compromise formula to assuage the fears and suspicions of domination among Nigeria's heterogeneous population. The social forces at work in Nigeria forced Nigerians to accept federalism as a form of government. Thus the foundations of Nigerian federalism are to be found in the pattern of colonial administration and in the responses of Nigerians themselves as they opted for federalism as a compromise formula in inter-group relations.

While it may not be useful to beat the colonial dead horse any longer for the ailments of Nigeria, it may be argued that ambivalent integration under colonial rule was partially responsible for generating fears and suspicions among Nigerians. After the amalgamation of Nigeria in 1914, the colonial authorities made no effort to encourage horizontal interaction among the various groups. As mentioned earlier such encouragement would have heralded the good riddance of the colonial masters from the scene as groups developed confidence and an anti-colonial psychology. Colonial rule encouraged a vertical relationship between the local administrative units and the colonial centres of power.

The resulting parochial nationalism in the terminal colonial period was born out of mutual fears and suspicions among the Nigerian groups. Related to this are two factors which heightened the fears: the structural imbalance in the federal system, and the differential spread in the pattern of Western education. It was John Stuart Mill who once said that in a federal system, "there should not be any one state so much more powerful than the rest as to be capable of vying in strength with many of them combined".[10]

We suggest that in the First Republic, the lopsided federal structure generated fears and suspicions among groups. The Northern Region was in a position to hold the whole country to ransom, as shown by the following figures: the Northern region had 79% of the country's total area as compared to the Eastern region's 8.3%, the Western region's 8.5% and the Mid-western region's 4.2%. According to the 1963 census figures, the regions accounted for 53.5%, 22.3%, 18.4% and 4.6% of the total population, respectively. It was not surprising that in the Southern part of the country there was always the fear of domination by virtue of the Northern Region's large population - *the tyranny of population* in the context of a democratic polity. The federal structure as it existed made it virtually impossible for the South to control political power at the centre, given the ethno regional politics of the country.

Similarly, given the Southern headstart in Western education (which had become a passport to occupational roles in the modern sector of the Nigerian political system), the Northern region feared Southern domination in the economic and public service sectors of society. The fear of *the tyranny of skills* from the South was fresh in the minds of Northern leaders. The North thus sought to protect its civil service from being swamped by the South. It may be suggested that there was a relative division of functions between the North and the South which maintained some delicate balance in the political system. The Northern control of political power was counterbalanced by the South's monopoly of economic power in the country.

We may even go further to argue that, contrary to Sklar's contention,[11] the military coup in January 1966 tilted what had been a delicate balance on which Nigeria had been able to survive since independence. The concentration of both political and economic power in the hands of Southern leaders altered the delicate Nigerian balance. Political power had been the North's safeguard against the South's economic and educational advantages. The South's advantage in the bureaucracy, which if anything was strengthened by the coup, was greatly augmented. The North reacted violently as it saw its last card - the political card - suddenly taken away or rendered ineffective.

These imbalances created problems for the federal system. Centrifugal forces continued to haunt Nigeria's federal balance.

Threats of secession by various regions in 1950, 1953 and 1964 climaxed in the abortive secession of Eastern Nigeria in 1967. This was a manifestation of extreme centrifugalism, and a challenge to the process of state-building. It took a civil war to return Nigeria to a position of relative balance between centrifugal and centripetal pulls.[12] This balance was, however, not to last for long as more recent experiences have shown. We will return to this point later.

The first military coup of 1966, and other events it triggered, culminating in the civil war, soon planted the military firmly in the Nigerian political soil. We shall now turn to a discussion of this crucial factor in the evolution of both the Nigerian state and federation.

Federalism under Military Rule

In much of Western Political Science literature, federalism is regarded as incompatible with military rule. Reasons adduced for this includes the fact that military rule does not provide for popular participation in plebiscitary forms. Military rulers are not elected and, therefore, are not accountable to the electorate. We would like to suggest that participation through plebiscitary mechanism is not the only form of participation. As Henry Bienen[13] showed clearly in his study of Kenya, the Kenya African National Union (KANU) did not offer as much opportunity for participation as the regional administrative structures. The political party was moribund between elections.

There are many dimensions of participation. It may be suggested that political participation takes at least two forms. It can be *political access*, an input into the decision-making unit from below. People come to participate in decisions which affect their lives through representation, expression of opinions, and involvement in community programmes. This may even involve anomic forms of participation, such as riots and rebellions. Participation in this respect is essentially access to decision-making units from below. Participation also has an output form. This is the *mobilization* of the people by government for specific activities. Thus, when the military government mobilized people for such activities as *Operation Feed the Nation* and the census exercise, it was mobilizing people for participation. The point of initiation was at the top. Our argument is that military rule is not necessarily incompatible with federalism. The nature of military regimes may be hierarchial and the constitution may be so amended that one may not have a strictly federal constitution, but that does not mean one cannot have a federal government. As Wheare wrote:

> "If we are looking for examples of federal government, it is not sufficient to look at constitutions only. What matters just as much is the practice of government."[14]

The crucial issue is the "working of the system." However, in its form, federalism thrives best in a democratic setting

In State-building, the impression is often created that the centre can penetrate the periphery with the little regard for heterogeneity at the sub national level. According to David Apter, a "mobilization system" is typified by a hierarchical authority structure emphasizing organization with "minimum accountability."[15] On the other hand, a "reconciliation system" emphasizes pluralism and a desire to reconcile diverse interests; it "mediates, integrates and above all, coordinates rather than organizes and mobilizes."

In Nigeria the military leaders found that a model of government that provided for mobilization or politically induced change from the centre without regard for the interest of sub national units was unsatisfactory in its operation (the reaction to Decree No. 34, 1966 illustrated this). As Nigeria's father of *military federalism*, General Gowon, put the issue:

> Our variety is such that you could not get the best out of people under a unitary system of government. You probably could, but at the expense of one group or the other or by being dictatorial and by forcing certain issues. I did appreciate that you could not do that in Nigeria and get away with it.[16]

Hence, the military leaders adopted a compromise solution between Apter's "mobilization" and "reconciliation" models. The disadvantage of the mobilization system, with its emphasis on coercion and non-accountability, is compensated for by the reconciling elements of the reconciliation system. The weakness of the reconciliation system is compensated for by the mobilizing aspects of the mobilization system. Under military rule, therefore, except for the brief periods mentioned before, Nigeria has always practiced some form of federalism, (no matter how warped). General Gowon emphasized this after the creation of 12 states: "I believe in a federation with a strong centre, but with states having enough powers to manage their own affairs."[17]

Let us therefore turn to the legal or constitutional provisions under military rule in Nigeria's *military federalism*. By the terms of the Constitution (Suspension and Modification) Decree No. 1, 17 January 1966, the federal government was given the "power to make laws for the peace, order and good government of Nigeria or any part thereof with respect to any matter whatsoever." All military administrations in Nigeria maintained this provision, except for the brief period under the Constitution (Suspension and Modification) Decree No. 8, March 17, 1967.

Technically, this provision made the Federal Military Government (FMG) the sole repository of power in the state. This violates the federal principle of non-centralization of powers among component federal units. Legally, Nigeria was unitary under military rule. One expects therefore that in this context, the FMG would merely delegate or devolve its powers to subnational units. However, these decrees also state that the Governor of a region or state cannot make laws with regard to all matters in the exclusive legislative list, and is precluded from making any laws with regard to the concurrent legislative list without the consent of the FMG. Yet the Governor of a region or state can "make laws for the peace, order, and good government" of the region or state.

There is deference to federal principles here. The federal military government had dual roles under these decrees. The FMG could make laws for the whole country and had specific responsibility for the running of the Federal Government. This will become clearer when we deal with the structures. The state governments were restricted to a residual list. In essence, Nigeria's military government never suspended the constitutions of 1963 and subsequent ones. Only sections of the constitutions were suspended and/or amended. The legislative powers of the FMG and the regions/states were expressed in the form of decrees and edicts respectively. Interestingly decrees suspending sections of the constitution, for example, Decree No.1, 1966, Section 6, and Decree No.1, 1984, Section 5, state clearly that: "No question as to the validity of this or any other Decree or any Edict shall be entertained by any court of law in Nigeria." In a way, this negates a cardinal federal principle of the role of courts, but the nature of military legislation and administration make this understandable.

The structure of government decision-making was also provided for by the decrees. Military regimes increased the political visibility and power of the executive branch. The actors in the executive branch had both executive and legislative powers. Under Decree No. 1, 1966, the Governors of the regions were members of the country's supreme legislative organ, the Supreme Military Council (SMC). The Supreme Military Council made legislation for the whole country and considered administrative issues involving both federal and state governments. It was usually chaired by the Head of Federal Military Government (HFMG).[18] The Federal Executive Council (FEC) exercised general "direction and control" over affairs of the federal government as contained in the exclusive legislative list[19]. While General Ironsi did not appoint political executives to head the various ministries, General Gowon did in 1967. This trend continued and also changed the composition of the FEC.[20] Most military governments in Nigeria had been run by both military and civilians, with the military having the veto.

The judiciary was left to operate in so far as it did not treat existing decrees with levity. The Nigerian military administration before 1984 did not blatantly tamper with the judiciary except on a few occasions. An illustration of this was the Federal Government's reaction to a decision of the court on the confiscation of the properties of an ex-politician. By the Federal Military Government (Supremacy and enforcement of Powers) Decree No. 28 of 9 May, 1970, the FMG reminded Nigerians that the government had no mandate from anyone and that the judiciary and all unabrogated parts of the constitution existed by its grace. It then stated that for "the efficacy and stability of government"

Any decision whether made before or after the commencement of this Decree, by any court of law in the exercise or purported exercise of any powers under the constitution or any enactment or law of the Federation or any state shall be null and void and no effect whatsoever as from the date of the making thereof.

This position was reinforced in 1984 after some ex-politicians (i.e. Governors) went to court to seek orders to prevent their having to face military tribunals. On many occasions the military did not obey court orders and often relied on retrospective laws, which grossly violated the rights of citizens.

In terms of federal-state relations under *military federalism*, two conscious features must be identified. The first is the military superstructure; a military regime in which institutions of popular participation were suspended. In the military hierarchy of authority, the HFMG and Commander-in-Chief of the Armed forces appointed all Military Governors, and they were responsible to him. This negated the traditional principle of federalism and fits into Apter's model of mobilization with a hierarchical chain of command and "minimum accountability" to the people.

Unlike a civilian Governor of a state who was elected or ousted from office through the ballot box, the Military Governor was appointed from the centre and only removable by Commander-In-Chief or Chairman of the Provisional Ruling Council (PRC) who appointed him. This is typical of the hierarchical nature of military rule. One negative impact of this in military administrations was that lapses of the Governors, unlike under civilian rule, reflected on the HFMG or Federal Government. The experience of General Gowon, whose Governors eroded his credibility, is still very fresh in the minds of Nigerians[21]. Similarly, under Generals Babangida and Abacha, Governors were reputed to have committed many acts of gross misconduct about which the people could do nothing. Often, they blamed the Federal Government which had appointed them.

On the other hand, these governors were autonomous in the running of the affairs of their various states. They had substantial powers over the affairs of the state. The degree of supervision of these Governors depended partly on the personality of the HFMG. While Gowon gave the states much autonomy and the Governors much latitude in the performance of their duties, General Murtala was more centralizing in his administrative technique. It was partly to cut the Governors down to size that the Murtala regime established the National Council of States (NCS), thus removing the Governors from the highest ruling body.

The National Council of States under General Babangida and General Abacha was under the supervision of the PRC [or the Armed Forces Ruling Council (AFRC)] through the office of the Chief of General Staff. The Council brought together all State Governors, the Head of State, and the Minister of the Federal Capital Territory (FCT) for deliberation over state issues. This body dealt with "policy guidelines on financial and economic matters" as they affected states, national development plans, such constitutional matters concerning states, and any other matters assigned to it by the PRC. The NCS under military rule was part of a functioning government structure and not a mere advisory body as was the case under the 1979 Constitution. It is pertinent to note that there were few changes in the names of these military political structures under the Babangida and Abacha administrations. The HFMG was called the "President" in the Babangida era but General Abacha preferred the use of "Head of State". The SMC became the Armed Forces Ruling Council (AFRC) under General Babangida and the PRC under General Abacha ; the FEC became the Council of Ministers (COM) under Babangida, and under Abacha, was called the FEC, while the Council of States remained the same.

Besides all of the above, other institutions of federalism existed, which were mainly civilian in terms of their incumbents. These included the federal and state bureaucracies and local government structures, the federal and state judicial institutions, and federal and state corporations - which retained autonomy in their respective spheres of operation, as contained in the constitution. Each state had a Civil Service Commission as distinct from the Federal Civil Service

Commission which took care of recruitment, promotion, discipline and welfare of their staff. Even the membership of the federal and state executive council was often dominantly civilian. The above fits into Apter's reconciliation model - especially when one takes cognizance of the near absolute powers wielded by the Governors. It is a reflection of Nigeria's past experiences, a recognition that there are "social limits to politically induced change from the centre"[22] and that penetration and control of subnational units "carried forward with disregard for local integrity, amount to no more than experiments in violence"[23]

In terms of the degree of autonomy wielded by the old regions, it is to the credit of military regimes that the new (even if highly centralized) federalism evident in Nigeria was effectively created by the military. The autonomy of the old regions under Ironsi and the early Gowon administration was indisputable. The Gowon-Ojukwu tussle in the process of state-building illustrated some of the problems of adjustment of federal pendulum even under a military regime. After May 1967, however, General Gowon, upon creating 12 states took a number of legislative and administrative actions that tilted the federal scale very much in favour of the centre[24]. This centralizing process was facilitated by: 1) The nature of military legislation by Decree; 2) The increase in "Petronaira" 3) The creation of smaller states; and 4) The civil war, which enabled the FMG to take certain measures which were not easily reversible. By the time General Gowon left office, he had successfully centralized the political system. No state was in a comfortable position to secede any longer.

The Murtala-Obasanjo regime further strengthened the centre at the expense of the states. The takeover of state television stations is an illustration of this trend in federalism under the military. On a symbolic level, state governments ceased to have coats-of-arms. The Buhari administration did go further in this centralizing trend. He detained, tried and imprisoned civilian State Governors, Commissioners and key persons, but allowed state tribunals to carry out detailed investigations of abuses of power in the public services of the various states. It also closely supervised the states thus re-emphasizing the locus of power at the centre. The Babangida administration seemed to prefer autonomous states. But in creating more subnational units (state and local government) which, like others before them, were not economically viable, dependence on the centre only increased. More states depended on their statutory allocation from the Federation Account, on grants from the Federal Government and on loans from the centre and private financial houses in order to operate. This trend continued under the Abacha Administration. The excessively powerful centre in the Nigerian federation is largely due to the hierarchical nature of military rule. Under Babangida (1990) and Abacha (1996) the federal government created local governments for the first time. This was usually a matter for the States.

The political process of *military federalism* is very interesting. There were no political parties, and as such Federal Ministers and Commissioners as were appointed were directly responsible to the Head of State or the Governor. Members of the statutory corporations were nominated, screened and appointed by the military. The military rulers were largely answerable only to themselves, since the highest decision making body, the PRC, comprised only the military except for a brief period under General Abacha[25]. However, there is no doubt that the military in Nigeria, as rulers, on occasions had to yield to the aspirations of Nigerians. Demands coming from the various groups often revolved around the same issues, thereby overloading the system. In reconciling these interests in the federal process, ironically, the military had to rely on its hierarchical mode of operation. Reactions to labour union or fuel price hike often tasked the capability of the military. It took a while for them to realize that force was no solution to problems arising between the governors and the governed.

The Abacha period was probably the most difficult in the lives of Nigerians. General Abacha showed little interest in governance and often kept away from the office while his subordinates played political lords. Unlike Babangida, Abacha was a bit of a recluse and could not easily break through his security cordon to get the "truth" about situations or feel the actual pulse of the people. He allowed his aides to hold him virtually hostage.

Many of these aides therefore committed many crimes against the Nigerian state, individuals and groups. At times security officers carried out violence against the state to convince General Abacha that the security situation in the country was really bad. As Abacha withdrew into his cocoon at the Aso Rock Presidential Villa, he became more distant from the people, tragically at a point he had wanted to transform himself into a Civilian President.

Thus, when General Abacha died on June 8, 1998, the country heaved a sigh of relief. His successor, General Abubakar scrapped all the political institutions which General Abacha had set up and embarked on a new transition programme to civil rule, which ended on May 29, 1999. Nigeria's former Head of State, General Olusegun Obasanjo who contested the election under the People's Democratic Party (PDP) defeated his opponent Chief Olu Falae who contested under the All Peoples Party (APP). Obasanjo was then sworn in as Nigeria's Second Executive President on May 29, 1999.

What has been the nature of Nigeria's federation since May 1999?

Federalism in Nigeria's New Democratic Polity

The politics of Nigeria's federation has been exciting but also frustrating. Its structure and its nature had generated very intense and interesting debates at the 1994 Constitutional Conference.

In 1993, this writer, based on the reactions of various groups to the Nigerian federation, generated the concerns of groups and governments at different tiers of the federation. Let us reproduce these for an evaluation to see if these concerns have changed.

The relations among tiers of government show how the operators of each order and levels of government perceive the other.

i) the *federal government's* powers are too sprawling and it is carrying out functions it has no business carrying out: its power should be curbed to allow the federal system to breathe a new lease of life from the squeeze imposed by years of military rule; the revenue formula must be reviewed to reflect these changes in functions; after all, we are closer to the grassroots and should have more resources to carry out development programmes: the fiscal dominance of the centre has made it so priced that politicians would do anything to get there;

ii) remember the period between 1960 and 1966? Do you want a weak *federal centre* unable to give the country a sense of security? It was a period in which the regional tails wagged the federal dogs. The trend all the world over is to have a strong federal government which can fiscally intervene to carry out fiscal and developmental equalization among component units of the federation; the states and local governments are complacent about revenue generation and must realize that autonomy in a federal association presupposes fiscal autonomy;

iii) *state governments* are still living in the past: they have not realized that local governments are now a constitutionally guaranteed third tier of government and are therefore autonomous of state governm ents; State Governors/Administrators must stop removing Local Government Chairmen as if they are bureaucrats; states should release appropriate statutory allocations to the local governments promptly: in fact states should be abolished because they have outlived their usefulness;

iv) *Local* governments comprise the most problematic tier in the federation; they lack executive capacity. Their leaders are inexperienced and mistake federally desirable autonomy for independence or sovereignty; they even forget the provision that the State House of Assembly can make laws specifying additional functions for them: they generate no revenue from internal sources and expect to be autonomous; really they need education on their roles; they have so much money which they are unable to manage properly because of their lack of executive capacity; money spent on local government is money thrown down the drain-pipe; give such money to the state government for a more productive performance. Autonomy for the local government is autonomy for excellence in wastage and mismanagement.

It is our suggestion that these issues still reverberate in the federation. Concern about the unfairness of the federal system to each group has led to the clamour in some quarters, especially in the Yoruba areas, for the restructuring of the federation and a Sovereign National

Conference (SNC). Other groups have also called for a national, but not sovereign conference. We shall return to this later.

Federal - State - Local Government Relations since May 1999

In terms of *Federal-State* relations, the conflicts have been complex. Initially the leaders at both levels exercised some caution, in order not to torpedo (and to use a Nigerian hackneyed cliché) the nation's "nascent democracy". Yet, at times, the conflicts simmered to the surface. One illustration of these conflicts is the National Minimum Wage (NMW). President Olusegun Obasanjo, on May 1, 2000 announced a national minimum wage of ₦5,500 for states and the rest of the society, and ₦7,500 for the federal government. Apparently acting under the pressure of the Nigerian Labour Congress (NLC), the President consulted neither the State Governors nor the National Assembly (NA).

State governors, for obvious reasons, were livid with anger. Governor Abdullahi Adamu of Nasarawa State reminded the federal government that Nigeria was no longer under a centralized military rule. He said:

> The federal government should realize that we are now operating a democratic government and the dictatorial era of the military should be jettisoned.[26]

He declared that no State Governor had been consulted and that no bill had been sent to the National Assembly. He announced that all the Governors got from the Presidency were fax messages. Governor Adamu, speaking on behalf of his colleagues, argued that "Nigeria is a federation of states. We are responsible for paying wages in our various states."[27]

Governor Lam Adesina of Oyo State rubbed the issue further when he said:

> In a federal set-up... the Federal Government has no power to negotiate on behalf of other states... The President was the person

who introduced the topic of minimum wage... We told him that in a federation there is never a central joint negotiating body.[28]

The complexity of the whole exercise was brought to the fore by Governor Abba Ibrahim of Yobe State. As he pointed out,

> It is the responsibility of the Federal Government to set the minimum wage, they have done that; it is their responsibility to agree with their workers, they have done that already... So it is for states and local governments to now start discussing with their workers from today on.[29]

Yes, that was the crux of the problem. The states found that in their negotiations with their workers, they could not afford to meet the demand of the labour force. Many of the states were spending up to 80% of their revenue on salaries. Works in many states were paralyzed as workers went on strike. Some state public servants could not understand why there should be a difference between federal and state government salaries for their respective workers – of course, in the shadow of the erstwhile homogenization of pay under military rule.[30] Since 1974, with the Udoji Administrative Reform, State and federal conditions of service were homogenized.

The State Governors made it clear that they had three options. The first is to retrench their work force, which in a democratic setting can have a popular backlash. They could also pay what they could afford in the context of the resource bases of their respective states. Finally, the federal government could increase states share of the Federation Account. As one governor put it,

> We were not elected to only pay salaries for four years. We were voted in by the people to develop our states and to positively affect the lives of everybody, including of course, the rural dwellers who are farmers, mechanics, traders and even the jobless. What happens is that salaries alone gulp over eighty per cent of what we get from the federation account. So what do we do?[31]

The Federal Government's reaction was that State Governments were receiving three times more revenues from the Federation Account than they were receiving. The Governors hit back that while there was an increase in statutory allocations to states, there were other competing demands. The labour force was unimpressed by these arguments and insisted that states should not pay their workers less than ₦6,500. Of course some states agreed with their labour force to pay, less than ₦6000 while others engaged in negotiations with their labour forces, even as at September 2000. In addition, federal civil servants did not get their July and August, 2000 salaries. According to government spokesman, this was because the Federal Government was checking out the exaggerated figures submitted by some ministries as part of the new increase in wages.

On balance, while the Federal Government has the constitutional right to set minimum wage, it should have consulted the states and the National Assembly. The National Assembly was even working on a bill for new minimum wage of ₦15,000 which if passed, would have messed up the finances of states which were already in trouble. Some analysts believe that President Obasanjo announced the NMW in haste to court the support of the labour force against the National Assembly with which he was having problems. But perhaps, this incident is illustrative of other cases in which the President's military background as a former military head of state (used to command and control) was at play. Residual militarism in his actions was not unusual, and there had been appeals to him to shed his erstwhile military cloak for a democratic one.

The other illustration of the frost in federal-state relations is the introduction of the *Universal Basic Education* programme. This programme is aimed at providing free universal basic education from primary school to the first three years of Secondary School. The Federal Government announced this programme and went ahead to launch it in Sokoto, before President Obasanjo had sent a bill to the National Assembly. State Governors complained of lack of consultation. They claimed that the matter was under the concurrent legislative list, and that since the Federal Government was going to depend on states for the implementation of the programme, states should have been adequately consulted.

In addition, some state governments were controlled by political parties different from the one at the federal level an each political party had its own programme on education. They therefore frowned on the 'military' fashion in which federal programmes were announced in areas of concurrent legislation, without regard to the priorities of states, especially where states were to be the implementing agency. The State Governors and the Vice-President met in September 2000 to harmonize areas of disagreement over this programme. Such consultations, if held much earlier, would have reduced tensions in federal-state relations.

Similarly, the issue of *law and order - the* role of the *Nigeria Police* have been sources of friction between the two tiers 'of government. Given the ineptitude and inefficiency of the Nigeria Police in the maintenance of law and order, governors of states with large urban centres and high rates of crimes, found themselves helpless in dealing with crimes. Police is a federal matter even though the Governor of a state is the Chief Security Officer of the State.

As happened in the Second Republic, many governors complained that State Commissioners of Police

> Ignored orders from them but took orders only from their boss, the Inspector-General of Police. In frustration, some State governors demanded for a review of the Constitution to enable the States establish their own police force. However, some State Governors are opposed to the idea of establishing State police forces and have said so. They expressed their reluctance to spend their meagre resources on maintaining State police. These governors opted for a greater level of decentralization of the Nigeria police to enable it respond to problems more effectively and promptly. In some States, the government officially resorted to using vigilante groups to maintain law and order.[32]

The former Lagos Governor, Bola Tinubu was at the fore of the demands for a state police force. The violence and crime level in Lagos State made Governor Tinubu's position understandable. Yet, there can be no state police force unless there is a constitutional amendment. Ironically, while some State Governors were asking for state police force, others rejected that option. The argument of the latter was that funds available to state governments from internally generated sources as well as statutory allocations were not enough for current demands, not to mention expending these on the establishment and maintenance of state police services. They argued that the federal government had a duty to protect lives and property and should therefore recruit and adequately train additional police officers and men, reorganize and decentralize the force, and properly equip it to cope with its numerous challenges.

In August 2000, while meeting with the leaders of Nigeria's Southwest Zone, President Obasanjo gave instructions that all Police Commissioners in the States should obey lawful orders from the Governors. He, however, warned the Governors not to use the police force in their states for private purposes. Evidence later showed clearly how President Obasanjo misused the police force in the illegal impeachment and removal of the Governors of Bayelsa, Plateau, Oyo, Anambra and Ekiti States. The courts declared the first four illegal. For those who therefore feared the misuse of the State police services it became clear, that the same could (and did) happen at the federal level, unless one had leaders who believed in the rule of law and valued integrity.

A variant of this problem of maintenance of law and order is the inability of the police force to cope with crimes in some urban centres, such as Onitsha (which has one of the biggest markets in Africa). Police officers and men have been accused of colluding with criminals, while at other times, were just plain inefficient. Of course, the Nigeria Police force has its problems which most Nigerians know. These include the neglect of the force for a very long period of military rule. In Anambra State, former Governor Mbadinuju invited the *Bakassi Boys* (a vigilante or neighbourhood watch group) to deal with accused robbers who had turned life into hell in the state. There were times when some people went to bed at 6.00pm, while some others took refuge in Churches for the night for fear of criminals.

The *Bakassi Boys*[33] (BB) in a short period cleared Onitsha and the state of the criminals and normal life returned to the state. Their style, however, was brutish and cruel. They gave instant judgements and often killed their suspects publicly. Some human rights groups reacted to this style of justice. The Federal Government therefore ordered that *Bakassi Boys* be 'flushed out' from Anambra State. There were widespread protests by the citizens of the State who dreaded a repeat of the situation before the use of the vigilante group. In response, the Governor of Anambra State got a bill passed through the State House of Assembly, recognizing the *Bakassi Boys* as a *vigilante* group to be paid as part of the public service. After all, the state had not established a Police force which would violate the constitution.

The quick reaction by Anambra State meant that only an Act of the National Assembly could render the State law null and void. The prospect of the Federal Government getting that kind of bill passed through the National Assembly was remote. It therefore settled for ensuring that the activities of the *Bakassi Boys* were within the rubric of the law.

Again, this is an issue of a matter exclusive to the Federal Government becoming a bone of contention between the two tiers of government. This was mainly because the Federal Government as the source of authority could not deliver expected services and the state government, as the closest tier of government, had to take action to protect the lives and property of its citizens.

One more illustration of conflict between federal and state government, is the issue of *power supply*. Under the constitution, only the Federal Government can generate, transmit and distribute electric power where there is National Electric Power Authority (NEPA) (now renamed Power Holding Company) grid. Lagos State is largely an industrial state. Power supply in Lagos State, as elsewhere in the country is epileptic. Frustrated by fruitless appeals to NEPA, Governor Tinubu sought for alternative sources of power. He was reminded that it was a federal matter. He then applied for permission to enable Lagos State supplement NEPA power supply in the State. Again frustrated, the Governor accused the Federal government of deliberately frustrating his effort to provide electric power to his state. The Federal government later authorized the state to go ahead with its arrangement for supplementary power supply in the state with EMRON Power Company. Since then, the Federal Government has

encouraged State governments to engage in supplementary programmes of power generation. Kwara and
Lagos States Governments have established power generation plants in their States.

A very important source of Federal- State conflicts was the *Electoral Bill* 2001, which had been passed separately by the Senate and House of Representatives. Two issues of conflict emerged from this Bill. First, the Electoral Bill extended the tenure of Local Government Chairmen and Councillors from three to four years. State governors felt that this was unconstitutional and vowed to dissolve local governments and conduct new elections in April 2002. Secondly, the bill provided for a new order of sequential elections, beginning with the Presidential elections through gubernatorial to local government elections. The governors opposed this new order as contained in the Senate bill. The House of Representatives had opposed one-day election for all elective positions. President Obasanjo, aware of the tensions within his political party over these issues, set up a committee to reconcile the issues of contention.[34]

Thus, while inefficiency in the process of implementation of matters under the exclusive list of the Federal Government had led to conflicts with state governments, on other occasions, federal arrogance and lack of consultation with the states on issues in the concurrent list have generated conflicts which could clearly have been avoided.

In the relations between *States and Local Governments,* there have been cold wars, with various battles fought at the subnational level. The moot-point between State - Local Government relations was the claim that there are no enabling laws for the operation of local governments. In 1999, while the enabling laws under the military were repealed by the out-going military government, some State Houses of Assembly had not made laws for "the establishment, structure, composition, finance and functions of such councils," as contained in Section 7(1) of the 1999 Constitution. The Attorney-General of the Federation argued that the old laws which had existed in the States were still in force. Secondly, local governments disliked interferences from state governments. As an illustration, the Sokoto State government was taken to court by 15 Local Governments in the State and the court restrained the state government from deducting 3% of its statutory allocation for funding the Sokoto Emirate Council as passed by the State House of Assembly.[35]

In addition, local government chairmen argued that State Governors, (especially where the chairman comes from a party different from the Governor's) always plotted to remove such chairmen by using the Audit powers of the state. State Governors were also accused of plotting with the State Houses of Assembly to shorten the term of three years of elected local government officials in order to put their supporters in office. In some States there were protests by elected local government officials against attempts by State Houses of Assembly to reduce their term to two years. Thus in lmo State, the police arrested 11 Local Government Councillors along with 300 others who had gone to the State House of Assembly to protest the reduction of their tenure from three to two years.[36]

However, many Governors claimed that a majority of Chairmen and Councillors of Local Governments, only sit down to share money and hardly embarked on development projects. President Obasanjo had publicly chided the Chairmen over this issue. The Governors were at pains to point out that the Chairmen of Local Government do not have the powers they had under the 1989 Constitution, and that they should be enlightened on this matter. In addition, the Governors were angry that the Federal Government relate directly with the Local governments which were operating under State governments. They argued that the 1999 Constitution, section 162(6) provided for the "States Joint Local Government Account" into which Statutory allocation from Federal and State Government accruing to the States' should be deposited. However, they were opposed to what they perceived as attempts by the Federal Government to relate directly to local governments under them. They cited the case of the Federal Government aiding the Local Government Chairmen to buy security vehicles and gadgets for the maintenance of law and order at local level without the knowledge and involvement of State Governors. The State Governors are the Chief Security Officers of the states and should be involved in this kind of arrangement.

Perhaps the most salient area of conflict between local governments and State governments revolves around the "State Joint Local Government Account". Many Chairmen of Local Governments complain that State governments i) do not regularly pay their mandatory 10% of the State budget into the account; and ii) divert and use funds due to local governments, without the permission of local governments. While many State governments deny this; there is enough evidence to show that some State Governments violated this constitutional provision.

It does seem that personality clashes and the lack of adequate culture of relations among the component tiers of government after long periods of military rule, have bedevilled relations among tiers of government. It is hoped that as a new democratic culture of consultations and the rule of law take root in the polity, unnecessary and abrasive conflicts will be avoided.

Let us now turn to revenue distribution in the Nigerian Federation.

Resource Distribution

Resource distribution includes both statuses and revenues. In fact, it includes the distribution of all scarce but allocatable resources. The location of government projects and/or offices as well as the pattern of recruitment into political offices and the public service are also yardsticks for measuring the fairness of leaders in the distribution process in Nigeria.

The 1999 Constitution provides in Section 162 (2) that the Revenue Mobilization, Allocation and Fiscal Commission has the function of tabling before the National Assembly a draft revenue allocation formula. The National Assembly shall then deliberate on this document, taking into account the principles of "population, equality of states, internal revenue generation, land mass, terrain as well as population density". The National Assembly shall note that the principles of derivation applied on all proceeds from all natural resources will not be less than 13%. Since the advent of the new democratic polity, State Governors have argued that a new allocation formula should be put in place giving the states, at least 40%. As a matter of fact, a delegation representing State Governors made the same point to the members of the Revenue Mobilization, Allocation and Fiscal Commission. This point was reinforced by the Governors' Forum, meeting in Abuja at various times between 1999 and 2008.

Generally, given the centralization of political power under the military, the centre became a financial titan, as military rulers altered the revenue formula as they deemed fit. They did not need to debate the formula at any legislative forum, except at the Armed Forces Ruling Council or the Provisional Ruling Council. There have been calls for the revision of the legislative list and accompanying tax powers in favour of local and State governments. The logic of this argument is that the federal centre has too much funds at its disposal, thus encouraging it to engage in policy adventures into areas which should belong to other tiers.

On the horizontal level, there have been cries of marginalization by all groups. The oil producing states of Niger-Delta are angry that while their area produces oil, the dividends go to other parts of the country. Basically, while oil accounts for over 80% of the country's annual revenue, it has not changed the lives of the Niger-Delta people. While the Constitution provides for 13% revenue (on the principles of derivation) to the oil producing area, the Governors of these states argue that the federal government refused to pay these funds to the oil-producing states between May - December 1999. In response the Governors of the South-South Zone decided to demand for the control of its resources. As Governor Ibori of Delta State put it:

> ...the Federal Government has not, and we believe does not intend to resolve that very provision of the constitution, so we are not asking for 13 per cent any more, what we are taking now is everything, the 100 per cent control.[37]

The point is that, as in Canada and Australia, the Revenue Commission should be tasked to carry out two functions, in addition, to its current functions. It should carry out a fiscal equalization on a vertical dimension, to ensure that funds are available to all three tiers of government to carry out their functions. Furthermore, its fiscal equalization measures on a horizontal level should carry out relative equalization among states in order to ensure some political stability.

In response to the complaints of neglect in the Niger-Delta, a new body *the Niger-Delta Development Commission* (NDDC) was established, to replace the old (OMPADEC). The NDDC is designed to alleviate poverty in the Delta area and embark on development projects aimed at improving the quality of lives of the average Niger-Delta person.

Similarly, states with solid minerals also complain that in spite of environmental degradation as a result of mining activities in their areas, they have not been adequately compensated. They are therefore calling for the establishment of the *Solid Minerals Producing Area Development Commission* (SOMPADEC). Interestingly, all the states from which hydro-electric power is generated have also called for the establishment of *Hydro Power Producing Areas Development Commission* (HYPPADEC) to compensate them for the consequences of any environmental damages caused by the activities associated with the generation of hydro-related energy.

Since the current quarrels are over the nature of distribution and not over the recognition of claims by contending parties, compromises will continue to be found. While the federal government went to court to seek the definition of the on-shore and off-shore minerals (or oil) in the context of resource distribution, there have been pressures for a political, rather than a legal solution of the matter. This was done when a law as passed merging off-shore and on-shore. Since then, however, some Northern states have gone to court to challenge this law. In addition, the politicians are likely to strike compromises over the percentage of resources in the federation account which should be allocated on the basis of derivation. Currently, all mineral resources belong to the federation, and the 13% of the proceeds return to the state of origin of such minerals (including petroleum). Given the centrifugal pulls in the federation, the percentage of the derivation principle may go up gradually within a decade.[38]

One disturbing trait in the politics of leadership and resource distribution is the extent to which actions of leaders (military and/or civilian) can be easily ethnicized. It is very easy for a leader's mandate to be ethnicized or geo-ethnicized by his people by the way they lay claim to him. It is also easy for a leader to ethnicize his mandate by his policies and actions. Usually, a leader's mandate being ethnicized by his people becomes more dangerous if the leader also ethnizes his mandate through, his official actions in government. The qualities of **fairness** and **justice** in a leader cannot be over-emphasized in the process of nation-building in a federal context. We shall discuss later in this volume. What are the prospects of federalism in the fourth Republic?

Prospects of Federalism in the Fourth Republic

It does seem that given the verdant memory of the last civil war, most Nigerian politicians know that Nigeria cannot survive a second civil war. Given the new freedom embedded in the democratic polity, after years of military rule, they want to test the system to see the extent to which they can go. They may even go to the precipice before finding a line of retreat into the centre of the polity. However, transforming democratic freedom into democratic licence can be very costly for any system and Nigerian politicians have to watch out.

This writer does not believe that Nigeria will break up in the foreseeable future. Nigerians, quite often, underestimate the common bonds which hold them together. Paradoxically Nigeria's complexity has been its saviour. It has made it more difficult for groups to easily pull out of the federation. The current complaints, in a way, are good for the system. They are part of the process of adjustment of the federal pendulum as it swings between centripetalism and centrifugalism. These adjustments can be painful and at times may put heavy strains and stresses on the federation.

Since federalism is about how to manage conflicts, it requires politicians and leaders with skills in effecting appropriate compromises and conflict resolution. It calls for a collective sense of patience, accommodation and tolerance. These are not the cheapest commodities to find in the market place when people operate under stress, yet they are indispensable. Perhaps even as important are such leadership qualities such as *Justice, Fairness* and *Equity* which are cardinal to the survival of any polity, not to mention a federal polity.

Conclusions

Our argument here is that while federalism is embedded with its own seeds of discord, the foundations of Nigeria's federal system are to be found in the nature of colonial administration and the responses of Nigerians to it. Therefore, the problems of Nigeria's federal compromises are also historical and multidimensional. We gave illustrations of these.

We also suggested that Nigeria's federation has become characterized by unitarist streaks as a result of almost three decades of military rule and its hierarchical structure. This long period of military rule has implications not only for the nature of Nigerian federalism, but also for the immediate post-military polity in the country. With the authoritarian lid of the military gone, violent reactions to many national issues bottled up for years, erupted. The bubbles are settling down, but it will take a while for Nigerians, exuberant about their democratic freedom, to realize that it does not mean democratic licence.

We also looked at some compromises effected in the Nigerian polity and concluded that the future threat to the survival of Nigeria is in the horizontal relations among Nigerian groups as they squabble over scarce, but allocatable resources. This subject matter is treated in greater detail later, under Nation-building.

Finally, it is our conclusion that leadership remains a vital factor in effecting the compromises that the federal process necessitates. Reconciliation is a basic component of this process and the leadership must be so inclined. The task of nation-building is complex and infinite. The leadership must therefore build the confidence of its citizens as it strives to balance conflicting claims. In the final analysis, structures and institutions alone cannot build understanding and cooperation in the polity. The attendant human values of *tolerance, fairness, justice and transparent honesty* are essential ingredients which the leadership must imbibe and promote. Let us turn to the issue of leadership and governance.

Notes

1.   James Coleman, *Nigeria: A Background to Nationalism,* (Berkeley: University of California Press, 1958), p.30.
2.   Ahmadu Bello, *My Life* (London: Cambridge University Press, 1962).
3.   Obafemi Awolowo, *Path to Nigerian Freedom,* (London: Faber and Faber, 1947), pp.47-48.
4.   Abubakar Tafawa Balewa in Nigeria, *Legislative Council Debates, 4 March, 1948, p.227.*
5.   See Nnamdi Azikiwe, *Political Blueprint for Nigeria,* (Lagos: 1945) for his speeches; In 1975, Zik explained the criteria he used in proposing the creation of units: "When I proposed that Nigeria should become a federation of eight regions in 1943, I was political, and not sociological in my approach. I did not necessarily overlook the tribal factor but, in my innocence, I minimized it" (*Daily Times Lagos,* 19 May 1975) p.5.
6.   Awolowo, *op.cit.,* 1947.
7.   Ethnoregionalism is used to refer to crystallization of identities of major ethnic groups with regional administrative boundaries.
8.   Interview with Aminu Kano, 1974.
9.   Clifford Geertz, *old Societies and New States, (Glencoe: The Free Press, 1963) p.155.*
10. *J.S. Mill, Representative Government* (Everyman edition,) pp.367-368, quoted in Wheare, Federal Government, op.cit., p.51.
11. According to Sklar, on the January 1966 coup, "political power had shifted away from the Northern rulers and their allies to a more progressive section of the population. The dangerous imbalance between legal and technological power had been corrected."
     a. In other words, the January coup corrected existing imbalance. Richard L. Sklar, "Nigerian Politics in Perspective." in R. Melson and H. Wolpe (eds.), *Nigeria: Modernization and the Politics of Communalism* (East Lansing: Michigan State University Press, 1970), p.50.
12. Even though Nigeria operated a military system, it was a military federal system of government. The military

governments of the regions/states were very powerful and autonomous, especially under the Gowon administration.

13.   Henry Bienen, *Kenya: The Politics of Participation and Control* (Princeton, N.J. Princeton University Press, 1974).

14.   Wheare, *op.cit.*, p.20.

15.   David Apter, *The Politics of Modernization* (Chicago: University of Chicago Press, 1965), pp.359-421.

16.   Interview with General Gowon.

17.   General Gowon, interview with *Drum* (Lagos), March 1968.

18.   By this decree, members of the council included 1) the HFMG, 2) the Head of the Nigerian Army, 3) the Head of the Nigerian Navy, 4) the Head of the Nigerian Air Force, 5) the Chief of Staff of the Armed Forces, 6) the Chief of Staff of the Nigerian Army, and 7) military governors of Northern, Eastern, Western, and Mid-Western Nigeria. After the creation of 12 states by General Gowon, the State Governors became members of the SMC.

19.   Note that the military administration centralized power between 1967-1975, many items, such as revenue allocation and university education, came under the exclusive list.

20.   Originally the FEC comprised 1) the HFMG, 2) the head of the Nigerian Navy, 3) the head of the Nigerian Army, 4) the head of the Nigerian Air Force, 5) the Chief of Staff of the Armed Forces, 6) the Chief of Staff of the Nigerian Army, 7) the Attorney General, and 8) the Inspector-General and Deputy Inspector-General of the Nigerian Police. The Federal Commissioners appointed in June 1967 became members of this body. See Constitution (Suspension and Modification) Decree No. 107, 1993, Section 8, for the current composition of the Provisional Ruling Council (PRC) and FEC.

21.   While Gowon was accepted as an officer and gentleman who was not a corrupt leader, many Nigerian were worried about the excesses and corruption of his governors. These eroded Gowon's credibility because they were his appointees.

22. Lewis, "The Social Limits of Politically Induced Change," in C.Morse etal. (Eds), *Modernization by Design*, (Ithaca,N.Y.: Cornell University Press, 1969), p. 24.

23. S.S. Harrison, India: *The Most Dangerous Decades* (Princeton University Press, 1960), p.11.

24. See detailed discussion of these measures in J. Isawa Elaigwu, "The Military and State-Building: Federal-State Relations in Nigeria's 'Military Federalism' 1966-76," *Readings on Federalism, op. cit.*, pp.155-181.

25. Membership of the PRC in the early days of the Abacha government (November 1993-March 1995) was made up of: (a) the Head of State and Commander-in-Chief of the Armed Forces, as Chairman; (b) the Chief of General Staff as Vice-Chairman; (c) the Chief of Air Staff; (f) the Inspector-General of Police; (g) the Minister of Foreign Affairs (civilian); (k) the Special Adviser on National Security (civilian); and (I) such members as the Head of State may from time to time appoint.

    b. See Decree N.107 "Constitution (Suspension and Modification) Decree, 17 November 1993", Section 8(2) a - 1 pp. A1503-4.

26. *Vanguard*, (Lagos) June 24, 2004, p.6.

27. *Vanguard*, May 4, 2000, p.9.

28. *Vanguard*, June 24, 2000, p.6.

29. *Vanguard*, May 4, 2000, p.2. In Plateau State, Governor Dariye indicated that government was ready to pay more than N6,500, but "Our concern is that we don't want to go back to the ugly past when workers were owed several months arrears of salaries." *(Vanguard* June 24, 2000 p.7).

30. *ThisDay*, August 1, 2000; August 10, 2000. In response to Governor Dariye's statement, William Alkali expressed the labour's worries about "the disparity between those who work for the Federal Government and their counterparts in the state and local government areas"... *(Vanguard,* June 24, 2000, However, Mr. Ayo Afolabi, Executive Assistant to Governor Akande on media, pleaded with labour leaders to understand that ".... the IGR and allocations to each state differs so it is fundamentally wrong for anybody to compare Osun State with any state whatsoever. More so, we are in a federal state and we

can only pay based on what we can afford..." *(Vanguard, September 7,* 2000, p.25).

31. Vanguard, June 24, 2000, p.6.

32. This is the case of Anambra State where the "Bakassi Boys" have become officially recognised 'Vigilante' to complement police efforts. Attempts by the Governor of Lagos to use OPC has been criticized by the Police, especially since the OPC is a banned organization. See *ThisDay* (Lagos) August 18 2000, p.13; August 2, 2000, p.1; July 30, 2000, p.1; July 27, 2000, p.1; July 26, p.5.

33. *ThisDay* (Lagos) August 18, 2000, p13; August 2, 2000, p1; July 27,2000, p1; July 26, 2000, p5

34. *Vanguard,* November 20, 2001

35. *Vanguard,* August 23, 1999, pp 1 & 2.

36. *Vanguard,* March 9, 2000, p.1.

37. *Vanguard,* July 19, 2000, p.2; also see *ThisDay,* July 28, 2000, p.7.

38. After all between 1964-1969, the percentage of mineral rents and royalties which went back to the States was 45%. It may go up again beyond the current 13%.

CHAPTER 2

LEADERSHIP AND GOVERNANCE

Introduction

The Twenty-First Century seems to have caught us unawares in our part of the world. The challenges of governance and development today are more complex and multidimensional than in the Twentieth Century. The leadership skills and styles required today are increasingly becoming more technocratic, yet more political and visionary.

What is leadership? What is governance? What is the relationship between leadership and governance? What have been Nigeria's experiences in leadership? What are the challenges of leadership in Nigeria? What are the prospects of effective and 'good' leadership in Nigeria?

To answer some of these questions we suggest that:

1. leadership is very important in the dynamics of governance in any nation-state;
2. the challenges of development in Nigeria, as in many African states, are multi-variable in causation, and multi-dimensional in nature;
3. Nigeria's experience shows that leadership skills and styles under the military and democratic polities as well as under multinational federal states and polyethnic unitary states are markedly different;
4. our leaders must develop new visions and new strategies; must summon new forms of determination and political will;
5. and demonstrate higher levels of patriotism, hardwork, selflessness, and responsiveness to the yearnings of the people, in order to deal with the challenges facing them; and
6. while the anxieties and agonies over our currently fluid setting tend to give an impression of dark clouds in the horizon, there are

rays of hope in the Nigerian tunnel of development, as we resolve to take our destiny in our hands.

Let us start with our first suggestion about leadership and governance.

Leadership and Governance

Leadership[1] presupposes followership. It presupposes a group of people who, from among themselves, have produced a leader, or from among whom a leader has emerged.

It was President Eisenhower of the United States who once defined leadership as the "ability to decide what is to be done and then to get others to want to do it".[2] President Harry Truman was even more vivid when he said – "A leader is a man who has the ability to get other people to do what they don't want to do, and like it".[3] These two leaders of the United States of America perceived leadership in terms of a man's ability to manage men in such a way as to get certain activities carried out willingly (even if initially they had any doubts). A leader is usually responsible for establishing clear-cut goals and organizing members of the community towards the achievement of these goals.

National leadership therefore involves a core elite group which must "develop the vision and authority to call the shots, "fully cognizant of the risk in taking initiatives", but realizing that "there are greater risks now in waiting for sure things,"[4] given the current unpredictability in our global setting. Such leadership as could claim to be 'National' must enjoy national acceptability and respect. It must also be noted that various organizations – private and public – have their own leadership. Leadership expectations in all cases would be determined by the organization and/or people.

In essence, leadership is a skill, that is, "the ability that comes from knowledge, practice, aptitude…"[5] A patterned exhibition of these ability or skills could be classified as style or leadership type. Studies of leadership, whether in private or public organizations, show that there are varied approaches and definitions. For our purposes, we shall narrow the scope of our overview in order to answer the questions we have posed, and react to our suggestions.

Leadership in a State refers to at least six elite groups – *political, economic, intellectual, bureaucratic, military, and traditional or cultural.* Their functions are also overlapping – the political elite seeks, acquires and uses political power; the economic elite deals with the economic and the business issues of the state; the intellectual class (which include many academics and professional groups, utilizes ideas for the functional benefit of the society and state; the bureaucratic elite helps to initiate and implement State policies; and the military protects the members of the society and defends the state against external aggression. Thus when the military stages coups, it engages in an elite form of instability, as it usurps political power in addition to its traditional role.[6] Traditional leadership symbolizes religious and cultural identity and help to maintain peace, law and order. In traditional society there was a fusion of political and traditional elites. Each elite group has leadership roles in the society. Herein lies the difficulty in the definition of leadership.

According to David Apter, there are four types of political systems—*mobilizational, bureaucratic, theocratic* and *reconciliation.*[7] Following closely along this line, Ali Mazrui identifies at least five styles among African leaders[8]: 1) *intimidatory leader,* 2) *patriarchal leader,* 3) *leader of reconciliation,* 4) *mobilizational leader,* and 5) *bureaucratic leader.* The intimidatory leader "relies primarily on fear and on instruments of coercion to assert his authority," and he specializes in the use and/or threat of the use of force to extract compliance from his fellow countrymen. The *patriarchal leader* is basically "one who commands neo-filial reverence, a near-father figure," such as *Mzee* Jomo Kenyatta in Kenya, and South Africa's *Madiba* Nelson Mandela. In Nigeria, Obasanjo attempted to tap from this patriarchial basis of legitimacy, by adopting *baba* or 'father' as a political alias—even from his biological elders. The leader of *reconciliation* relies "for his effectiveness on qualities of tactical accommodation and capacity to discover areas of compromise between otherwise antagonistic viewpoints. He remains in control as long as he is successful in politics of compromise and synthesis".[9] The reconciliation is quite often between antagonistic political interest groups. But in the present African situation, the reconciliation leader may have to perfect also the art of reconciling the military with the civilian sectors of authority.

Examples of the reconciliation leaders are Milton Obote of Uganda before the Amin coup in 1971, and Abubakar Tafawa Balewa who was killed in the January 1966 coup and General Gowon of Nigeria.

The *mobilizational* leader has ideology as his main drive, with an undercurrent of charismatic qualities which buttress his ability to mobilize the populace for particular kinds of social action. Nigeria's Murtala Mohammed, Mozambique's Samora Machel, Sekou Toure of Guinea and Ghana's Kwame Nkrumah displayed this kind of leadership. The fifth kind of leader, the *bureaucratic leader*, is the low-key type who relies on "efficiency rather than evocation, procedure rather than passion"[10]. General Buhari of Nigeria fits into this model.

Let us make another distinction—between *transactional* and *transformational* leadership. According to Bernard M. Baas, a *transactional leader* motivates "followers by exchanging with them rewards for services rendered[11]. Usually he/she operates within the traditional or existing political institutions and policies. Fundamental changes are not in his normal domain of actions.

On the other hand, *the transformational leader* "sharply arouses or alters the strength of needs which may have lain dormant"[12] among his followers. Often, he raises the awareness of his followers to higher essences of consequence. Operating within existing structures, he may effect moderate changes in institutions and policies. On the other hand, he may clear out old institutions in order to effect fundamental changes to policies. Revolutions owe much to transformational leadership.

It is our argument that transactional leaders who merely seek to maintain the system, have less problems than transformational leaders who seek fundamental changes in the system. Often transformational leaders in heterogeneous or multinational states are faced with complex problems which tax their skills as dynamic leaders of reconciliation and leaders of societal transformation.

For our purposes, *democratic governance* refers to control or management, or how authority is exercised in the governance of the society, in accordance with the democratic principles of *authority,* the *rule of law, legitimacy, choice,* and *accountability.* How have our political elites in power governed in accordance with democratic principles to achieve the ends of the state — the *maintenance of law and order, the welfare of the people, and the pursuit of national interest in a competitive global setting?*

It is thus clear that if the ends or goals of the state are—the pursuit of 1) law and order; 2) welfare of the people; and 3) national interests in the global setting, leadership is important. The quality of leadership partly determines whether a government can achieve these goals or not. Thus, leadership and governance are intertwined in the dynamics of the polity.

The environment in which a leader finds himself can partly determine the skills he deploys or the styles he employs. A society with a history of inequity in the distribution of scarce but allocatable resources, may suddenly have a leader with transformational zeal. Such a leader may use radical strategies for effecting relative equalization policies. Thus, Nasser in Egypt in his early days; Mao Ze Dung in China (Beijing) especially during and immediately after the cultural revolution; the military leaders in Peru in the early days of land redistribution – are all examples of how environmental history determine the leadership styles. These leaders embarked on radical policies such as land redistribution.

Quite often, a country with a history of gross break down of law and order, political instability or threats of such, may see the emergence of an *intimidatory* leader. The intimidatory leader may have moved from a guardianship role of maintaining law and order to heavy reliance on the use of coercion to extract compliance. The Pol Pot regime in Cambodia, Mobutu Sese Seko in Zaire (now the Democratic Republic of the Congo), and Pinochet regime in Chile, are examples of this leadership styles.

Yet in some other societies or states, years of oppression, graft and indiscipline can lead to the emergence of a transformation leader, intent on effecting fundamental changes in the state. The Soviet and Cuban revolutions are examples of how the ecological setting can determine the nature or styles of leadership in a state. Often, when in power such leadership may change their styles depending on their perception of political and other exigencies. It is not unusual to see transformational leaders change into transactional leaders, and gradually drift into patriarchal leaders.

In complex societies of multinational states, the leadership skill required may not be mobilizational, but reconciliatory. Thus, Abubakar Tafawa Balewa and Yakubu Gowon of Nigeria, and Nelson Mandela of South Africa utilized reconciliation styles of leadership to cope with problems of ethnicity, religion, ethnoregionalism, race and class in their countries. *Madiba* Mandela still plays the role of a patriarchal leader in his country. Fidel Castro of Cuba has gradually moved from transformational, through transactional to patriarchal leadership.

Often, the use of particular styles of leadership would depend on the exigencies of the time. A good leader would know when to go mobilizational or reconciliatory, transformational or transactional.

Challenges of Governance for Nigerian Leaders in the Twenty-First Century

The Twenty-First Century poses many challenges of governance in the process of development. What is the setting of the Twenty-First Century?

The Challenges of the Twenty-First Century

The Twenty-First Century provides a complex setting with changes in means and/ or techniques of pursuing national interests. Increasingly the position of the nation-state is being severely threatened. *The technological revolution, which began after the World War II with its attendant communication revolution, has changed the face of the world, the fortunes of nation-states and the options available in nation-building.*

The 21st Century is marked by technological revolution, with its attendant communication revolution. There is the movement from cords to fibre optics; from micro-cards to microchips; mechanical time to aggressive commodity time. The global system has entered the age of the information superhighway where computer and communication technology; microchips and fibre optics are converging to promote computer-mediated networks. Integrated services and digital networks allow the transmission of even ultrasound scans for a more effective medical evaluation in better-equipped hospitals by specialists. When registered on internet, subscribers could use it for e-mail, file transfer, research and even advertising.[13] Computer pornography or cybersex has made a bang on an already sliding base of morality in many societies around the globe. May be, John Herz,[14] was correct to envisage in the 1950s the "demise of the nation-state".

The implication of all these, is that actors in the global system who possess these skills also have a headstart over those who do not. They can penetrate the boundaries of the nation-state and make a real mockery of the sovereignty of nations. Paradoxically, technological revolution has undermined the sovereignty of nations and violated the privacy of the individual and groups, at a point when the sovereignty of many African states is still very fragile.

The visual and air waves of the global system are now being ruled, by various satellite networks. They transmit programmes every second, across national boundaries, affecting or changing the values and culture of many people. The culture of violence transmitted across borders from a country like the United States has taken a toll on the values of sanctity of human life in Nigeria. Like everything else, man is becoming a commodity in the market place. From the *Coca-colonization* of the world, we have arrived at the *CNNization* and *Aljazeeranization* of the world. American values, politics, and business are being powerfully transmitted across nations. Western (especially American) values of 'democracy', human rights, sound market economy and life-style, are being disseminated around the globe as models. Yes, there is a successful attempt at the homogenization of the world from the perspective of the West. This enables them to even set conditions for international trade, membership of multilateral institutions such as the International Bank for Reconstruction and Development, otherwise known as the World Bank, and the International Monetary Fund. *Technological skills are giving new powers to the owners.* Aljazeera cable service seeks to challenge the domination and provide the world an alternative and powerful viewpoint to CNN.

Using the satellite technology, conferences involving various people from different countries can be organized without any of the participants meeting physically. We have also entered the age of hyper-speed economy where economic systems function at much faster speed than at any point in time in history. Economic transactions are now increasingly conducted without the money. We now have electronic banking. The Twenty-First Century is witnessing refinement of electronic money and "electronic banking-in-your-wallet which contain microchips allowing the user to check his or her bank balances, buy and sell shares, make airline reservations, and perform a variety of other tasks".[15] Currently telephone banking has added to the new technology of jet-speed economy. The use of paper money is likely to fade out and give way to the electronic money in the 21st Century. Transactions involving millions of dollars can now be conducted across boundaries through computer and communication networks. More time is being conquered and converted into money, and the ability of nations to do that increasingly, will determined their *power base* in the global system of the 21st Century.

Thus, of all the changes in the global system, technological revolution has been the most profound in its impact. Like a knife, modern technology can be used to save life as well as destroy it; beautify environment as much as pollute it; and improve the quality of life as well as to adulterate and dilute it. Technological revolution has impacts ranging from saving lives from within the doctor's operation theatre and intensive care units in the United States to the shreds of human lives and environment at Nagasaki and Hiroshima in Japan. Similarly, the same technological revolution which facilitates the building of a global hamlet through more sophisticated communication equipment has helped to alienate one human group from the other at times creating more opportunities for misunderstanding one another. Whoever says that the technological revolution we have witnessed, especially since the 1940s, is not a double-edged sword? The rate at which impoverished nations talk about and yearn for some forms of technology gives one the impression that their leaders are more fascinated by these items than they comprehend their functional utility.[16]

In addition to these *Globalization*, refers to the relative liberalization and homogenization of the globe as a result of the technological revolutions since 1940s. Global or world economy is being liberalized rapidly. There is a "widening and deepening of international flows of trade, finance and information, in a single global market."[17] The assumption is that the liberalization of national and global markets would enhance the free-flows of trade, finance and information, which would produce the best outcome for "growth and human welfare". Is this necessarily so?

> Similarly, added to these trends, which question the relevance of states, is an on-going paradox. While within the nation-state, there are explosions of cultural identities (ethnic, racial, religious and others) and self-determination, there is the serious challenge to national sovereignty as multinationals penetrate national boundaries and demonstrate little or no sensibility to local conditions or jurisdictions. Indeed, States seem to "have become too big for small things, and too small for the big".[18]

As the United Nations Development Programme (UNDP) report of 1997 observed, "Today's global integration is wiping away national borders and weakening national policies. A system of global policies is needed to make markets work for people, not people for markets".[19]

As the process of globalization renders national borders fragile, and exposes the inadequacy of individual states to cope with the challenges facing them, nation-states are becoming more insecure. The result is that there is a big shift from bilateral to multilateral diplomacy. This insecurity has led to the formation of supranational groups and organizations to find collective solutions to those challenges, which transcend the capability of individual states.

While the concept of development and *modes of development* are still under debate, certain challenges of political development had been identified by the *International Social Science Research Council*. Among such challenges of political development are four basic ones which all nations tend to experience. These are the challenges of: - 1) authority or State-building; 2) unity (nation-building); 3) participation; and 4) distribution[20].

The challenge of *authority or State-building* refers to the problem of the political centre penetrating or controlling the periphery to make its presence felt and to maximize its authority.[21] This is crucial given the fragility of authority in most developing countries.

The second challenge is one of *creating unity* among heterogeneous groups in the State. In a multinational State, such as Nigeria[22] it involves attempts at integrating the various groups in order to build a nation out of the state. This process is often referred to as Nation-building.

The challenge of *participation* highlights the extent to which people influence decision which affect their lives. The *identity explosion* all over the world has led to demands for greater participation in decision-making process, especially- in developing countries.

Finally, the challenge of *distribution* deals with the ability of a system to distribute scarce, but allocatable resources relatively equitably among various groups in a state. It has become a very salient indicator of the performance of most political system.[23]

If earlier developers such as Britain and the United States had the luxury of treating these challenges sequentially, African states found out that that technique had become a luxury. The technological revolution had not only created a smaller globe, thus denying these states the relative isolation within which to sequentially tackle these problems, but had made simultaneous solutions to these challenges a political imperative. Thus new leaders who took over the reins of government soon found their decision-making units overloaded with demands and expectations but with few capabilities and resources to meet them. The globalization process has further complicated these challenges for leaders of new states.

Often, governments were overthrown as a result of frustration with incumbents whose 'delivery of the goods' in an impatient political environment was rated very low. It was soon found that a change of government was only a cosmetic strategy for coping with problems of development that are more deep-rooted. Industrialized countries did not help matters by setting up high and difficult yardsticks for attainment by Africa's leaders— forgetting the sequentiality of their European history of development. African leaders have not yet realized that, simultaneity of crises of development create contradictions which need to be sorted out. As an illustration, while African leaders in Liberia and Burundi have problems centralizing authority, they are expected, in a democratic spirit, to offer avenues for participation. Historically, the process of centralization of authority was never a democratic process.

It is, therefore important to note that a new and important impact of technology has been the simultaneity of challenges of development for Africa. It had robbed Africa of the luxury that countries like Britain, for example, had to centralize authority before expanding participation, and turning to distribution and unity. The sense, therefore, is that Africa miserably lacks the luxury of sequential development and strives in throes of simultaneity of challenges of development. The import here is that of perspective, and the fact that the new milieu provides a wider and yet more difficult scope for dealing with development problems.

The Challenges of Governance

In this 21st Century context, there are many challenges of governance for our leaders. Currently, we all know that Nigeria's economy is still in bad shape; our infrastructure are dilapidated; our educational system is collapsing; our health sector is severely in pains; unemployment is soaring and helping to heighten our feeling of insecurity; and manufacturing sector has continued to experience closures inspite of our privatization process. There seems to be a greater *invasion* of our market by external forces than *investment*; our economy is monocultural; and *deregulation* and *privatization* policies are hardly neither transparent nor accountable. The average citizen is experiencing hardship while governments continue to boast about soaring contents of our foreign reserves.

The challenges of governance are even amply demonstrated by our inability to achieve the Millennium Development Goals (MDG), to which we have committed ourselves. These MDGs, projected to be achieved by 2015 include:

i)   eradication of extreme poverty;
ii) achievement of universal primary education;
iii) promotion of gender equality and empowerment of women;
iv) reduction of child mortality;
v)   combating HIV/AIDS, malaria and other diseases;

vi) ensuring environmental sustainability; and

vii) development of partnership for development

How have Nigerian leaders performed so far? We are all leaders—from the family, through schools, to our work places. For our purposes, we shall concentrate on political leaders at the federal or central level. Often these yardsticks are applicable at lower levels. We shall avoid going statistical in our analysis of leadership performance here.

Nigeria's Experience In Leadership

> Nigeria is a cast iron, which has to be gently anvil led and slowly bent to prevent the breaking or doing damage to the body-work, not to talk of the ever-present possibility of fatal damage to the ornamentor[24].

Nigeria has experienced both democratic and military leadership. It is our contention that there is a difference between the leadership styles of military officers serving as political leaders and civilian leaders operating in a democratic context. In Nigeria's 50 years, 30 years have been under military rule and only a chequered period of about 20 years can be referred to as a period under democratic rule.

Let us start with years of military rule.

Leadership Skills/Styles under Military Rule

Under military rule, "might is right" and as Jean-Jacques Rousseau once pointed out, in such situation, every might that is greater than the first succeeds to its rights. [25] This is why treason dares not prosper in military regimes, for if it does, none dare call it treason. [26] Military rule always derives its ultimate "authority" from the use or threat of the use of instruments of violence. Their cardinal concern, therefore, is the maintenance of law and order. Chaos threatens military rule.

As most military regimes find out after some time in office, the master is not always able to remain master unless he transforms might into right and obedience into duty. This is the political economy of power.

Claude Welch (Jnr) and Arthur Smith, identify three forms of leadership under military rule – *military guardianship, reformist or radical military-based regime.*[27]

The *guardian* role is when the military regime's major preoccupation is the maintenance of law and order – a greater concern with political stability than with effecting social changes. Very often this concern emanates from the general political climate the military inherited. Such a regime relies heavily on coercion. [28] The *reformist* military regime is concerned mainly with 'creating a national identity and promoting orderly economic development. [29] For such a regime, economic development and industrialization are highly functional to the achievement of national and military power. Very often reformist regimes are idealistic and their programmes are based on their military faith 'in problem-solving by command decision...' It is not unusual for successful reformist military regimes to drift gradually to a guardianship role as demands for greater participation makes them rely more on coercion.

Radical military regimes very often act as 'the linkage of interest between military officers, who are essentially of the middle and lower classes, and the masses, who previously had been unintegrated into national political life'.[30] Very often this sort of action requires a very high level of political consciousness which goads radical military regimes towards mobilization of the masses. The radical military must organize the masses towards the achievement of their goals. That is why very often it has to organize political parties for such purposes. Yet military values contradict the radicalism which facilitates its incursions into political arena. The military's antipathy for politics means that radical military regimes are very often short-lived. The military leader usually has charismatic qualities which must be routinized quickly to enable him perform. Such regimes have appeared in Libya, and briefly in Nasser's Egypt, Argentina, Iraq and Peru. The contradiction between military professionalism and sense of mission on the one hand, and the mass mobilizational structure, in the form of a revolutionally political platform, on the other, dilutes the radical contents of such regimes which then drift towards guardianship roles.[31] Libya's Gaddafi has been in power for over 40 years, and many observers claim that his erstwhile radical posture has gradually changed to one of a guardian leader.

It is our contention that Nigeria has never had radical military regime. We shall briefly look at military regimes to prove our point. Space prevents elaborate treatment. The Ironsi regime was obviously, neither reformist nor radical. It played a guardian role of restoring law and order and maintaining some level of political stability. Coming after the violence and the breakdown of law and order during Nigeria's First Republic, this was natural. His program announced on January 17, 1966 did not indicate that he was going to embark on any social and economic reforms. He was only going to establish structures for returning to civilian rule in 1969. The Decree No. 33 enforcing law and order and proscribing ethnic associations was not a reformist measure but an indication of guardianship role. The major reformist measure was decree No. 34 which would have changed the form of government. The communal and intra-military instability which followed this, were reflective of the resistance to the imposition of a unitary system of government, inspite of military rule.

Ironsi was a good military officer but a bad politician. Despite the military's self-delusion that it is possible to play

apolitical politics, Ironsi was a politician in uniform who was immobilized at the end, in part because of his lack of political sagacity and in part because of the socio-political circumstances in which he found himself.

The second military regime under General Yakubu Gowon started out like as a guardian regime. It was begotten in the throes of conflict and for a long time survived amidst crises. It was obviously more concerned about the restoration of law and order, and relative level of political stability. The period 1966-67 was one in which Gowon and his colleagues sought for an appropriate form of government to respond to Nigeria's problems which were grounded on mutual fears and suspicions of domination among various Nigerian groups.

However, by mid-1967, the regime had taken on the first direction of political reform with the creation of twelve states. The creation of states which opened the avenue for additional states later was a major step in political engineering and reform to which Nigerians can now attest. The numerous demands for more states were an indication of the impact of this exercise done at the peak of Nigeria's crises. The country was later hardened in the crucible of a bloody civil war after which it emerged as a single entity.

Gowon was a *military reformer*. He was also a *reconciliation* leader. He was not a radical nor could one detect radical pretensions in his actions. At the end of the civil war he announced a nine- point programme 'to guarantee peace, stability and progress in the country. . .'[32] These included (i) reorganization of the armed forces, (ii) the implementation of National Development Plan and repair the damage and neglect of the war, (iii) the eradication of corruption in our national life, (iv) the settlement of the question of the creation of additional states, (v) the preparation of the new constitution, (vi) the introduction of the new Revenue Allocation formula, (vii) conducting a national population census, (viii) the organization of genuinely national political parties and (ix) the organization of elections and installation of popularly elected government in the states and at the center.

Like military reformers Gowon was really idealistic. Some of his programs could never have been achieved in his life time. Nor could the repairs and neglect of the civil war be completed before 1976, his target date for quitting the stage. Similarly he underestimated the problems of the census exercise in Nigeria.

There was no doubt that Gowon did effect many changes in Nigeria. The numerous transport infrastructures in Nigeria – network of roads and airports – were initiated and started by his regime. Some of thisprograms were completed by his successors. The expansion in the number of universities also owed much to this regime. Similarly, other changes such as decimalization of currency, and the change to right-hand drive were to his credit. Thanks to petro-naira, Gowon had stored some foreign reserves for Nigeria (over two and half billion naira) which was later expended by his successors. He successfully completed the Second Development Plan, 1970-1975 which had laudable reformist objectives of building, (i) a united, strong and self-reliant nation,(ii) a great and dynamic economy, (iii) a just and egalitarian society,(iv) a land full of opportunity for all citizens, and

(v) a free and democratic society. He also initiated a Third National Development Plan, 1975-80.

From an armed forces battered in 1966, Gowon mobilized an army to fight a successful civil war and came out with an army better organized than he had inherited. He did not grapple with the issue of demobilization which became a difficult one to handle. His loss of contact with his military constituency in the period between 1973 and 1975 gradually eroded his credibility and his inability to continue the reconciliatory role of affecting a balance between military and civilian sectors of society, later led to his ouster.

Similarly, the conspicuous consumption of his lieutenants and the sheer display of arrogance of their power further eroded his credibility. Corruption in his regime was so pronounced that many doubted if he could even minimize the extent of corruption, not to mention the eradication of corruption. With the benefit of hindsight succeeding military regimes were even far more corrupt that the Gowon regime, thus making corruption under his regime a mole hill. Gowon was not seen as personally corrupt to most Nigerian observers. One of the greatest shockers and dilemmas from which Gowon hardly recovered was the extent of politicization of the 1973 census exercise. It influenced his decision on revenue allocation which, he announced in 1974, would no longer be a constitutional issue. The public outcries about corruption, the census exercise and apparent indecision on Gowon's part to respond to these, drove his regime from the reformist one to that of guardianship–relying increasingly more on coercion. Once he lost his capability as reconciliation leader with reformist objectives, and moved to a guardianship role, his regime drifted. Hence Gowon was subsequently gracefully eased out of the political arena.

His successor General Murtala Mohammed, was fiery and unconventional, but a dedicated soldier. Again, Murtala, like Gowon, was a *social reformer* and not a radical military ruler. It is our contention that any regime which came after Gowon would certainly grapple with certain problems which Gowon found insoluble and quietly tucked away under the *carpet*, waiting for the more conducive time for decision. The census issue, the reneging on the promise to return to civil rule, the creation of additional states, the widespread corruption among public officers and apparent inept handing of the Festival of Arts and Culture (FESTAC), are illustrations of these.

Using radical, clean-up and legitimizing technique of the new regime, Mohammed took actions on all these issues which nine years of political leadership had mollified Gowon from taking. The new break with an on-going drift gave the impression of radicalism. No doubt Mohammed was a man of action and did give the country a new sense of direction, but his programs were aimed at demilitarization of the political system rather than one of mass mobilization or for effecting social and economic changes in the society at large.

In his broadcast on October 1, 1975, General Murtala Mohammed announced a 'five stage programme designed to ensure smooth transition to civil rule by those elected by the people of this country.'[33] In the first stage the committee on the creation of additional states was to be set up, and to submit its report on December 1975. Preliminary steps towards establishing the new states were to be completed by April 1976. During this stage, also, a Constitution Drafting Committee was to be appointed and was expected to complete drafting a constitution in September 1976.

The second stage in the process of demilitarization of politics included the creation and establishment of the new states; the reorganization of Local Government throughout the country and the conduct of local government elections without party politics; and the establishment of Constituent Assembly (partly elected and partly appointed) based on the local government councils. This second stage which was to last two years, was expected to be completed by October 1976. This was the reformist stage of Murtala's programme.

The lift of the ban on political activities to enable the formation of political parties, constituted the third stage. The ban was to be lifted on October 1978. The fourth stage comprised elections into legislatures at state level as prescribed by the nation. And the fifth and final stage included elections to legislatures and offices at the federal level. These two last stages were to be completed by October 1, 1979. General Mohammed emphasized that his administration did 'not intend to stay in office a day longer than necessary, and certainly not beyond this date.' Thus the regime had no programmes for economic and social reforms. Worried about its institutional cohesion after the Gowon administration had refused to demilitarize, the new military regime worked out a clean package for disengagement.

In line with his promise, Murtala set up a panel on creation of states in August 1975. The report was submitted to him in December 1975 and he took a decisive action by creating seven additional states in February 1976. In reaction to widespread corruption he purged the civil service, giving it a real shock therapy. The implementation of the exercise could have been better handled. The public service is still recovering from the shock. In essence Murtala's was not a radical regime. It could have been reformist but never lived to demonstrate it. The states creation was certainly reformist. His early days in office were preoccupied with clearing legacies he had inherited. Perhaps the greatest problem of Murtala was that he used mobilization technique without mobilization structures such as parties, and others. In addition, he used mobilization technique in Nigeria which despite its pretensions is a reconciliatory system.

His successor General Olusegun Obasanjo might have given the impression that he was intellectually sound and cool headed, but he lacked charisma and leadership dynamism. His regime was colourless and banal. It was uneventful, except that he meticulously kept to his predecessor's programmes of action. His greatest achievement was the meticulous supervision of the military disengagement process from the political arena. It is our contention that given dissatisfaction under Obasanjo regime, the military would have been badly battered in the process of another coup. It is in the self-interest of the military as a cohesive institution (albeit, with some cracks on its wall) to have withdrawn quietly.

Obasanjo's was essentially a *guardian military regime*, it carefully relying on its coercive capabilities to ensure its exit in 1979. The regime could not be absolved from corruption. Given the relatively shorter period in office than the Gowon administration, the allegations of wrong doing were too difficult to be dismissed with a wave of the hand. Allegations of massive siphoning of public funds to private coffers went unattended. It was also a very insensitive regime; highly unresponsive to public outcries. It took the jumbo loans for which Nigerians had to pay for many years, without much evidence of the functional utility of the loans. But the regime did pave the way for democratic government for which Nigerians must be grateful. It was reliably understood from some of Obasanjo's friends and aides that he became lukewarm or reluctant about handing over power to civilians as the date drew nearer. He had to be pressured to accept the wisdom of the transition.

Major-General Muhammadu Buhari became the Head of State after the military coup which overthrew President Shehu Shagari in 1983. Disgusted with the level of indiscipline and patriotism in Nigeria, Buhari tried to instill a sense of discipline and purpose in the society. He launched the *War Against Indiscipline* (WAI) to carry out value re-orientation among Nigerians. In addition, the regime deprecated corruption under its predecessor government and tried politicians for their political 'sins' of corruption at various levels.

Buhari was a *guardian* military ruler who emphasized law and order, with a streak of intimidatory style. The long jail sentences for politicians, his decrees on public policy, and his reaction to freedom and democracy gave these impressions. His 20-month regime produced no political transition programme. It is therefore difficult to ascertain the kind of polity his regime wanted to bequeathe to Nigerians. A deeply religious man who is strong on principles, Buhari has been regarded by some observers as rigid. He has even been accused of being a regional or religious champion. His later stance in Nigerian politics shows that this impression is probably wrong. Essentially, Buhari could also be regarded as a *bureaucratic* leader who emphasized "efficiency rather than evocation". A combination of societal and intra-military factors led to his overthrow in August 1985.

General Ibrahim Badamasi Babangida succeeded General Buhari, in what was apparently a palace coup. Perhaps, more than any military leader, General Babangida understood the Nigerian polity and society. Like the Murtala's, he realized that a political programme was the life-line of his administration. The lack of political programme had tolled the death-knell of his predecessor's administration. It was thought that a transition programme, in part, provided a guarantee of survival for the military government. After all, who would be stupid enough to interrupt a programme for a transition to civil rule. The April 1990 abortive Orkar coup brutally challenged this assumption.

In his first populist action, General Babangida embarked on the liberalization of the polity by abolishing Decree No. 4, which had curtailed the liberty of the press. In addition, he threw the debate over IMF loan to the public domain. His first political transition action was the setting up of the *Political Bureau* to make recommendations on Nigeria's political future. On the basis of the Report, the Armed Forces Ruling Council issued a *White Paper*, which formed the basis of his political transition programme.

The transition programme which spanned the period 1987-1992 gave details of the various steps towards full democratization, from local government to the federal centre. As part of this transition programme, which was to be "a learning process", Babangida established many institutions, which changed the political landscape. Illustrations of these include the Directorate for Social Mobilization (otherwise called MAMSER); the National Electoral Commission; the National Population Commission; the Code of Conduct Bureau, and Tribunal; the National Revenue Mobilization, Allocation and Fiscal Commission, and a number of other agencies which are still functional in the political arena.

His Structural Adjustment Programme (SAP) was criticized for its impact on the people, even if it was seen to have had some macro-economic advantage, which the people did not immediately feel. His government successfully carried out a census exercise in 1991.

However, his transition programme ran into trouble by 1991. A number of adjustments had to be made to the programme. While elections were successfully held at local and state levels, the elections into the Presidency were fraught with problems. Although the National Assembly was in place, it had no job because there was no elected President. The June 12, 1993 election was annulled because of societal and intra-military factors, leading to the establishment of an Interim National Government (ING) under Chief Ernest Shonekan.

General Babangida was a *reformist* military ruler, who used a combination of reconciliation and mobilizational styles of leadership to carry out his policies over the eight-year period. His charm and charisma are traits of a mobilizational leader. He probably lasted long in power because of his ability in reconciliation and mobilizational skills, as circumstances dictated. In certain circumstances some analysts have described IBB as a transactional leader, in view of his use of the carrot and stick' tactics to achieve his ends. This led to his nickname as 'Maradona'—a dribbler in the Nigerian political terrain. His inability to continue to efficiently balance his military and civilian constituencies, led to his stepping 'aside' from office in 1993.

While Babangida had boasted that his would be the last military regime (because he had hoped that his transition programme would have had such impact), the ING was overthrown by General Sani Abacha in about three months.

General Sani Abacha was the Defence Minister under Shonekan's ING. Between 1993 and 1994, General Abacha essentially played a *guardianship* role. He embarked on political reforms and established his own transitional programme, his leadership style became more coercive or *intimidatory*. A reticent and courageous officer, General Abacha created six states and additional local governments in 1996. His transitional programme saw the emergence of five major political parties, which were in the process of adopting him as their 'consensus candidate'. As the Abacha regime executed its political transition programme, the more intimidatory he became. General Abacha enjoyed being Head of State, but did not enjoy governing. He spent less time in office and on the affairs of government. This gave his aides the opportunity to carry out many illegal and heinous activities in the society. General Abacha probably did not know much about many cases of detention and killings. In fact, it is alleged that knowing his weakness, his aides executed some of the bomb blasts to create a feeling of insecurity for General Abacha. The more insecure he was, the greater the leverage of the aides, or at least as they were alleged to have believed.

Thus, General Abacha came across rightly or wrongly as Nigeria's *intimidatory* military ruler. However, Abacha's management of the economy and attempts at rehabilitating infrastructure and social services especially through the Petroleum Task Force (PTF), gives some reformist taint to his regime. No Nigerian leader seemed to have had such a firm grip of Nigeria under the shadow of the threat/or actual use of violence. His natural exit in June 1998, therefore, led to so many changes in the Nigerian polity.

General Abdulsalami Abuabakar, who succeeded him, made no pretensions towards being a radical or reformist leader. He was essentially a military *guardian* who used reconciliatory style of leadership to usher in a transition from military to civil rule. His position was similar to Obasanjo's after the death of Murtala in 1976. However, while Obasanjo inherited a transition programme, Abubakar had to embark on his on transition programme. His 10-month transition programme ushered in a new 'democratic' polity on May 29, 1999, with the emergence of General Olusegun Obasanjo as new President.

Essentially, the military came into politics with a messianic and idealistic fervor— to cleanse the polity of all its political 'dirt' or 'sin' and withdraw to the barracks. Often, as they found out, the military in politics is a paradox of political rectitude versus the politics of poverty; institutional political hygiene versus the dilution of professionalism; and the transformation of the political physician to a political patient suffering from an overdose of the ailment they had set out to cure.

On balance, it is unfair to blame the military leadership for all of the country's problems. We are all collectively responsible. The military has been part of Nigeria's problems but it has also been part of their solutions. The military fought and kept Nigeria as a single country. Our ability to create a sustainable democratic polity, capable of tackling the challenges of development, will determine the future.

Let us look at the civilian leadership.

The Leadership Skills/Styles of Civilian Leaders

Unlike military regimes, most of the civilian regimes in Nigeria were supposed to be *democratic.* A democratic polity, with its checks and balances, requires different kinds of leadership skills/styles. The setting is usually different.

Democracy

For our purposes, it is possible to identify some of the salient characteristics of democracy. Among these characteristics is the locus of *authority* in a democratic polity. Authority emanates from the people. Any authority that does not emerge from the consent of the people is not democratic. How consent is operationalised may vary from one system to the other. Secondly, a democratic polity must be based on the *rule of law.* Law cannot be arbitrary in a democracy. There are specified limits to power and how it can be used. In addition, there should be an acceptance of the "rules of the game" of politics by all the players, if arbitrariness is not to creep in at a later stage.

The third characteristic of a democratic polity is that it must be *legitimate.* For our purpose, legitimacy involves two processes. One of these is that the leader has the *right to rule* – that is to say – that given the law of the rules for accession to power he is the right person to be there. The institutional mechanism for this accession to power would depend on the particular country and people. The other is that he is *ruling rightly.* This is to say that he is performing well, given the ends for which he has been elected or chosen. He must be bound in his action by constitutional pressures.

In addition to these, is the fourth, the element of *choice.* The people should have the right to effect changes in the leadership or the government of their country, given available alternate leadership. In some countries the plebiscetarian system is used. In some others, other mechanisms for providing choice are used. Choice also includes all basic human freedoms— of thought, movement, association, worship, and others in relative terms. Fifthly, there must be *accountability.* Leaders must be held responsible for their actions as representatives of the people who are trusted with power to achieve particular ends and must so account for such actions periodically.

These five principles may be seen as the minimum characteristics of democracy. However, the institutional framework for their operation may differ from one country to the other.

In a democratic polity, leaders are products of popular choice by the people. Often, there are checks and balances on their authority. Unlike military regimes, the assumption of executive and legislative authority by the incumbent leader or the Commander-in-Chief, is unacceptable. The emphasis on the rule of law means that even the Head of State is subject to the laws of the state. This is Western democracy as inherited by Nigeria.

Unlike military rule, democratic polities emphasize the opportunity for the people, who are the repositories of power, to effect changes in the leadership, if they so feel. The leadership must also periodically account for its stewardship and the trust bestowed on it by the people. In a military regime, the leaders are responsible to the military constituency which keeps the leadership in power.

Thus, it is not surprising that Nigeria's first executive President, Alhaji Shehu Shagari complained about the legislature immobilizing the executive in the Second Republic. Similarly, the experience of General Olusegun Obasanjo with the legislature, civic groups, including the Nigeria Labour Congress (NLC) is a far cry from his experience as a military leader. The *supremacy of the constitution* (rather than the supremacy of the *incumbent ruler*) is the cardinal element of democratic politics.

For democratic leaders, *bargaining, negotiation* and *compromises* are the very essentials of the stability of the polity. Responsiveness and effective constituency relations are important to leaders, as they collate feedbacks. Similarly, the role of political parties in mobilization, aggregation and articulation of interests, is more a collective and reconciliatory effort than under military regime.

Yet, leadership skills in a federal multinational state can be daunting.

Leadership in a Federal State

For our purposes, a *polyethnic state* refers to a state which has many small ethnic groups, none of which lays claims to subnational autonomy enough to challenge the autonomy of the center by asserting its subnational self-determination. No ethnic group in such state regards itself as a nation. Thus, Tanzania, Senegal, The Gambia, Guinea (Conakry), and the Congo (Brazzaville)— illustrate polyethnic states in Africa.

On the other hand, a *multinational state* comprises ethnic groups who not only vary in size but also in the distribution of power, influence, and resources. Such a state is marked by aggressive ethnic nationalism as various groups push for the realization of their subnational self-determination. Often their demands for subnational self-determination directly challenge the centre's demands for national self-determination: Nigeria (Ibo, Yoruba, and Hausa); Zaire (the Kongo, the Mongo, Luba and Kivu ethnic types); Ethiopia (the Galla and Tigre types); The Chad (the Arab and Sudanic types); and The Sudan (Arab and the various Southern clusters) – illustrate multinational states in Africa. It is our contention that problems of integration and leadership are less intractable in polyethnic state than in multinational states. Both systems may call for different structures for the distribution of powers in the state, and for styles of leadership in responding to their peculiar problems.

In polyethnic states, the tasks of integration and state-building are not as daunting as in multinational states. Most polyethnic states adopt unitary systems of government. In some multinational states, such as the United States of America, Canada, Nigeria, old Soviet Union and Brazil, *federalism* is adopted as a technique for managing conflicts.

The very nature of federal compromise means that there is always a constant adjustment of the political pendulum between centripetal and centrifugal forces in the system, at any given point in time. Therefore it is not unusual in the system to find the pendulum swing in favour of subnational units (or centrifugal forces) at another point in time. The degree to which a delicate and appropriate balance can be struck between centripetal and centrifugal forces is usually related to the skill of the national leadership in social management.

What is the relationship between leadership and federalism? For our purpose here, the leadership of the federal State refers to the actors at the centre.

If federalism involves adjustment and compromises, it requires a leadership that is committed to ensuring a delicate balance which protects the identity of all subnational groups while maintaining an effective political umbrella over all, thus symbolizing national self-determination. On the other hand, if centrifugal forces are not to be allowed to lead the nation into disintegration, such national leadership must always reassess the issues of compromises, the nature of compromises and how adjustments can be effectively made without threatening the consensual basis of the society.

What kind of national leadership does a federal system such as Nigeria's require? It requires a leadership that is acceptable to the majority of the members of the state as having the 'right to rule' that is legitimate. In its performance, it must visibly demonstrate fairness and justice to all communities, and generate a sense of inclusiveness or belonging to the political community, rather than foster a sense of alienation or exclusivity.

The political leader must have the charisma and the skills of a reconciliation leader, as he deftly reconciles various demands and interests, strikes a delicate balance between centrifugal and centripetal forces, and mobilizes followers into positive actions in order to achieve the ends of the state. Such a political leader must have many and differing attractions to varying groups. Various groups should have various reasons for identifying with him/her and his/her cause, and these would also be embellished by his charisma.

This leader must, like the leader of any state, exhibit minimum number of human personal weaknesses. As an illustration, *he cannot, in a complex society, be a religious fanatic, and ethnic champion, geo-ethnic 'nationalist', a nepotist or a self-opinionated bigot. His personal standards of incorruptibility must be unquestionable. In other words, the ideal leader must exhibit integrity, dedication, magnanimity, (and fairness), openness and creativity.* These are traits which a good leader needs to have - in unitary or federal state.

Nigeria's political setting imposes "social limits to politically-induced change" [34] from the centre. The national mobilizational leader, utilizing hierarchical authority structure of organization to penetrate the periphery is not appropriate for a federal polity. He must be a reconciliation leader who, in recognition of social pluralism, *mediates, integrates and coordinates, rather than organizes and mobilizes.* [35] The leader relies "for his effectiveness on qualities of tactical accommodation and a capacity to discover areas of compromise between otherwise antagonistic viewpoints."[36] He must operate within a pyramidal structure, but he needs not necessarily be a weak leader. Such a leader must constantly bear in mind the basic reasons for the adoption of a federal system.

He does not deny or repress conflict, but sees it as an opportunity or challenge. For "once everyone has come to see it that way, they can exchange their combative posture for creative stance, because they don't feel threatened, they feel challenged".[37]

Civilian Leaders

We shall use Heads of the Federal Government as our illustrations of civilian leadership. The First Republic was a parliamentary form of government with a split executive. The President, Dr. Nnamdi Azikiwe was a ceremonial President from October 1, 1963 to January 15, 1966. The Head of Government was Sir Abubakar Tafawa Balewa, the Prime Minister.

As a politician, Azikiwe was a pragmatic actor who was very cautious about when to fight, to withdraw, and to strike compromises. As President of the Senate and later President of the country, Azikiwe tried to give an image of a national leader. This image was almost entrapped in the electoral crises of 1964. He hearkened to advice against his wishes, to call Sir Abubakar Tafawa Belewa, of the Northern Peoples' Congress (NPC) to form a government in January 1965. It will not be fair to evaluate Azikiwe either as a transactional or transformational leader, since he was not a Head of Government.

Sir Abubakar Tafawa Belewa, was acclaimed as the 'golden voice of Africa', given his reputation as a broadcaster. An amiable, gentle but strong-willed politician, he was very conscious of constitutional provisions and the complex nature of the Nigerian federation. He had good relations with even opposition politicians, and was nationalistic in his outlook. Unfortunately, he was the deputy leader of his political party, and was therefore, not always in charge of his party position on national affairs.

Abubakar was essentially a *transactional leader*. He tried to keep the country together in the context of three and later four powerful regions, in a federation in which the "regional tails" wagged the "federal dog". His reconciliation skills delicately managed to keep Nigeria together in those days of dual federalism. A reconciliation leader, he realized that there were limits to socially induced changes from the center. Thus, when the North rejected Israeli scholarships, he allowed the Eastern and Western regions which had accepted it to utilize them.

Most of his political colleagues (whom one had interviewed), agreed that he was a *reconciliation* leader. An abstemious and contented leader, he was not corrupt, and barely had any property beyond his personal home in Bauchi. He died a poor but dignified man. The Nzeogwu coupists had referred to the corruption of politicians in the First Republic, as one of the reasons for the coup. With the benefit of hindsight, politicians of that Republic may be regarded as 'saints' today, given how monstrously corruption has grown in Nigeria.

Alhaji Shehu Shagari, succeeded General O. Obasanjo as the first Executive President of Nigeria. A humble man with unassuming disposition, Shagari believed in the supremacy of the constitution.[38] While some observers saw him as a weak President, it seems that one often forgets the circumstances of his administration. His political party had only a slim majority in the National Assembly in which the Unity Party of Nigeria (UPN), the Great Nigeria Peoples Party (GNPP), the Peoples' Redemption Party (PRP) and the Nigerian Peoples' Party (NPP) also had sizable representations. Shagari had to be cautious in order to carry the National Assembly along. His initial attempt to form a broad-based national government of all political parties failed.

In addition, as Shehu Shagari later complained, he was virtually immobilized by the National Assembly on many occasions.[39] However, many Nigerians believed that there was too much of a mixture of Tafawa Balewa's weakness and Gowon's over-consideration of the feelings of others in Shagari's character for decisive presidential action in policy making and implementation. For Shagari, however, it was more important to be constitutional in his actions, than to be crude and apparently decisive. This situation became clearer later when Obasanjo became an Executive President, with little regard for the rule of law. However, many Nigerians were worried about some members of his Presidential entourage who were apparently more interested in acquisition for the self than in the service of the nation. Shagari and

Ekwueme (his deputy) were both cleared of allegations of corruption by a military tribunal, after they had left office.

> Shagari was sensitive to intergovernmental relations in the federation, and respected the autonomy of states even when there were differences. Some states took the Federal Government to court on the 1981 Revenue Allocation Formula and River Basin Development Authorities.[40]

On balance, Shagari was a *reconciliation* leader who operated a complex federation in a democratic context. He attempted to be transformational, but these did not catch on. His crusades on the *Green Revolution* and *Ethical Revolution,* laudable as they were, did not make much impact on the populace. His housing programme, popular as they were, remained uncompleted in many states, before he left office. Some of these have been allocated to people in different states. Shagari was essentially *transactional leader* who used *reconciliation* techniques to deal with the complexities of the Nigerian policy. His inability to balance delicately the demands of the ballot box and the barracks, partly led to his ouster in 1983, after the post-reelection squabbles of that year.

Chief Ernest Shonekan, a quiet and unassuming gentleman, found himself thrust with national leadership, with Babangida's decision to step aside in August 1993. Chief Shonekan's role was essentially to restore confidence in the electoral system, after the annulment of the June 12, 1993 election. His government was to organize new elections and hand over to a popularly elected Nigerian.

Chief Shonekan was doing his best possible in the circumstances. Unfortunately his efforts were attenuated by Sani Abacha's military coup of November 17, 1993. He spent barely three months in office before he was overthrown because of a combination of intra-military and societal sources of military intervention in politics.

Chief Shonekan was to use his *reconciliation* skills to make another national election acceptable to Nigerians in order to produce a new leader. His was a *care-taker government* which was immobilized and ousted before he could carry out his role.

General Olusegun Obasanjo was imprisoned by the Abacha regime. The Abubakar regime released him, pardoned him, and influenced his being the Presidential candidate of the Peoples' Democratic Party (PDP). He was elected as President and sworn in on May 29, 1999. In his inauguration, he made anti-corruption crusade the main plank of his regime. Nigeria witnessed the return of General Olusegun Obasanjo as a civilian leader. If Obasanjo had been a *guardian* military leader, were his eight years in office as a civilian President a reflection of a social reformer or a transformational leader? Was Obasanjo a reconciliation leader?

Nigerians had high hopes that the new President was going to turn Nigeria around and effect fundamental changes. After all, he had promised that governance was not going to be "business as usual". After May 29, 1999, Obasanjo tried to launder Nigerians image and attract investments. Nigeria heaved a sigh of relief as they experienced greater freedom of speech, thought, worship, movement and association. Political parties operated freely, albeit, amidst a high dosage of intrigues. For a while the queues at the petrol stations vanished, only to reappear two years later. Government introduced its deregulation and privatization programmes and promised to encourage foreign investment and tourism. The military went back to the barracks, with new programmes for reprofessionalization. The boundaries between the barracks and ballot box became more distinct.

After four and half years, the Federal Government introduced its economic blue print— the *National Economic Empowerment and Development Strategy* (NEEDS), which was praised by the World Bank and Western countries because the programmes were perceived to be in accordance with their basic liberal economic principles. Obasanjo's regime managed to secure debt relief for Nigeria (even though some people have argued that much of that loan was gotten and wasted by his military regime). Nigeria made a long-trek from her erstwhile *pariah* status. Nigeria remains a sub-regional power and continues to serve at peace missions abroad. On balance, the Obasanjo regime did quite much between 1999 and 2007. Did these make him a transformational leader?

Obasanjo's second coming in *mufti* could be described as a blessing and yet a disaster. We have just listed some of the blessings. There is the other side to the Obasanjo story. The most visible were his exhibition of *messianic arrogance and residual militarism.* He exhibited a big and fragile ego, with claims of encyclopaedic knowledge. He therefore found it difficult to take advice. In the democratic polity, he profusely recorded *democratic deficit.* The violation of numerous court orders illustrates this. President Obasanjo did not believe in the existence of the legislature as a check on his powers. He manipulated the leadership of the Senate and influenced a rapid turn-over of its leadership. Obasanjo's relation with the judiciary was also terse.

As a leader, he was insensitive to Nigeria as a reconciliation system. If the old Obasanjo had thought that Nigeria was an anvil which could do damage to the ornamentor, the new Obasanjo believed in constantly overheating the polity with controversial statements and decisions in order to bend the hot iron. Hardworking as he seemed to be, his energies seemed to be scoundrelously dissipated in pursuing perceived enemies, and grafting himself sturdily in the polity. His attempt to amend the constitution to get a third term in office was one of such adventures.

Obasanjo operated as a 'military' leader in *mufti.* He was not a democrat. He treated State Governors as his prefects, and hardly encouraged desirable intergovernmental relations among tiers of government of the federation.

His anti-corruption crusade became hollow by the time he left office. Agencies of anti-corruption crusade, such as the *Economic and Financial Crime Commission (EFCC)* were used to pursue his enemies. The quarrel with his Vice-President exposed the corrupt side of Obasanjo, as cheque copies made for personal and political purposes littered the pages of newspapers. There have been various calls for him to be probed since he left office.

Perhaps Obasanjo's worst legacy was in the electoral process which he copiously adulterated, bastardized and prostituted, with glee. The 2003 and 2007 elections were seriously and variously flawed. He even appropriated his party (the PDP) and called the 2007 election a "do-or-die" affair. He personalized disagreements with other arms of government, and demeaned the office of the Presidency by his statements and actions.

By the time of his exit, Nigeria was still experiencing darkness inspite of the billions of naira allegedly spent on the power sector. The roads were in a total state of disrepair as illustrated by the shameful case of Benin-Lagos road; the railways had stopped functioning. The Nigerian telecommunications (NITEL) had collapsed and had been sold out to Transcorp. Yet Nigeria was looking for investment when its infrastructure was in disrepair. The educational system was in decay and the health sector was severely in pains. His economic reforms seemed to have been more 'deforms' in their impact. Later on a visit to Jigawa State after leaving office, Obasanjo rationalized his failure in the area of infrastructure. He claimed that Nigerians had elected him to unite the country and not to develop infrastructure. Unfortunately the country remained even as divided when he left office, as when he came in.

Perhaps, Obasanjo's second coming was anti-climax. His image as leader would have been better preserved if he had left office in 2003. Obasanjo's was an avidly *transactional* regime which motivated 'followers by exchanging with them rewards for services rendered'. Unfortunately he resorted to using *intimidatory* techniques in a *democratic* and *reconciliation* federal system. It is hoped that history will be kinder to him than Nigerians seem to be.

Out of the flawed election, emerged Alhaji Umaru Musa Yar'adua as the new President. Alhaji Atiku Abubakar of the Action Congress (AC), and Gen. Buhari, the All Nigeria Peoples' Party (ANPP) candidate, went to the court over Yar'adua's declared victory. After his emergence, like Murtala Mohammed, he tried to deal with knotty issues of inheritance from the predecessor regime. His first act or action was to deal with the booby traps set for him by the Obasanjo regime. His first task was to deal with pump price of petrol which had been raised by Obasanjo on the eve of his departure from N65 to N75 per litre. He also had to revert VAT to its 5% status instead of 10%, as had been raised by Obasanjo on the eve of his exit.

Perhaps, the most annoying to Nigerians was the sale of Port Harcourt and Kaduna refineries by the Obasanjo regime. These, Yar'adua also reversed. Yar'adua's mark is in the area of the *rule of law*. Conscious of the deficit in this area by his predecessor, he vowed to obey court orders and had so demonstrated. As an example, he returned to Lagos state the Local Government funds intercepted by

Obasanjo, inspite of Supreme Court orders. Unlike his party (PDP), Yar'adua had accepted that the 2007 elections were flawed, even though he believed he would still have won, without these. He therefore, set up an *Electoral Reform Committee* under Justice Mohammed Uwais to make recommendations for comprehensive reforms in that area. Yar'adua also sent some bills to the National Assembly on the electoral reforms, even though many Nigerians were not satisfied with them and some of these bills were thrown out by the Senate. Some of these bills were thrown out partly for reasons of poor drafting. Many Nigerians believe that the hawks of the Peoples Democratic Party (PDP) would not allow for any meaningful electoral reforms to take place before 2011 elections. Yar'adua believed in the grafting of democratic institutions in the Nigerian political soil. While many Nigerians had felt he would rule under the shadow of Obasanjo who made him President, Yar'adua demonstrated remarkable independence in his actions.

Yar'adua, as a former Governor, respected the autonomy of states and encouraged intergovernmental relations. His collaboration with the Governor of Lagos State (from a different party) on the development of Lagos as a megacity, was an indication of the new trend of intergovernmental relations in the Nigerian federation.

Yar'adua was a decent, amiable gentleman, a transactional leader with reformist zeal who was committed to Nigeria's democracy. His electoral reforms would have propelled him to the level of a reformist. Unfortunately ill-health and ultimately the pangs of death did not give him the chance to prove himself. But his amnesty deal with Niger-Delta militants was a reformist move, which he did not live to conclude. Yar'adua died in office on May 5, 2010.

What are the main challenges for the Nigerian leader today?

Challenges of Nigerian Leadership

Our fourth suggestion is that the challenges of the 21st Century are enormous. Therefore, our leaders must develop new visions and new strategies; must summon new forms of determination and political will; and demonstrate higher levels of patriotism, hardwork, selflessness, and responsiveness to the yearnings of the people, in order to deal with the challenges facing them.

In governance, the leadership must have a collective vision of the future or its goal, and the path to the achievement of these goals. It must always carry the people along. In the Nigerian context, given the challenges enumerated earlier, the leadership must:

1. develop the *capabilities for societal transformation,* and *reconciliation* of different groups in the State. The challenges are higher in the multinational States such as Nigeria in which such a leader must reconcile the demands of various ethnic groups, build bridges across religions and gender, and establish a legitimate basis for new forms of nationalism;

2. maintain *law and order, protect lives and property* of all citizens, without becoming autocratic. There can hardly be development without political stability or relative peace;

3. increase the *productive capability* of the state, while establishing modalities for a *relatively equitable distribution of scarce but allocatable resources* and statuses;

4. have *clear and effective programme for poverty eradication* – must tackle rural poverty and urban unemployment;

5. *aggressively embark on social development* - the educational and health sector are probably the most important foundations for development in other sectors. In addition, it is necessary to arrest the current "brain drain" or is it "brain hemorrhage", through deliberate government policies. We need these skills in the country and should not drive away our best brains because of political intolerance or ineptitude.

6. *establish and maintain infrastructure* such as roads, rails, and airports, as well as power or energy necessary for industrial development.

7. be *transparent and accountable.* Leadership must account for the democratic mandate given to it. It must not only be transparent in its actions but must be accountable. The personalization of national assets and the blatant corruption or rent-seeking

behavior of some leaders must be checked to enable the people, (not only the leaders), benefit from these resources.

Specifically, our leaders must take a number of urgent actions to prepare us for the great tasks ahead. In addition to the issues raised above, there are five other cross-cutting issues about leadership we must deal with immediately.

First, *decentralization of authority* is important, because it involves the devolution of powers to lower levels to carry out policies which affect their lives. The European policy of subsidiarity is important, if the people are to be carried along in the development crusade. The concept of subsidiarity emphasizes that the closest and the most effective level of government in the delivery of services should be given the relevant functions to execute.

Second, the *democratic polity must be stabilized,* while democratic culture is imbibed. Authority must emanate from the people through free and fair elections; the rule of law must prevail; the people must have the choice to select or elect their representatives; and such representatives or leaders must be accountable and transparent in their actions. The essence of *legitimacy* is also very important. Not only must the leader have the *right to rule,* he/she must *rule rightly.* The people as the repositories of power, must be the ultimate judge of this. Political parties, interest and pressure groups, civil society organizations (CSOs) must be allowed to operate relatively freely in the polity.

Third, leaders must *build the institutional capacity to manage development,* because such capacity in the executive, the judiciary, and the legislature; the political parties, CSOs, and others - are important for development.

Fourth, Nigerian leaders must *invest more funds in developing human "infrastructure",* than in grandiose projects. While investments in *education, health, and water* may not be as visible as a big viable structure in the capital city, these are the areas of strength of the country.

Fifth, the *recruitment of political leaders through political parties and the electoral process must be democratic, free and fair.*

What kind of leaders does Nigeria need now?

Prospects

We have tried to come back from the brink. We can still turn things around. We have made appreciable gains and Nigerians should be honest enough to accept this. But we can still do much better because we have leaders in different sectors of the society who can launch us powerfully into the 21st Century. We need more of the few that have demonstrably distinguished themselves.

Unfortunately, the younger generation seems to be engrossed with materialism without being commensurately productive. They do not value the dignity of labour. It does seem that members of my generation are condemned to taking care of their parents and yet fending for their adult offsprings. As parents, we have also failed our successor generations. The avarice, greed, crass materialism and corruption of our generation is a bad learning experience for the younger ones. We even encourage them to embark on the wrong route to self-development, such as buying exam results and other forms of examination malpractices.

For those of us who had/have been in position of leadership in the public, we have failed to build on the good foundations we inherited from our founding fathers. We have thus deprived the generations after us of the comfort and pride of being citizens of a great Nigeria.

I believe anybody above fifty (in 2010) has an experience to share on how he or she benefitted from relatively free and qualitative education that was provided by our past political leaders; the discipline and selflessness they displayed for us to emulate; the friendliness they preached; the hardwork and the dignity of labour they cherished and tried to inculcate in us; the humility they treated us with in the belief that we shall be better than them. But here we are. We did not live up to the expectations of the past generation and we are failing to meet the aspirations of the future generations.

Yet, we believe that it is not too late to turn things around. Nigerians need leaders who:

a. *listen* and are *sensitive* to the people's plight;

b. *accommodate* differing viewpoints and do not exhibit messianic arrogance and residual militarism;

c. are *just* to all groups, and are not nepotistic, especially in appointments to state statuses;

d. *do not use the instruments of state power* to persecute political opponents, but behave as genuine statesmen in a State House;

e. are *fair to all* in the sharing of scarce but allocatable resources, and do not favour their geopolitical zone at the expense of others;

f. have the *humility* to *accept superior views* and do not allow their egos to becloud their judgement on national matters;

g. are *religiously* tolerant and genuinely God-fearing in their speeches and actions; must be *transparent;* and

h. *predictable* in their public actions; and eschew demonstrable political hypocrisy; and

i. must be concerned, all the times, about the *welfare* of the people.

Conclusions

Leadership is a very important variable in the transformation of the Nigerian society. We need such transformation to avoid Nigeria being de-linked from the global train of the 21st Century. This country is abundantly blessed by God. Our leaders must mobilize all citizens to take appropriate place in the 21st Century. Yet, there can be no leadership without followership. It is the followership, which makes leaders. As the saying goes, a society gets the leaders it deserves.

Here, we have argued that leadership is very important in the dynamics of governance in all nation-states, including Nigeria. We tried to show that the challenges of development in Nigeria, as in many African countries, are multivariable in causation and multi-dimensional in nature. In addition, we tried to briefly delineate Nigeria's experiences in military and civilian 'democratic' leadership and the differences in skills and styles of leadership.

It is our contention that Nigerians and their leaders must develop new visions and new strategies; must summon new forms of determination and political will; and demonstrate higher levels of patriotism, hardworks, selflessness, and responsiveness to the yearnings of the people, in order to deal with the challenges facing them.

Our final argument is that while anxieties and agonies over our currently fluid setting tend to give an impression of dark clouds in the horizon, there are rays of hope in the Nigerian tunnel of development, as we resolve to take our destiny in our hand.

We must not play the whining children drowned in the vortex of self-pity. We must not play the role of professional 'grumbletonians' — grumbling about everything but doing nothing. The challenges mentioned above are challenges for all Nigerians. We are leaders at different levels, starting from the family level.

Our leaders must be more patriotic, hardworking, and selfless. Candidly, we are the only ones responsible for cleaning our stables; to do that we must, in order that we can walk hand-in-hand with other nations as we seek to improve the quality of our lives as a people. Our past experiences, have shown that old paths must be abandoned and new ones found, and old traits and values must be reassessed and some discarded, while new ones are imbibed. Nigeria has a bright future if its citizens decide to work to achieve that dream.

What are the challenges of nation-building for national leaders? This is our next focus.

NOTES

1. The literatures on leadership are now so many that one can compile a book of bibliography on it. See interesting discussions in the following – Berneard M. Bass, *Leadership and Performance Beyond Expectations.* (New York: Free Press, 1985); John P. Kotter, *The Leadership Factor* (New York: Free Press, 1988). Jay Alden Conger, *The Charismatic Leadership: Behind the Mystique of Exceptional Leadership* (San Francisco: Jossy-Bass Publishers, 1989); E. Rosenbach and Robert L. Taylor (eds) *Contemporary Issues in Leadership* (Boulder: Westview Press, 1989); Manfred F.R. Kets de Vries, *Prisoners of Leadership* (New York: Wiley,

1989); Warren G. Bennis, *Why Leaders Can't Lead: The Unconscious Conspiracy Continues* (San Francisco: Jossy-Bass Publishers, 1989).

2. Eisenhower in A. Larson, *The President Nobody Knew* (New York; Popular Library, 1968) quoted in Bass, *op.cit*, p.17.

3. H. S. Truman, *Memoirs* (New York: Doubleday, 1958), quoted in Bass *op.cit* p. 17.

4. Warren Bennis, *Why Leaders Can't Lead, op.cit* p.154.

5. *The Hammond International Dictionary* (New Jersey: Hammond, 1964), p.731

6. See interesting discussions in Donald Morrison, Robert Mitchell, John Paden and Hugh Stevenson (eds.) *Black Africa: A Comparative Handbook* (New York: The Free Press, 1972). Also see D. Morrison and H. Stevenson, "Integration and Instability: Patterns of African Political Development", *American Political Science Review*, LXVI, no.3, September, 1972. This role of the military is in Western liberal model of civil-military relations.

7. David Apter, *The Politics of Modernization* (Chicago: University of Chicago press, 1965), pp. 359-421.

8. Ali Mazrui, *Soldiers and Kinsmen in Uganda: The Making of a Military Ethnocracy* (Beverly Hills, California: Sage, 1977), p. 7.

9. *Ibid.*, p. 8.

10. Bennis, *op. cit*, p. 158.

11. Bass: *op. cit*, p. 11.

12. *Ibid* p. 17 – Bass contends – that "To achieve follower performance beyond ordinary limits, leadership must be transformational. Followers altitudes, beliefs, motives and confidence need to be transformed from a lower to higher plane of arousal and maturity" (p. xiii).

13. Michael Batty and Bob Barr. "The Electronic Frontier: Exploring and Mapping Cyberspace" in *Future*, 26 (7), pp. 699-712.

14. John Herz, *International Politics in the Atomic Age*, (1969); and "The Territorial State Revisited: Reflections on the Future of the Nation-State" in James N. Rosenau, (ed.) *International Politics and Foreign Policy: A Reader in Research and Theory* (New York: The Free Press, 1969), p. 257.

15. Alvin Toffler, *Power Shift: Knowledge, Wealth and Violence at the Edge of the 21st Century* (Great Britain: Bantam Free Press, 1990).

16. Dennis Goulet, *The Uncertain Promise: Value Conflicts in Technology Transfer* (New York: North American Inc., 1977) for a very interesting analysis of this topic.

17. United Nations Development Programme, *Human Development Report 1997* (New York: Oxford University Press, 1997), p. 82.

18. UNDP, *Human Development Report 1997*, p. 91.

19. *Ibid;*

20. See G. Almond and B. Powell, *Comparative Politics: A Developmental Approach* (Boston: Little Brown, 1962) and L. Binder, *Political Development in a Changing Society* (Berkeley: University of California Press. 1962).

21. However, it must be noted that there are many ways to centralize political authority. Lewis, warned that "national programmes of unification disrupt and undermine the existing patterns of authority of local units", thus creating problems of authority which "impose restraints on politically induced change". Unconscious reorganization of a society "may aggravate or produce numerous impediments to the exercise of leadership" see John Lewis "The Social Limits of Politically Induced Change" in Morse, et al. (ed.) *Modernization by Design* (Ithaca: Cornell University Press, 1965) p. 24.

22 See Sheldon Geller, *State-Building and Nation-Building in West-Africa* (Bloomington: International Development Centre, Indiana University, 1972).

23. See the problems of this as analyzed by David Apter, *Choice and the Politics of Allocation* (New Haven: Yale University Press 1971).

24. Olusegun Obasanjo, *Not My Will* (Ibadan: University Press Limited, 1990) pp. 130-131.

25. Jean–Jacques Rousseau, *The Social Contract or Principles of Political Right* (ed.) With running commentaries by Charles M. Sherover) (Cleveland: Meridian Books) p 11.

26. *Ibid;*

27. Claude E. Welch, Jr. and Arthur K. Smith, *Military Role and Rule* (Massachusetts: Duxbury Press, 1974) pp. 55-70.
28. *Ibid;* p. 255.
29. *Ibid;* p. 63.
30. *Ibid;* p. 65.
31. *Ibid* "The thought of actually mobilizing and organizing the masses as a political resource is antithetical to their ingrained contempt for politics and to their sense of mission as professionals."
32. Benue-Plateau State government, *Unity, Stability and Progress: The Second Decade of Nigeria's Independence* (Jos: Government Printer, n.d.), p.2.
33 Federal Republic of Nigeria, *A Programme For Political Action* (Lagos: Government Printer, 1975).
34. John Lewis, "The Social Limits of Politically Induced Change" in C. Morse, et al. *Modernization by Design* (Ithaca: Cornell University Press, 19650 chapter 6. This is to say that penetration of the periphery through mobilizational techniques are difficult to carry out in Nigeria's setting with aggressive subnationalism of groups.
35. David Apter, *The Politics of Modernization* (Chicago: University of Chicago Press, 1965) pp. 359-421 – identifies four types of political systems – Mobilizational, Bureaucratic, Theocratic and Reconciliation. Nigeria is a reconciliation system – emphasizing the need to reconcile diverse elements and interests. Thus a reconciliation system calls for a reconciliation leader.
36. Ali Mazrui, *op.cit.* p. 7
37. Bennis, *op.cit.* p. 158.
38. See Shehu Shagari, *Beckoned To Serve* (Ibadan: Heineman Nig., 2001).
39. Shehu Shagari, "The Power and Limitation of the Executive and the Legislature in the Presidential Experience," in J. Isawa Elaigwu, P.C. Logams and H.S. Galadima (eds.) *Federalism and Nation-Building in Nigeria: The Challenges of the Twenty-First Century* (Abuja: NCIR, 194), pp. 135-144.

40.   See J.Isawa Elaigwu, *Nigeria's Federal Balance: Conflicts and Compromises in the Political System* (Monograph) (Jos: University of Jos Post-Graduate School Lecture Series, 1984), No. 4, p.40.

---

* *The original text was given at* The Commandant's Annual Lecture, *2007 at the Nigerian Defence Academy, Kaduna: November 17, 2007.*

CHAPTER 3

NATION-BUILDING

Introduction

In this chapter, we will discuss Nation-Building. A very polemical term, it has been at the centre of discourse in Nigeria. While for some Nigerians, we have done well in the process of nation-building, others believe that we are at the brinks of the precipice and that Nigeria would soon disintegrate. The issue of nation-building has taken many forms. For some, it is the *national question* – should we stay together as a nation, and if so, on what terms?

For our purposes, we believe that the Nigerian nation is being built and that Nigeria will not disintegrate. It is with this optimistic perspective that we discuss *"The Challenges of Nation-Building in the Twenty-First Century: The Nigerian Experience"*. This topic raises some questions. What are the Challenges of the Twenty-First Century? What is a Nation? What is Nation-Building? What are the basic challenges of nation-building in the new millennium? What have been Nigeria's experiences in nation-building?

We do not pretend to have all the answers to these questions. In fact, as one studies the process of nation-building, from comparative perspective, there are usually more questions than answers. But for our purposes, we suggest that

i) the Twenty-First Century poses many challenges of nation-building to Nigeria;

ii) Western models of nation-building are not really available to Nigeria as options, at this point in time;

iii) the problems of Nation-Building in Nigeria are historical and multi-dimensional;

iv) Nigerians have made significant efforts to transform the country from *a mere geographical expression* to *an organic state*. She now needs to integrate the organic state into an organic nation;

v) echoes of the past are still very much around (like a bogy cloud hanging over the country) even if heard within different structures; these often detract from efforts towards national unity; and

vi) unless we substantially overhaul the ship of the nation-state, we shall find ourselves as inept cripples in the Twenty-First Century of high speed information technology and services.

Let us take a brief look at the Twenty-First Century, which provides the new context for our nation-building and the kind of challenges contained therein. In chapter three, we have sketched some of the challenges of the 21st Century for the nation-state. These challenges are multidimensional and are enormous for those building new nations from new states.

Basically the 21st Century is the context in which nation-building in Nigeria is taking place. The international context of the Twenty-First Century further compounds the challenges of nation-building. Given the new technological and communication revolution, there is a greater *explosion of identities,* at precisely the time we are trying to partialize subnational identities to build a new political community called a nation. The explosion of identities in Europe in the 1990s with the aggressive tribalism which created new states with a concatenation of violent crises, illustrates this point.

Similarly, those leaders who worry about the territorial identity of nation-states, watch helplessly as *the boundaries of the nation-states are violated* blatantly everyday by information technology and satellites. Related to this is the adulteration of cultural values. If China, in the 1960s and 1970s could control the impact of Western values on its culture, it is becoming more difficult to do so. In Nigeria, aspects of the ghetto culture in the Bronx, New York, USA, find their ways into the life systems of youngsters who have never traveled beyond the town of their birth. So also do the cultures of violence in the USA or South Africa get transmitted to many unemployed youths who now embark on daredevil robberies in the daylight.

How do these pose challenges for nation-building in Nigeria? What is Nation-Building?

Nation-Building: Towards A Definition

For our purposes, the concept of a nation may refer to at least three categories of human groups. First, it may refer to "a stable, historically developed community of people with a territory, economic life, distinctive culture, and language in common". Second, it may refer to "the people of a territory united under a single government; country; state". Third, a nation may refer to "a people or tribe".[1]

Often, scholars in attempting to define the concept *nation* make distinctions between objective and subjective properties of a nation. Among such objective indicators of a nation usually mentioned are: language, history, territory, culture (at times including religion), political organization, and economic life. The subjective indicators include a common sense of identity and commitment or loyalty to the group. These psychological variables are not easily measurable. M.G. Smith, however, did a good job of combining both the objective and subjective variables when he defined a nation as:

> ...usually a single inclusive group whose members—or the majority of them—share common traditions, institutions, history, and ethnic identity.[2]

By our first definition, a nation may refer to the Ibo, Yoruba, and Hausa-Fulani in Nigeria; the Kikuyu or Luo in Kenya, the Hutu in Burundi; or the Tswana in Botswana. For our purposes, however, the operational definition of a nation is the second one, which states that a nation is "the people of a territory united under a single government", country, or state. By this definition, we should be talking about Nigeria, Kenya, Burundi, and Botswana as *nations*—not the various "nations" within the nation-state or state-nation.

Much of the literature on nation-building refers to this process "whereby people transfer their commitment and loyalty from smaller tribes, villages or petty principalities to the larger central political system".[3] From their own experiences, Western writers also create the impression that state- and nation- building processes are two separate processes which eventually lead to the establishment of a nation- state. Nation - State is the highest point in the process of state- and nation-building. Thus, in Western experience, the *nation* was established before the state, and nation-state forms the end-product of those processes. In essence, the process of nation-building is the cultivation by a people, over time, of political "attitudes, beliefs and values—the development of a political culture".[4] The emphasis in nation-building is thus on the "congruity of cultural and political identities".[5] It is a "trend toward cultural homogeneity (nationhood)".[6]

For us, the process of nation-building does not involve the *transfer* of "commitment and loyalties" from narrow or parochial levels of ethnic groups to larger political units such as Nigeria. That you are an Ibo, a Yoruba, Efik, or a Kikuyu is a matter of identity. You cannot transfer it. You cannot cease being an Ibo or a Hausa or a Kikuyu or an Efik simply because you so declare. For us, it involves the widening (rather than transfer) of horizons of identity of parochial units to include larger units such as the state.

By *nation-building* we refer to two dimensions of identity. One is closely linked to state-building. We refer to the progressive acceptance by members of the polity of the *legitimacy* of a central government, and identification with the central government as a symbol of the nation. This is the *vertical* dimension of nation-building. In this case, you not only have a *state*, but the people accept the authority of the state (and not merely its coercive powers) and see its government as the symbol of their political community. Thus, secessionist bids in *Nigeria, Ethiopia, the Sudan* and *Zaire* were challenges to the authority of the central government and a denial of a shared sense of identity. The end of the civil war in Nigeria not only indicated the renewed acceptance of the Nigerian state by its citizens, but also an acceptance by Nigerians that the central government should be the symbol of an emerging Nigerian *nation*.

On the horizontal dimension, nation-building involves the acceptance of other members of the civic body as equal fellow members of a "corporate" nation—a recognition of the rights of other members to a share of common history, resources, values, and other aspects of the state—buttressed by a sense of belonging to one political community. It involves the feeling that all members of the polity are entitled to a share of the *sweet* and the *bitter* in the process of political development, not only the sweet. Nation-building, therefore, *is the widespread acceptance of the process of state-building; it is the creation of a political community that gives a fuller meaning to the life of the state.*

Both processes of a state - and nation- building can take place concurrently, and often do overlap. For many ex-colonial African states (including Nigeria) the State preceded the nation. Many groups of peoples were arbitrarily sandwiched into a territorial unit, which then formed a geopolitical entity called the state. To many of the peoples of these states, there was no identification with the State as a symbol of a people or a political community. In fact, most of these groups became exposed to one another in the terminal colonial period, as the colonial masters folded their political umbrellas and rolled their flags.[7]

For these peoples, there was no sharing of common "values, beliefs, and attitudes" among the people of new states that would have created a political culture. In addition, emerging mainly after the 1960s, the period of state-building for many African states have been short. As experiments in state-building go on, so also have experiments in nation-building. These add to the strains on the capabilities of the political systems in all African states. Rajni Kothari was correct when he observed that in the Third World, "the concept of nation itself tends to draw less from cultural and linguistic notions which were the origins of national consciousness in Europe and more *from a transcendent notion* of statehood which coincides with nationhood".[8]

Furthermore, as Sheldon Gellar persuasively argued, the processes of state-and nation-building have witnessed the development of "state-nations" which recognizes the paradox of national integration, that is, "diversity in unity" and not only "unity in diversity".[9] The process of nation-building could thus entail the creation of "state-nations" as well as "nation-states" as end-products.

Does nation-building necessarily involve the homogenization of cultural and political identities? As Clifford Geertz observed, any attempt at simple replacement of primordial ties and identifications by civil ones is "sheer impossibility". [10] He contends that the compromise is to be found in "adjustments between them", so that the processes of government can proceed "fully without threatening the cultural framework of personal identity". Whatever discontinuities occur as a result of this would, therefore, "not radically distort political functioning". Perhaps Ali Mazrui is correct in suggesting that what nation-building implies is "substantial cultural homogeneity" to enable the sense of nationhood to stick.[11]

It may be argued, therefore, as Edmund Burke did, that "the love of the whole"

> is not extinguished by... subordinate partiality... to be attached to the subdivision, to love the little platoon we belong to in society, is just the principle...of public affections.[12]

Perhaps it is the degree of attachment to the sub-national loyalties, which may threaten the whole. The process of nation-building consciously attempts to widen the horizons for sub-national loyalties to coincide with State boundaries, and ultimately partialized the level of commitment to the parochial groups.

It may be argued that nation-building involves a process of making a 'salad bowl'. The various contents of the salad bowl – carrots, eggs, cabbages, lettuce and others, are partialized in identity (they do not remain as whole entities) in order to accommodate others in the bowl. We may even go further to argue that the 'salad cream' (or the collective experiences of thepeople) binds all the contents of the bowl together. Thus, the nation is like a salad bowl. It is the sum total of partialized identities of members of the political community, as each group widens the horizons of parochial identities to include others. While Americans in the United States may boast of their 'melting pot', the reality shows clearly that identities have not really melted – what with Italian-Americans, African-Americans, Jewish-Americans, Irish-Americans and other subnational identities. These identities have visible political consequences for the country.

Finally, we hasten to argue that the processes of *nation- building* in African *States* have been punctuated by conflicts and crises. Given the diversity of the groups involved in this process, conflict is inevitable. It is not just the conflicts, but the intensity of the conflicts, without threatening the consensual values on which the association is grafted, that are important in the process of nation-building. As Ali Mazrui has suggested, "an accumulated experience of resolving conflicts between antithetical forces is, after all, one of the great indices of national integration". [13] After all, Lewis Coser has argued that conflicts may be positively functional to group solidarity.[14]

Let us now turn to two important theoretical issues. The first is the distinction between *polyethnic* and *multinational states*. Except for Somalia, most African states are either multinational or polyethnic states. For our purposes, polyethnic states refer to those states which have many ethnic groups, none of which lays claim to subnational autonomy enough to challenge the autonomy of the centre by asserting its subnational self-determination. No ethnic group in such states regards itself as a nation.[15] Thus, Tanzania, Senegal (inspite of the Casamance), The Gambia, Guinea (Conakry) and Congo (Brazzaville) illustrate polyethnic states in Africa.

On the other hand, *multinational states* comprise ethnic groups, which do not only vary in size but also in the distribution of power, influence and resources. Such states are marked by aggressive ethnic nationalism as various groups push for the realization of their subnational self-determination. Often, the demands for subnational self-determinaiton directly challenge the centre's demands for national self-determination: Nigeria (Ibo, Yoruba, and Hausa); The Democratic Republic of the Congo (DRC) (The Congo, the Mongo, Luba and Kivu ethnic types); Ethiopia (the Galla and the Tigre types); The Chad (The Chad and Sudanic types and the Sudan (Arab and various Southern clusters). It is our argument that nation-building in polyethnic states (such as The Gambia or Tanzania) are less intractable than in multinational states (such as Nigeria or the DRC).

The second theoretical issue we need to raise at this point, is that the process of integration or the building of unity in a heterogeneous society is *infinite*. There may be, at least, four identifiable stages of integration. Ali Mazrui[16] in his study of political integration identified four stages of national integration. First is the stage of *coexistence*— which is the '*minimum degree of integration.*' At this stage, groups merely coexist within the same borders and need not know of one another's existence. At the second stage of *contact*, groups at least have "minimum" dealing with one another. They communicate with one another, even though these interactions need not necessarily be one of cooperation or friendship. They may be interactions of conflict or hostility. But at least they are aware of the existence of one another and are in contact.

The third stage, is one of *compromise*. Here Mazrui claims that "the dealings between groups have become sufficiently complex, diverse, and interdependent to require a climate of peaceful reconciliation between conflicting interests".

Even though groups still have distinct identities, "the process of national integration has now produced a capacity for constant discovery of compatibility".

The fourth and final stage in Mazrui's categories is the stage of *coalescence* in which identities coalesce, "rather than merger of interests". The society is getting more "technically complex and functionally integrated". There may be diverse interests emerging with blurred identities, but "conflict of interests is no longer a conflict between two identities".

Thus at different stages of nation-building, there may be identifiable characteristics. No multinational state ever fully achieves coalescence of identities, but they could attain different sub-stages of coalescence of identities, as they continue to refine relations among members of the political community.

Let us now turn to our third suggestion—that the problem ofnation-building in Nigeria are historical and multidimensional.

Nigeria's Nation-Building in Historical Perspective

The Colonial Antecedents

At the risk of over-flogging the colonial horse, it may be suggested that the British colonial superstructure had great consequence for state- and nation-building processes in Nigeria. As noted in chapter one by 1900, what later became known as Nigeria comprised three colonial territories under the umbrella of British colonialism, but administered separately, and receiving orders direct from the metropolis: London. These were the Colony of Lagos and what came to be known as the Protectorates of Southern Nigeria and Northern Nigeria. In 1906, the Colony and the Protectorate of Southern Nigeria were unified under a single administrator. The year 1914 witnessed the amalgamation of the Colony of Lagos and the Protectorates of Northern and Southern Nigeria—as the Colony and Protectorate of Nigeria.[17] In 1939, Nigeria was divided into the Colony of Lagos, and Northern, Eastern and Western Groups of Provinces, with each group of provinces having a Chief Commissioner who was responsible to the Governor in Lagos.

If the amalgamation of 1914 was aimed at a political fusion of the North and the South, it did not have the objective of building a unified state, nor did the British envisage, by the remotest stroke of imagination, that a 'nation' would emerge from this 'geopolity'. This British attitude was not unique. Most colonial regimes hardly gave any thought to granting independence to their subjects, and as such, they gave little thought to the form of government and administration that would best suit the people of a particular colonial territory. Nor did they encourage understanding among different groups in the colonial state. This would of course, place colonial rulers at further disadvantage. They were usually numerically inferior to their subjects, and could not gamble on encouraging horizontal interaction among groups. This would only hasten their good riddance from the territory.

It was therefore, not surprising that between 1914 and 1946, the British hardly made efforts to integrate the Northern and Southern provinces. As a matter of fact, these provinces were administered separately, and colonial officials in these administrations zealously fought to keep each group of provinces separate. As James Coleman once reported, this led to the quip that "if all Africans were to leave Nigeria, the Northern and Southern administrators would go to war". [18] In some other African colonial states, colonial officials even encouraged inter-ethnic quarrels, competitions and hostility— the old 'divide-and-rule' strategy.[19] Thus, except for the amalgamation of some essential departments, such as customs, education, railways, police, and prisons, little effort was made at integration.

It was not until after the introduction of the *Richards Constitution* of 1946, that Nigerians ever had the opportunity to sit at a single platform to deliberate on issues which affected their lives. The Northern Province, until 1947, had no representation in the central legislature. This separate political development of the North and the South might have been suitable for colonial rule, but it was not suitable for the development of a *State* and *Nation,* especially given Nigeria's multiethnic composition. The impact of this was to be felt much later. Colonial administration encouraged vertical relations between colonial centre of power and the relevant periphery—district, divisions, provinces, and regions. It did not encourage horizontal interaction among groups. Most Nigerian groups hardly knew of the existence of one another. Only the colonial administration knew of, and interacted with, all ethnic groups in the country.

We also suggested in chapter one that the period between 1914 - 1946 was one in which colonial Nigeria only experienced mere *co-existence* of groups. They hardly knew of one another's existence beyond the geoethnic colonial administrative units. Where they knew of such groups, these groups had little relevance for them because they hardly interacted.

However, in 1947 when Nigerians began to interact with one another at the Legislative Council, a wave of nationalism was sweeping across the southern part of the country. The aggressiveness with which nationalists attacked the Richards Constitution illustrated the upsurge in political awareness in the country. At the same time, a concatenation of national and international events, demonstrated to Nigerians that the struggle for autonomy, self-government or independence was on the right track. Curiously too, these Nigerians who had come together to 'fight' colonialism - whether these were members of the National Council for Nigeria and Cameroons (NCNC-formed in 1944), *Egbe Omo Oduduwa* (formed in 1945), the *Jam'iyyar Mutanen Arewa* (the Northern People's Congress as a cultural group) in 1949 or the Northern Elements Progressive Union (NEPU—formed in 1949) — soon realized that the colonial umbrella would soon fold up.

They became keenly aware that there was going to be a political vacuum in Nigeria and that they had to compete with one another in order to fill this vacuum. This realization came as Nigeria's ethnic groups were establishing contacts with one another. They had started to interact with one another, but soon realized that they were strange bed-fellows in the same polity. They had not interacted with one another long enough to work out mechanisms for conflict resolution.

Given the competitive setting in which they found themselves, Nigerian politicians withdrew into their ethnic, ethnoregional or geo-ethnic[20] cocoons in order to mobilize effectively for competition.

An interesting trend at this time was the appeal to ethnic loyalty and the crystallization of ethnic identity around the regions. After the 1951 elections, the Action Group (AG) became the dominant party in the West (with a strong NCNC opposition) in the predominantly Yoruba Western Region, while the NCNC controlled the government of the predominantly Ibo Eastern Region. The NPC soon became the party of the dominantly Hausa-Fulani Northern Region. Thus, gradually, Nigerian political parties became identified with particular regions and often appealed to the ethnic groups in those regions for support in their competition with political parties from other regions. In a way, Azikiwe's lack of a regional base in Nigeria's ethno-regional politics had led to his exclusion from the Western legislature. That he returned to his home region in the East later was a realization of the ethno-regional basis of Nigerian nationalism. His displacement of Prof. Eyo Ita as Chief Minister created inter-ethnic animosity in the Eastern region for a while.

Furthermore, the Yoruba-Ibo rivalry, which ensued in the South, only accentuated the pace of aggressive ethnic nationalism. Statements reflecting inter-ethnic animosity were often made with reckless abandon. One of such statements was made by a member of the *Egbe Omo Oduduwa*, who said, "we were bunched together by the British who named us Nigeria. We never knew the Ibos, but since we knew them we have been friendly and neighborly... we have tolerated enough from a class of Ibos and addle-brained Yorubas who have mortgaged their thinking caps to Azikiwe and hirelings". [21] This statement was a reflection of Yoruba feelings: an appeal to members of that group to organize so that "the Yoruba will not be relegated to the background in the future".[22]

On the other hand, the election of Azikiwe as the President of the Ibo Union and his speech at the 1949 Ibo State Union Conference may be regarded as an appeal to his ethnic bedfellows for support in the emerging Yoruba-Ibo competition for jobs in the modernizing sector. In his speech, Azikiwe had told the conference that "it would appear that the God of Africa had specifically created the Ibo nation to lead the children of Africa from the bondage of the ages... The martial prowess of the Ibo nation at all stages of human history has enabled them not only to conquer others but also to adapt themselves to the rule of the preserver... The Ibo nation cannot shirk its responsibility.[23]

No matter the intentions of Azikiwe, the speech could not have been more ill-timed. It came at the height of Yoruba-Ibo competition and was quickly used by some nationalists to dismiss Azikiwe's pan-Nigerian claims.

Once nationalists turned to their ethnic bedfellows to canvass for support in competition with members of other ethnic groups, *Nigeria nationalism became interpreted as ethnic nationalism.* This trend was strengthened because of the fragile sense of identity of Nigerians with the concept of the Nigerian nation. Thus, Awolowo described Nigeria as a *mere geographic expression.* There are no 'Nigerians' in the same sense as there are 'English', 'Welsh', or 'French'.[24] A similar statement was made by Alhaji Abubakar Tafawa Balewa, the deputy leader of the NPC, when he told the Legislative Council in 1948, that Nigerians did not "show themselves any signs of willingness to unite.... Nigerian unity is only a British intention for this country".[25]

In the absence of any strong sense of unity, the process of decolonization created feelings of suspicions and fears as ethnic groups interacted with one another in a competitive process. Emergent identities crystallized around the regions as effective units for competition. Intra-regional ethnic differences were often "driven under the carpet" to present a homogeneous front for competition with other regional groups, and political parties assumed regional labels (consciously or unconsciously

Thus the period between 1951-1954 saw the gradual decentralization of the colonial central government.[26] Not only had regions established their legislatures, their civil services had taken on their own dynamics. The Marketing Board even became regionalized. Since groups did not understand one another well, there was hardly a basis for trust or confidence. Regional and ethnoregional platforms held greater attractions than the national level for political mobilization.

As the regions developed a comfortable base for competition, federalism became attractive as a form of government. Thus, the Lyttleton Constitution of 1954 indicated the trend of events, which were confirmed at subsequent constitutional conferences leading to independence in 1960. In essence, federalism as adopted later in Nigeria was a compromise formula to assuage the fears and suspicions of domination among Nigeria's heterogeneous population during the colonial period. Of course, one cannot ignore British flair for a legacy of federalism in her ex-colonies such as Australia and the federation of Rhodesia and Nyasaland. At different times, the colonial state, got shocks from the regions. In 1950 the Northern Nigeria threatened to secede unless she had equal representation with the Southern regions in the central legislature.[27] The Western Region also threatened to secede if the Colony of Lagos was not merged with that region and if revenue allocation formula did not weigh overwhelmingly in favour of the principle of derivation.[28]

In the context of aggressive ethno-regionalism between 1951-1959, there was a false impression created of homogeneous regions. It took the prospects of independence to expose these fallacies. As prospects for independence became increasingly a reality, minority groups in the regions expressed their fears of discrimination and domination in the various regions. These fears derived mainly from the multi-ethnicity of Nigeria, the size, nature and composition of subnational political units, and the desire by each group to protect its interest as power passed to Nigerians from the British colonial rulers. Demands for new subnational states or regions emerged in the polity.

The Midwest State Movement demanded the creation of a Midwest State from the predominantly Yoruba Western region. In the North, minority groups from the MiddleBelt section formed various associations[29] to mobilize opinion in favour of the creation of a Middle-Belt State. In the Eastern Region, the Calabar-Ogoja-Rivers (COR) State movement sought for a separate existence outside the predominantly Ibo Eastern Region.

These pressures subsequently led to the establishment of the *Willink Commission* which was empowered by the colonial administration to investigate the fears of minority groups. The Report of this Commission confirmed that there were bases for fears among minorities—but that a "separate state would not provide a remedy for the fears expressed."[30] Moreover, the creation of new states would delay the proposed granting of independence to Nigeria. It made a number of recommendations for ameliorating the situation. The colonial government later opted for the inclusion of a 'human rights' clause in the 1960 Constitution.

By Independence in 1960, two basic but interrelated issues remained unresolved: i) the fundamental imbalance in Nigeria's political structure which fanned the embers of suspicion, fear, and aggressive ethno-regionalism after independence; and ii) fears by minority groups of domination by majorities in the context of Nigeria's three regional structure. As a former Military Head of State of Nigeria once pointed out,

> "There has always been fear of domination in Nigeria - domination by size, population, or religion. There was even the fear of domination through skill. In some parts of the country, people would say that because of the size or population of a particular region, it was dominating the rest. In other parts, they would say that because people from another part of the country were educated as a result of earlier contact with Europeans, they were dominating the less educated ones"...[31]

Independent Nigeria

The Nigerian State at Independence was already bedeviled by problems arising from mutual suspicions and fears of domination among various groups which had established *contact* with one another during the terminal colonial period. These suspicions were really not unusual; they were also understandable.

For Nigeria, the processes of state and nation-building ran concurrently. The problems which pestered the process of state-building also provided obstacles for nation-building. The imbalance in Nigeria's federal structure was one of such potent sources of fear among groups. Federalism had been adopted as 'compromise' formula to deal with problems of national and subnational self-determination. Yet the very structure of federalism escalated mutual suspicions among groups rather than dampened them.

A federal structure in which the Northern Region accounted for 79% of the total geographic area and 54% of the population, made groups from the Southern regions[32] feel seriously disadvantage. In the context of Nigeria's ethno-regionalism and democratic framework of one man, one vote, the South saw Northern *tyranny of population* as detrimental to their political interest. It may be pointed out that many citizens of the Southern regions never believed that the North actually had the large population that was attributed to it by the 1963 census office.[33]Thus the fear that the North would continue to provide political leadership in the country created an intense sense of political deprivation in the South. The North-South dichotomy became sharper and clearer. Thus, a dichotomy created by the nature of colonial administration was even widened by Nigerians as they operated within inherited colonial structures.

On the other hand, the North was disadvantaged educationally. The Southern regions had had a headstart in Western Education, which had become a passport into the modernizing sectors of the society—parastatals, federal civil service, and even in private economic sectors.   The North was very keenly aware of this handicap. As Sir Ahmadu Bello described the situation;

> "We were very conscious indeed that the Northern Region was far behind the others educationally. We knew that individually the educated Northerners could hold their own against the educated Southerners, but we simply had not got the numbers they had, nor had we people with the University degrees necessary as a qualification..... for some higher posts".[34]

It was therefore not surprising that the North adopted a *Northernization Policy* of recruitment into her public Service. The other regions virtually did the same thing but they did not need to enunciate a policy such as the North did.   Northern suspicion of Southern *tyranny of skills* made her feel more insecure, with the fear of economic domination from the South.

Essentially, while the North had political power, economic power resided in the South. In addition to these issues (which did not make for harmonious horizontal relations among groups) was the fear among minorities that they could not effectively protect their interests within the regional structures as existed then. These groups continued to press for separate existence outside the existing regional framework, which favoured the majority groups.

It had become clear that the regions were the bases of power in Nigeria. Constitutionally the 1960 and 1963 Constitutions had effectively distributed political authority among the component tiers of the federation. But centrifugal forces were so active in the system that the regions became very powerful. As one Nigerian Head of State once observed, the regions became so powerful that they even exhibited pretensions of sovereignty.[35] it was therefore not surprising that a constitutionally powerful centre became a weak centre in the context of constitutionalism in Nigeria.

The period between 1960–65 witnessed blatant violations of the constitution. The regions quarreled over the 1962 and 1963 census exercises, the 1964 Federal Elections, the Binn's Commission Report on Revenue Allocation Formula in 1964, and the Western Regional election of 1965. At various points in time, compromises were found among politicians to enable the system move on. Some of these compromises were really negative in their impact on the system. As an illustration, the 1962–68 Development Plan had included the establishment of a steel and iron ore smelting industry in Nigeria. At one of the meetings of the National Economic Council (NEC) in 1964, the North requested the siting of the industry at Idah, the Eastern leaders wanted it at Onitsha, while the Western Region pressed for it to be sited at Ikare. In the ensuing squabble, the Western Region withdrew its request (a sign of its weakness at that point in time) and the NEC decided that the industry be split between the North and the East, with a plant at Idah and another in Onitsha—an imprudent decision.[36]

The process of state-building which by our definition entails centralization of authority, was often punctuated by conflicts. The regions at various times had threatened to secede as was shown above.

In 1964 the Eastern Region also threatened to secede over the census exercise and the Federal Election of 1964.[37]   In addition, the regions often interfered in areas of exclusive federal preserve, such as in foreign policy.[38] In fact, the federal centre under Balewa exhibited such signs of weakness that its relations with the regions was often described as one of "regional tails" wagging "federal dog."[39]

The nation-building process was often tension-charged because of the relations among ethnic groups within the regions. As mentioned above, the regions often presented homogeneous fronts in their competition with other regions. Internally, the regions had their inter-communal problems. These problems were worsened by the region-based political parties and the utterances and performances of politicians.[40]

By 1965, the graph of Nigeria's political temperature had risen very high. The rules of the game of politics had been ruthlessly violated, and corruption and conspicuous consumption of politicians amidst the abject poverty of the masses became very glaring. Census exercises were inflated and politicized because of mutual suspicions among groups. The rigging of elections disenfranchised the Nigerian masses. In fact, it was not unusual for a pregnant woman to go into the polling booth and re-emerge 'unpregnant'— having emptied her 'entrails' into the ballot box. As the temperature of the polity rose without any outlets for ventilation, politics became dangerous for both players and spectators. In fact, with *operation wetie*[41] in the Western region, and riots in Tiv land of the Northern region, politics became a 'battle', not a game.

It was in this context that Major Chukwuma Nzeogwu and his fellow military colleagues imploded into the political arena, on January 15, 1966 the military intervened in politics.

In the 'compromise' among the soldiers Major-General Aguiyi-Ironsi emerged as the new Head of State and the Supreme Commander of the Armed Forces of Nigeria.

When the new politicians in 'khaki' uniforms came in, they tried to cope with some of the problems which had plagued the Nigerian political system. By Decree No. 1 1966 *Constitution (Suspension and Modification)*, the Federal Military Government (FMG) assumed "the power to make laws for the peace, order and good government of

Nigeria or any part thereof with respect to any matter whatsoever".[42] But in practice the regions retained their autonomy under the new military governors despite the hierarchical military structure.

Given the problems of state-building in Nigeria, one would have thought that Ironsi would have tackled the issue of federal-state relations immediately. It took Ironsi five months before he made up his mind to centralize political power in Nigeria. The Decree No. 34 of 24th of May 1966 which he promulgated, abolished the regions, established 'groups of provinces' and introduced a unitary form of government. Furthermore, certain grades of public officers were now to be absorbed into a national civil service. Feeling grossly threatened by this action, the North reacted violently in one of the bloodiest forms of communal instability this country had witnessed. People from the Eastern Region (especially Ibos) were killed.

Then came the second coup of July 1966, which was the North's vengeful coup against the apparent insult by the Ibos in January 1966. Like the January coup it was only partially successful. The Eastern Region had not been involved in the coup. From then on the political crisis took on additional dimensions of hostility between the Eastern Region and Federal Government. The Federal Government virtually lost its control over the Eastern Region. It was an effective challenge to the authority of the federal centre and therefore a challenge to the process of state-building. At the same time, it demonstrated the fragile nature of the cords which bound Nigerian groups together in her early stages of nation-building. Attempts to get Nigerians to work out another framework of association at the *Ad Hoc Constitutional Conference*, failed.[43]

At the instance of General Ankrah of Ghana, Nigerian leaders met at Aburi, Ghana, in January 1967. This led to a new political experiment in Nigeria's quest for an appropriate form of government. By Decree no. 59, 1966[44] Nigeria returned to 'federalism' under the military. On March 17, 1967, Nigerian leaders found that they had to grapple with a confederal system as introduced by Decree No. 8, 1967.[45] By the terms of this decree the federal government was effectively cut down to size—at the mercy of regional governments. Major decisions on policies and appointments needed the concurrence of all Military Governors and the armed forces were decentralized into Area Commands under each regional military governor.

For all practical intents and purposes, Nigeria became a confederal system. It took a 'coup' by General Gowon on May 27, 1967[46] to end this impasse. Gowon created twelve states in Nigeria, thus attacking effectively one of the basic problems of Nigeria's state-and nation-building processes - the imbalance in Nigeria's federal structure. However, this political initiative came on the eve of secession and did not solve the immediate political problem, even though it had long-term effect. The Nigerian state had been so badly shaken that a part of it no longer recognized the authority of the central government; nor did this part any longer have any sense of belonging to Nigeria's inchoate nation. Hence, the former Eastern Region seceded on May 30, 1967.

Nigeria then became embroiled in a 30-month fratricidal war which began on July 6, 1967 and formally terminated on January 15th 1970. It was a grueling saga of bloodbath of erstwhile bedfellows in the same country. Yet like all such conflicts, the Nigerian state learnt some major lessons. From 1966 to 1975 when he was overthrown, the Gowon regime had effectively centralized political power. He took legal, fiscal and other practical measures to centralize political authority.[47] It can be argued that given the geopolitics of Nigeria's federal structure, no single state is in a position to secede any longer.

After Gowon, came the Mohammed regime which shocked Nigeria out of its lethargy and gave a momentary sense of direction to the system. He succeeded in further strengthening the powers of the centre at the expense of states. As noted earlier the take-over of television stations is an illustration of this trend in state-building under the military. On the symbolic level, state governments ceased to have coats-of-arms. Obasanjo continued this centralization process and followed the programme of demilitarization of the Nigerian polity to its conclusion by a return to civilian rule, October 1, 1979.

With the surrender of *Biafra* in 1970, secession had ended. This surrender symbolized triumph for Nigerian state-builders. It is our contention that the Nigerian state has come to stay. The Nigerian state has been built, even though the nation is still being built. The re-entry of Biafra into Nigeria was a recognition of the authority of the central government. By the end of military rule, the authority of the central government was no longer in doubt. If it had been relegated to the background in the period 1960-66, the central government was now a political titan.

The year 1970 was also important in a more fundamental sense. If Nigerian politicians had referred to Nigeria as a mere geographical expression, that year marked the transformation of the Nigerian State from a mechanical state to an organic political community. Having shed about a million lives to keep Nigeria together, it would be erroneous to argue that Nigeria is still *mere geographical expression*. Few people if ever, would shed their blood for a mere geographical expression to which they had no commitment. The war showed us how interwoven the destiny of Nigerians had become over the years. It exposed the inter-dependence of Nigerians on one another. Not only were the Ibos of the Eastern region deprived of the Fulani's cattle; palm oil became scarce in Northern markets. Moreover the impounding of the rolling stock of the Nigerian railways by Ojukwu deprived the Northern Nigerian Marketing Board of its much-needed stocks. He also stopped the sale of petroleum products from the refinery at Port Harcourt to the North.[48] Similarly, while Kolanuts were produced in the Western region, the Hausa-Fulanis of the North were the greatest consumers. Much of the food crops of the country came from the Middle Belt area.

Having watered the tree of nationhood with their blood, a new Nigerian nation began to emerge after 1970. The period between 1960 and 1969 was a period which saw Nigerians still at the terminal phase of Mazrui's *contact* stage. As Nigerians related to one another and competed for scarce but allocatable resources, conflicts ensued. It climaxed in a civil war out of which emerged a state grilled and seasoned in the crucible of developmental process. More than any group of leaders, Nigerians owe the military leaders immense gratitude for the emergence of a strong state.

From 1970 we saw a Nigeria moving into the beginning phase of the stage of *compromise*. Interactions among Nigerian groups became more "complex, diverse and interdependent" and Nigerians tried to find mechanisms for reconciling conflicting interests. While conflicts still abound in the system, at least Nigerians have gradually developed the "capacity for constant discovery of compatibility". Thus as the military made their exit out of the political arena they handed over a new constitution to Nigeria - a constitution drafted and ratified by civilians.

Shehu Shagari became the new President under the 1979 constitution.[49] He was overthrown on December 31, 1983. The new Head of State, Major-General Muhammadu Buhari ruled Nigeria between 1984 and August 1985 when he was overthrown by General Ibrahim Babangida, who became a Military President from 1985 to August 27, 1993. Chief Ernest Shonekan succeeded him as the Head of the Interim Government. Again, he was overthrown by General Sani Abacha who became Head of State. Sani Abacha died on June 8, 1998 and was succeeded by General Abdulsalami Abubakar, who carried out a transition to civil rule which terminated on May 29, 1999. General Olusegun Obasanjo became the President of the Fourth Nigerian Republic. Nigeria's history is thus replete with forms of elite instability in which governments at the centre changed quite often.

The Military and Nation-Building

It may be relevant here to make a few specific remarks about the military and nation-building. In terms of state-building, the command structure of the military made centralization of the polity quite easier than under civilian rule. But a few factors contributed to the strengthening of the federal centre at the expense of the states or subnational units.

Concerned that the structural imbalance of Nigeria had led to a lop-sided federation, successive military rulers created additional subnational states. Gowon created 12 states out of 4 regions in 1967; General Murtala Mohammed increased the number to 19 states out of 12 in 1976; Babangida made the structure 21 states in 1987 and 30 in 1991. General Abacha added six additional states in 1996, thus changing the federation to a structure of thirty-six states and the Federal Capital Territory (FCT), Abuja. The creation of states reduced the prospects of subnational threats of the central government. In addition, it created states with less resource bases, which became more dependent on the centre for financial interventions. The creation of additional states meant that there were no longer states which were "so powerful that they even exhibited pretensions of sovereignty."

While for purposes of state-building, this was useful, there were implications for nation-building. States creation which was a structural prescription to the problem of structural imbalance in the federal structure soon came to be regarded by the aggrieved as an *elixir* to solve all political problems. There were many demands for the creation of additional states - almost an avoidance mechanism for dealing with problems of inter-group relations. In some states from which new states were created (such as Anambra and Enugu states) there were demands by the public services of those states that wives should follow their husbands to the new states, even though they originally hailed from the old state. In addition, with every creation of additional states, there are *new majorities* and *new minorities* with new and accompanying problems.

As a result of the divisive dimensions of the creation of states, some elder statesmen such as Chief Anthony Enahoro and Dr. Alex Ekwueme, have canvassed for the merging of states into bigger regions. Have the numerous states helped to reduce our problems of nation-building, or are these mere "political rashes" resulting from the creation of states? There are currently more demands for additional states.

The second issue of relevance here is the nature of military rule. The command structure and the hierarchical nature of the military impose a unifying and unitary superstructure on the polity. The Military Governors/Administrators were appointed by the Head of State and Commander-in-Chief, from whom they have their marching orders. Since the Gowon regime, the autonomy of successive military regimes had been progressively eroded. In essence, subnational dissent in relations with the centre was non-existent and would have been seen as disloyalty, rebellion or indiscipline.

Related to this is the military's mode of legislation by *decrees* at the federal level, and *edicts* at the state levels. Such debates, as existed, took place within the confines of the Supreme Military Council or the Armed Forces Ruling Council (AFRC) or the Provisional Ruling

Council (PRC) as the case may be, or in the State Executive Council at the state level. It was therefore easier to legislate under military rule than under a democratic setting.

In addition, there were a number of centralizing actions, overtime, which only strengthened the centre at the expense of states.[50] As an illustration, by Decree No.14, 1967, the Gowon administration created 12 States, but Decree No. 27, 1967, limited the power of the new states only to residual matters in the amended constitution. Similarly the military homogenized income or salaries of Federal and State public servants starting from the Udoji Commission Report in 1974. The closure of the Regional Deputy High Commissions in Britain was also part of this centralizing act. The abolition of Local/Native Authority police and prison department also robbed subnational units of agencies of law enforcement and correction. Essentially, the sense of patriotism of the military, especially after having fought a civil war, meant that they were very uncomfortable with subnational autonomy. The mode of military legislation only helped in this centralizing process.

The *civil war* provided an opportunity for the military to usurp certain powers of the states which they never cared to restore. Decree No. 17, 1967 (Newspaper Prohibition Of Circulation) 1967, for example, gave the Head of the Federal Military Government the power to "prohibit the circulation in the Federation or in any state thereof, as the case may require, of any newspaper." This decree was used by succeeding military leaders to deal with dissenting publishing houses. Thus, the military mode of legislation, its hierarchical structure of command, and its sense of nationalism goaded military rulers on a centralizing path. This strengthened the federal centre and certainly did make the centre a symbol of emerging nation.

The fourth factor in this centralizing trend was the advent of petronaira, with profit tax accruing to the centre. Over time, successive military regimes tinkered with the revenue formula in favour of the Central government. By May 1999, the central or Federal Government had become a financial titan.

There was no doubt that the military saw itself as a national institution and believed that the centralization of authority was the best thing for Nigeria. By May 1999, there were numerous complaints about over-centralization of the Nigerian Federation; popular agitation for a more decentralizing structure; dissatisfaction with the nature of the distribution of scarce but allocatable resources; communal conflicts and violence; and demands by some subnational groups for greater autonomy, and in some cases, for self-determination. There were even calls for a national and/or sovereign national conference to assess the nature of association within the federation.

What really happened between 1967 and 1999? Why did we have such a dramatic transition between a federation in which the 'tail' was said to be wagging the 'federal dog', and which called for the creation of states and centralization of power, to one in which subnational groups are complaining about the suffocating grip of the federal centre? Did we over centralize political power under military rule?

Perhaps Nigerians have really gotten enmeshed in the integrative stage of *compromise.* Yes, relationships among various groups have become more "complex, diverse and interdependent". Nigerians have more confidence now in discussing their future without the fear of the political community necessarily breaking up. Over time, they have acquired and are still acquiring skills in reconciling conflicting interests, even if these escalate into violence at times. They are gradually discovering areas of compatibility, even though the rhetoric of interaction may, at times, give the opposite impression. More networks of interaction have to be established, and better conflict resolution mechanisms have to be evolved as the country tries to strike desirable compromises.

Let us now turn to the challenges of nation-building currently facing the Nigerian Nation.

Nation-Building in Nigeria's New Democratic Polity.

Federalism

In Nigeria today, there are some Nigerians who believe that part of the problem of political stability in the country is the emergence of a *titanic* centre from the crises of the 1960s and almost three decades of military rule. Some of those who ascribe to this view see the future of the Nigerian federation as one which would divest the central government of its powers through the devolution of powers.

Some of these problems derive from lack of mutual confidence in one another among Nigerian groups, and suspicions of domination by one group or the other. In 1993, I summarized some of the problems of power relations in the Nigerian Federation along horizontal dimensions – viz:

- Why should one group of Nigerians tend to monopolize the leadership of Nigeria, (that is the Presidency or Head of Government) we must have it this time or we will assess our relations within the federal association;

- Why is it that the major resource which gives blood to the Nigerian federation comes from my area and yet there is no evidence of the impact of this wealth on the lives of my people?... We must discuss the adequate sharing of this and other resources now or pack it up;

- What makes some parts of Nigeria attract more   federal presence in terms of industrialization and the location of major federal projects to the exclusion of our area? Is this a federation? If so, should there not be more equitable distribution of resources? Should the federal presence not be felt all over the country? Or are we federally *pariah*?

- Why is it that some Nigerian groups think that they must concentrate political and economic powers in their hands? Do they realize that federal compromise involves sharing and not concentration? If we lose our political guarantee against their economic powers, we shall have to re-assess our position in this federal association.

- In the context of a relatively primitive capitalist system with a dominant state role in the economy inspite of privatization, the powers of the centre are very important, therefore, you cannot divorce the political from economic power; to rob us the access to political is tantamount to undercutting our economic power; this we shall not accept; the principles of June 12 must therefore be adequately addressed.

- Those of us who fought over the nature of the federal association are not fools; we are watching the greed of others as they share political and economic powers; we shall not originate the excision from the polity this time, but we shall not allow anyone to go; those who betrayed us the last time, cannot do it twice and if they try to go, we shall force them to stay. To 'keep Nigeria one' is a task that was accomplished, and must continue to be done, so let us sit down and discuss; and

- What makes our bigger brothers behave as if they do   not need this country and that only those of us who are small need it; are they saying they have milked the system enough and now that there is nothing to exploit, they must quit? What have we gained in our areas from this federal association? – nothing; yet the smaller groups are in the majority... we must discuss our new pattern of relationship in the federal system to take account of our grievances."

Candidly, these are genuine concerns expressed by patriotic Nigerians. The fact is that the Nigerian federation today is very highly centralized. As mentioned earlier, a number of factors are responsible for this - i) the nature of military rule (almost thirty years) and its mode of legislation made it easy to centralize authority; ii) the civil war and its emergency powers which enabled the centre to assume functions of subnational units, functions which were never reversed after the war; iii) the creation of states which gradually reduced the resource bases of states; iv) the advent of petronaria which, through profit tax, strengthened the   financial strength of the centre; v) international trade, globalization, and the need for relative homogeneity across subnational boundaries, which give added functions to the central government in all federations.

Given this situation, many Nigerians have legitimately expressed concerns about the unitarist streaks in Nigeria's federation. In fact the *Report of the Constitutional Conference Containing the Resolutions and Recommendations*, volume 11, recommended 'innovation' to the Nigerian federation thus:

It should be true federalism with clear demarcation of powers and functions among the levels of government in the exercise of those powers and functions assigned by the Constitution, each level of government should be autonomous.[51]

However, as Ranjit Sarkaria of India correctly observed:

The classical concept of federation which envisaged two parallel governments of coordinate jurisdiction, operating in isolation from each other in watertight compartments, is no where a functional reality now. With the emergence of the Social Welfare State, the traditional theory of federation completely lost its ground. After First World War, it became very much a myth even in the old federations... By the middle of the Twentieth Century, Federalism has come to be understood as dynamic process of cooperation and shared action between two or more levels of government, with increasing interdependence and centrist trends.[52]

The complexity of modern government, the need for homogeneity within the nation-state, as well as the nature of foreign trade (among other reasons) have contributed to the power of the central governments in most federal states, except for Belgium. While the Swiss Constitution is legally decentralized, Switzerland is administratively quite centralized, even though it is very sensitive to its plurality and minority groups. Similarly, the powers of the Federal (central) Government in the United States have increased at the expense of states. The globalization process further strengthens the central government.

In essence, the old sense of autonomy of component units in their areas of jurisdiction, have given way to cooperation, interdependence and interaction. That there is still a call for a return to a nostalgic classical K. C. Wheare model of federalism, however, is a reflection of the extent to which centrifugal forces are at work in the current Nigerian federation as groups seek greater autonomy or self-rule at sub-national state level to liberate themselves from suffocating federal clutches in order to control their destiny. Paradoxically, the greater the number of states we create, the less 'autonomous' the content of this self-rule.

Given the dissatisfaction with the federation, a number of individuals and groups have argued for the restructuring of the federation into larger and more autonomous units. I grant Nigerians the right to change their minds, given new challenges. Otherwise, it is interesting to note that as late as 1995, Nigerians were asking for additional states. Even people from the same lingo-cultural groups were at daggers drawn, as they demanded their separate states.

Since 1967, the demands for additional states have continued, as 'new majorities' and new 'minorities' emerged. Often the new majorities are even more vicious and intolerant than the old majorities. Our point here, is that the restructuring of the federation as a prescription to our problems of inter-group relations, cannot be used as elixir to solve all our human problems of co-existence, accommodation, participation, and equitable distribution of resources. What are the major arguments for restructuring the federation? The major arguments include – i) Reducing the power of distribution of scarce but allocatable resources by the centre; ii) Giving more autonomy to the subnational units to enable them operate more 'independently' in the Federation, and iii) Making it possible for the key central political office (i.e. the Presidency) to rotate among more Nigerian groups. Are the solutions to these issues to be found only in the restructuring of the Federation? Or are we seeking a structural prescription to issues that are not really structural, but human and processual?

Perhaps it is time for us to move away from unidimensional solutions and search for multidimensional approaches to providing solutions to our problems of coexistence - which in any case defy quick-fix formulae, as in any society.

We should perhaps look at the aggressive subnationalism and the challenges of self-determination since May 1999, to see the level of accommodation and tolerance in our federation.

The general mood of the nation in 1967 was that if Nigeria was to survive, there must be a strong Federal Centre. Since 1999, there have been calls for a return to the loose federal association among Nigerians. What happened? Why did Nigeria move in the direction of a federal system with a strong centre in

1967 and yet by the year 2001, various groups were calling for a national conference to review the federation? Why is Nigeria's *federal pendulum* swinging from centripetal towards centrifugal forces?

Many years of military rule, the emergence of a fiscally and politically titanic centre has questioned the basic sense of security of groups, as we had pointed out earlier. Under General Sani Abacha, and as a result of the Constitutional Conference of 1994, Nigeria was informally divided into 6 geopolitical zones.[53] These zones were regarded as development zones, from the Abacha days had pressed for a Sovereign National Conference to discuss the restructuring of Nigeria. In essence, it was asking for a return to the old regions with their accompanying autonomy. This demand was partly predicated on the assumption that the federation was too centralized and that those who controlled political power at the centre also controlled resources, including their extraction and distribution. They therefore opted for the old regional autonomy in order to control their resources and pace of development.

After May 1999, the *O'dua People's Congress* (OPC) declared its stand for the freedom of Yoruba to go it alone as an independent unit. It declared its desire to protect and defend Yoruba interests in Nigeria. The first eruption of crisis was in Shagamu between OPC-backed group and Hausa settlers. Many people were killed and goods were destroyed. The corpses of Hausa men, which were carried back to Kano, generated a retaliatory wave of violence in that city against Yorubas. In response, Northern youths formed the Arewa People's Congress (APC) to challenge OPC violence.

OPC violence at Ketu and other places in Lagos angered the Ibos who also set up the Ibo People Congress (IPC) to deal with what they considered OPC's unwarranted meddlesomeness and violence. The OPC violence in Lagos got to a point at which the President threatened the Governor of Lagos State with a declaration of a State of Emergency in the State, unless he could restore law and order. Lagos had become extremely unsafe. Many people saw OPC's espousal of Yoruba nationalism as the reason why OPC leaders were being shielded from the police. The leader of a wing of OPC who was declared wanted for about two years had been arrested and charged for multiple murder and treason. But his bail was construed by Northern leaders to mean selective justice, since Northerners such as Major Mustapha and Gen. Bamaiyi have not been allowed bail despite allegations of murder, which, in their view, was less than that of the OPC factional leader. Infact Gen. Bamaiyi openly declared that the Oputa Panel is a separate justice for the Northerners and the Yorubas in Lagos, thereby giving his case ethnic colouration even when the processes are completely dependent on the judicial interpretations of the individual judge presiding. The OPC took into its hands the functions of a *vigilante* group too. President Obasanjo was accused, in some quarters, of treating OPC with kid's gloves when he had wasted no time in razing Odi, in Bayelsa state. Right or wrong as the accusations may be, the Nigerian federation had become such that ethnoregional interpretations of actions of political leaders, were not unusual.

If OPC activities were not properly curbed by President Obasanjo, because of the logic of federal autonomy of Yoruba espoused by that group, why would Obasanjo deal with political manifestations of autonomy in other states? The North, then chose to use Sharia to declare it federally desirable autonomy. Since May 1999, it was clear that the old North had lost political power, even though it had voted massively for General Obasanjo. After the announcement of the introduction of Supreme Sharia[54] in Zamfara, the Sharia was adopted in, at least, ten other Northern states. The Governors of these states have created a new factor in the federation. 'Yes', they argued we run a federal system in which State House of Assembly can, within their areas of jurisdiction, make laws. Zamfara claimed to have utilized these provisions. A similar attempt to introduce *Sharia* in Kaduna State's multi-ethnic and multi-religious society led to gross violence, with many people losing their lives earlier in Kaduna and in Gwantu, the headquarters of Sanga Local Government Council Area of that State.

Was Sharia, as introduced by the political (rather than religious) leaders, a political card? Was it a new bargaining chip in Nigeria's federation? The killing of Ibos and others in Kaduna extracted reciprocal killings of Muslims and Northerners in Abia and Imo States. In fact it led to the call by the Governors of the Southeastern States for a confederation. As a State Governor put it:

114

The Northern governors started it by adopting Sharia. We asked the president to intervene he refused until the situation got out of hand and Igbo people were killed. We really have to sit down and talk about the future of this country[55]

The governors rose from their meeting with a communiqué which made the following points: -

We the governors of the South East Zone still affirm our faith in the corporate existence of Nigeria... We endorse the decision of the National Council of state to suspend the Sharia Law passed in some state of the federation... We condemn in its entirety without any equivocation, the unprovoked and unwarranted attacks and killings of Easterners in Kaduna... That based on the realistic appraisal of the recent events in Nigeria and taking advantage of the setting up of a constitutional review committee by the Federal Government, we endorse the principles of confederation as the basis of our continued existence in corporate Nigeria[56]

In no time the Yoruba Afenifere leader, Chief Abraham Adesanya backed the position of the Southeastern Governors. He argued that there was hardly any difference between "true federation" as demanded by Yorubas and "confederacy which the Igbos are now demanding". In his reaction, President Obasanjo[57] called the demand for a confederation as "highly mischievous and extremely unpatriotic".[58] But the Governor of Abia described Obasanjo's views as "his personal opinion".[59] The demand for a confederal Nigeria sent shivers through the political spine of the North, which then sent emissaries to the Southeast on reconciliation trips. Meanwhile, the Governors moved to see that the state Houses of Assembly in their state passed the confederation resolution, similar to the passage of the Sharia laws in Zamfara, Sokoto and Kano Houses of Assembly.

Following closely this development was the announced intention to declare a Republic of Biafra by the Movement for the Actualization of the Sovereign State of Biafra (MASSOB), on May 27, 2000. Disowned by Ojukwu and the pan-Ibo *Ohaneze* the group hoisted a Biafra flag, while the leader escaped on motorcycle during the so-called ceremony. In May 2001, Ojukwu opened the *Biafra* Office in New York. Was the call for confederation, like the Sharia, political card? If it was, other zones were soon to put their card on the political table.

As mentioned, the governors of the South-South complained about the non-release of 13% derivation fund to their states. From the days of the military rule, the Niger-Delta had always been an area of violence. Devastated by oil exploration, inadequately touched by the benefits of oil, overwhelmed by an army of unemployed youths, the area has seen violence aimed at extracting a positive response from the Federal Government and oil companies.

In fact, pipelines had been sabotaged at various times, while communities involved in illegal oil bunkering had suffered tragic consequences resulting from unexpected explosions and inferno.[60] In a demonstration of anger, Bayelsa youths in Odi had ambushed and killed four soldiers. The military's reaction was to raze Odi village. It was wanton military operation, illustrating clearly the need for Nigeria to establish a para-military unit for dealing with civil disobedience.

With this background of restiveness among the youth and what was seen as the refusal of the federal government to release the 13% derivation fund from May-December 1999, political leader of the South-South zone met and issued a communiqué stating:

> Conference, in consultation with the people of the zone had decided to set in motion, the machinery to assume full control of its resources within the framework of true federalism. Accordingly, it requests the National Assembly through the State Houses of Assembly of the South-South zone to pass an Act empowering the states to take full control of their respective natural resources on behalf of the people.[61]

Was this constitutionally possible? As the former Governor of Sokoto State, Alhaji Yahaya Abdulkarim, (who is opposed to South-South resource control) opined- "If the Federal Government allows their suggestion, that means everybody is going his way".[62] However, as Governor Duke of Cross Rivers State clarified – there are constitutional hurdles, when we have worked this out, we shall make things clear, but it's currently a mere statement of intent.[63] Could this resource control plank be a political card for the South-South? If it was, it was a powerful one, for it sent some concerned leaders of the country reaching out for a reconciliatory line.

However, the Governors went beyond the expression of intent, to increase their collective power to influence the destiny of their people. The six states floated Oil Company BEDROCK OIL for exploration and production of oil in the country. In addition, each state set up its own company. Governor Attah of Akwa Ibom explained the rationale of these actions:

> We can acquire the required technology, we can acquire the financial ability to go for a major off-shore block and that is what we intend to do with it and I think that it is about time Nigerians started developing themselves. That is what democracy is all about.[64]

There is no doubt that the South-South plank, which also involves a call for national conference, reflects the dissatisfaction of the states with the pattern of resource distribution in the Federation.

However, the prospects of a review of the legislative list in favour of subnational units are high. The future is most likely to witness a relatively less strong centre than Nigeria has now.

But it is unlikely that Nigerians would revert to the loose Federation they had between 1960-65, or even adopt a confederal constitution.[65]

The Middle-Belt (MB) zone, (which includes the North Central Zone) also reacted to a number of issues in the federation. The trigger for the Middle Belt was the complaint by the core North that the Service Chiefs of the Armed Forces came from the Middle belt and not the core North. There were spontaneous reactions to what was regarded as Northern hypocrisy – using the Middle Belt when it was convenient, to fight its war, and turn around to dump them. The Middle belt Forum made it clear that it was no longer interested in being part of the old Northern geopolity, or share Northern identity with the Hausa-Fulanis.[66] The Middle Belt supported a federation with a strong centre, with equity in opportunities for all. It called for equity in the distribution of resources and the need to encourage solid minerals, agriculture and industrial development in the zone.

The Middle Belt search for identity started in the 1950s and had seen the zone as the major seat of opposition in the old Northern Region. Both the Middle Belt Forum and the Middle Belt Progressive Movement also called for a conference of ethnic nationalities to redefine the Nigerian Federation. The Sharia riots aggravated the demands for separate identity and political course from the Hausa/Fulani. In response to the Middle Belt demand for a separate identity, late Alhaji Wada Nas (Abacha's Minister) accused them of "suffering from inferiority complex". He further stressed that "as far as we are concerned, we are in a democratic system where only the majority can have its way. So nothing can be done about this".[67] One wonders what majority Wada Nas was talking about. Did he forget that the various minority groups form a majority? Did he forget the indispensable role played by minority states in the elections of Presidents Shehu Shagari and Olusegun Obasanjo?

In the search for greater political muscle, the Middle Belt Forum and Niger-Delta formed a new alliance of Northern and Southern minorities. The alliance was aimed, according to Chief David Dafinone , at bringing together like-minded people of both regions, refocus their energies, create an economic haven where human rights are respected, and advocate for the restructuring of the federation to effect equitable distribution of powers, resources and opportunities.[68]

Alfred Horsfall, (former Chairman of the Oil Mineral Producing and Development Commission) succinctly made the case for this alliance:

> ...The Igbos, Hausas and Yorubas have dealt with minorities. All the same, when the Hausas want to fight a war, they will go to the Middle Belt and recruit soldiers. When they want to exploit them, the Middle Belt is part of the North; in this place, when they want to marginalize us, we are part of the East. But when the time for sharing power and resources comes, we are seen as slaves. We have therefore come together to take over our destiny into our hands... We have come to the conclusion that we cannot fight that war alone. The only way we can fight and win is by fighting together. They call us minorities, but we are giants of this country.[69]

The participants at this Middle Belt/Niger-Delta Conference basked in their new found bases of political strength. As Obong Akpan Isemin, the former Governor of Akwa Ibom State put it:

> ... The issues of self-determination and control of resources are not negotiable ... Nigeria fought the civil war with the resources from the Middle Belt, and reconstructed the country with resources from the Niger-Delta... the hallmark of the struggle is the coming together of the two wealthy but marginalized regions, the Niger-Delta and the Middle Belt.[70]

In a similar search for alliance, the former Baifran leader, Chief Odumegwu Ojukwu, has been canvassing for Ibo – Yoruba alliance in order to tackle the North. He believed very strongly that the current contacts between *Ohaneze* and *Afenifere* would produce a new alliance, possibly *Ohanifere*.[71]

While one would have thought that this vigorous assertions and inter-zonal solidarity sought among Nigeria's ethnic groups will not stretch beyond the above demands, a new dimension of identity explosion had been brought heavily unto the delicate balance of Nigeria's Nation-building process. In the light of the above, there was a re-definition of aggressive boundary relations among ethnic groups and conflagration resulting from strong claims to citizenship, indigeneship and non-indigeneship by these groups. These agitations stretched the capacity of our police force to almost unimaginable heights. The invitation of the Armed Forces and their subsequent over-reaction (given the unspeakable act of gruesome murder of their comrades by ethnic men) in the troubled Taraba-Benue boarders, reinforces the argument for the National Assembly to pass a law establishing a security agency charged wholly with the responsibility of identifying, preventing, controlling and managing internal conflicts. This will go a long way in combating ethnic, religious and youth restiveness, while safeguarding a relative balance of federal pendulum.

Let us give an insight into these incidents and how they affect our Nigeria's federation.

Fighting between ethnic Tiv and Hausa-speaking Azara people erupted in Nassarawa State on June 12 after an Azara leader was killed and the Tivs were blamed. What followed from claims by both parties to land in Nasarawa, led to the death of several hundreds of people and the displacement of others who became refugees in our country. Jos the capital of Plateau State was a relatively peaceful town until September 7, 2001 when it became embroiled in a crisis which left several lives and property destroyed. Again the crisis was traced to the rivalry between the Muslim Hausa/Fulani and Christians in Jos North local government.

In describing the mayhem in Jos and its environs, a newspaper put in:

Religious zealots, defying a dusk to dawn curfew by the state government, embarked on a daring mission, squaring up with the police in shootouts, and venting unprovoked anger on luxury buses, passengers and residents.[72]

There have been many violent conflicts in Jos since 2001. Similarly, in October 2001, fighting between Tivs and Jukuns in the Benue-Taraba boundaries had reached its climax following sporadic attacks by both Tiv and Jukun militia men on each other's territory. What started as a result of conflict over land between the Fulanis and Jukuns on one hand, and the Tiv on the other soon escalated, leading to the abduction, dehumanization and subsequent murder of 19 soldiers, by Tiv ethnic militiamen including an Army Captain deployed along the Taraba-Benue boarders in the wake of renewed clashes between Tivs and Jukuns. Failure to produce the killers of the soldiers, the remaining bodies of the slain soldiers and their guns by the Benue State government as directed by the Federal Authority, attracted reprisal attacks from the Army which left 5 villages and several properties destroyed. Many lives were also lost. While it is most condemnable for ethnic militia men to kill soldiers on peacekeeping, it is equally atrocious for the Army to undertake such reprisal attack on innocent civilians.

In Kano, on October 12, 2001 what was meant to be a peaceful demonstration against United States reprisal attack on Afghanistan by Muslims, was soon overtaken by another group made up of religious fanatics who openly looted and harassed non-indigene traders. After their shops had been looted, some non-indigenes began to retaliate by killing the religious fanatics.

Following the mayhem in Kano, in their assessment, both Tijjani Bala Kalarawi, and El-Zakzaky, renowned Islamic preachers said, "the crisis had nothing to do with religion". They said "most of those who carried out lootings and killings did so because they had no jobs and no means of livelihood."[73]

While it is possible to attribute some of the causes of these conflicts to the economic inequalities among citizens, it is also necessary to state that most of the root causes of these violent agitations are not unconnected with the lack of adequate mechanism in our constitution for handling such and the inability of our leaders to appropriately apply the techniques of dialogue and compromise.

Importantly, while the various ethno-regional assertions could be viewed as political cards for ensuring equitable distributive bargains in the federal polity, can the same be said of the various inter-ethnic and aggressive identity explosions across the nation? These explosions of subnational identities in our federal arrangement require compromises from the conflicting parties, the re-definition of our citizenship rights by the National Assembly and the establishment of specialized security agency for managing violent internal conflicts.

In essence, the violent protests in the Niger-Delta over perceived injustice in resource distribution; the Itsekiri-Ijaw violence in the Delta; the resumption of the Ife-Modakeke communal violence; the menace of Odu'a Peoples' Congress (OPC) and the accompanying violence in Lagos and Shagamu areas; the formation of the Arewa Peoples' Congress (APC) and the Igbo Peoples' Congress (IPC); the MASSOB's feeble attempt to resuscitate Biafra; the Sharia crisis and the demands for a confederation; the South-South demand for the control of its resources; and all the recent inter-ethnic/religious conflicts in various states across the country are all part of the bubbles of the Nigerian Federation in the process of nation-building.

That these political bubbles worried former President Obansanjo, is reflected in his address to the members of the Obasanjo Leadership Forum when they paid a courtesy call on him. Obasanjo claimed that the Sharia, OPC and Niger-Delta crises were all programmed to destabilize Nigeria. According to Obasanjo;

... some people want to secede. Some people want to break away from Nigeria while others want a stronger federation.[74]

Would Nigeria break up?

I do not believe that Nigeria would break up in the nearest future. The reasons for the adoption of the federal form of government by our founding fathers are still very much around. While political leaders in their rhetoric, may dramatize their cases by strutting up to the precipice, they are likely to walk back to the center stage for negotiations. Nigerian leaders are aware that there is an intricate network of interdependence among Nigerians. Moreover, they know that Nigeria may not survive a second civil war, and that there is no need tempting our collective fate.

Also, with the threats of disintegration, Nigeria will be swimming against the strong global tides, which increasingly demands larger regional units—for economic and non-economic interests. I strongly believe that despite our differences, we can still create some harmony amidst our myriads of conflicts. Such conflicts are normal, in the face of the challenges of nation-building in a world of globalization. Let us not forget that we must agree to disagree.

We shall now turn to the challenges of nation-building in Nigeria.

The Nigerian ship of nation-state faces a number of challenges. These can be summarized as i) the challenge of the politics of federalism ii) challenge of democracy and good governance and iii) challenge of attitudinal re-orientation. Some of these challenges are not new. They have been there but at times, their echoes are heard within different structures

1. The Challenge of the Politics of Federalism

Given the analysis of the dynamics of our federation, there are thorny issues, which attract our attention.

a) *The Challenge of Distribution of Resources*

All the systems have this problem. In Canada, Ontario, British Columbia and Alberta are the more viable provinces. Through process of fiscal equalization, funds are transferred to other states that are less well-to-do without necessarily robbing the rich states of their funds. In Australia, the Australian Lands Grant Commission carries out fiscal equalization among component units of the Federation.

It is recommended that Revenue Mobilization, Allocation and Fiscal Commission should collate available data and embark on vertical and horizontal fiscal equalization among the component units of the Federation. This should be an annual event, which would still take cognizance of the Revenue Formula. Fiscal equalization would transfer funds to less well-to-do states for the purpose of national development. At the same time, it retains funds in states from where resources are extracted.

Our experience is such that an Economic Emergency Fund should be set up for Niger-Delta area to enable the people of these communities raise their quality of life and appreciate the benefits of their contribution to the Federation. The National Assembly may allocate a certain percentage of the Federation Account to this account in the next 5 years. The Niger-Delta Development Commission and other relevant agencies can be funded from this account.

b) *The Challenge of Cooperative/Competitive Federalism*

The concept of dual federalism as we practised in our First Republic, is everywhere, now becoming history. New federal associations are going cooperative, collaborative, competitive and interdependent. Those who shout "true federalism" may do well to remember that there is hardly anything like that now, especially the classical model espoused by K. C. Wheare. [75] The advent of the Welfare State after the Second World War has changed the nature of federal states and rendered them more interdependent. [76]

It is true that years of military rule, in part, contributed to the centralization of the Nigerian Federation- a far cry from 1965. Candidly, there is need for the revision of the legislative list to give states and local governments more functions. In addition, tax powers of each tier of government should be reviewed to reflect new responsibilities so acquired.

So far, the Federal Government seems to have so much funds that it dabbles into any area of its fancy. Candidly, housing, water, agriculture, primary schools and rural development should revert to state and local governments, which should have enough resources to carry out these functions.

Political leaders should be sensitive to constitutional provisions. The Obasanjo administration treated the running of the Federation under democracy as if we are under military rule. The constant summoning of the Governors to Abuja was reflective of military rule. The Governors are Chief Executives of their states, responsible to their electorates, and must therefore be left alone to do their jobs. The use of the National Council of States (NCS) to legitimize government decisions is unconstitutional. NCS is an advisory body to the President. The President should relate more actively with the National Assembly, to give the Federation and our democracy the proper nudge forward. There are obvious areas of greater inter-governmental relations, which the large ego of President Obasanjo prevented him from exploiting.

c) *The Subnational Challenges*

From the creation of four regions in 1963, we now have 36 states. Over the years, the fears of minorities in each region or state have led to the demands for additional states. The demands were often replete with complaints of injustice, unfairness and domination by the large ethnic groups. Often these requests for new states are responses to these complaints. They expect that the new states would provide them with new forms of autonomy and opportunity to exercise self-rule. However, the truth is that each new state creates 'new majorities' and 'new minorities'. In many cases the new majorities are even more vicious than the old majorities. They may also find that the new states have less resource bases than the old ones and new lines of cleavage often emerge. Perhaps, the solution to these challenges is that leaders at all levels of government should endeavour to be fair, just and equitable in relations with their electorates.

1. Challenges of Democracy and Good Governance

While laws, structures and processes are useful in the operation of federalism as a mechanism for managing conflicts in the process of nation-building, the **HUMAN DIMENSION** poses the greatest challenge to the polity. It does not matter what laws and structures are in place, human beings must run the system. Human operators must imbibe the values of justice, equity and accommodation of opponents, as well as operate in the same polity. We all cannot share one viewpoint or opinion. We come from different backgrounds and must appreciate and respect these differences without lionizing them. We must focus more on our commonalities, without ignoring our "diversity". We must accept that even though we operate in one polity, our interests do not always coincide, and when they are in conflict, we must find appropriate mechanisms of resolving them.

a) *Politicians*

We have made a transition from military to civil rule. So far, many of our politicians are still learning democratic values. They exhibit 'residual military' psyche in their actions. We do not seem to be ready for democratic practices. Our politicians see democracy in instrumental terms. They are more concerned with the perquisites that politics provides under a democracy.

This is why we have three groups of politicians- politicians, political contractors and political touts- in the political terrain. The politician is one who is dedicated to politics and seeks to acquire and use power in the interest of his electorate— for the maintenance of law and order, provision of welfare, and the pursuit of the interest of the State in relations with other states in the international system. There are very few of these available in Nigeria today; even these have become an endangered specie.

The political contractor is a businessman in the political terrain. For him, democracy is tolerable nuisance, which provides greater access to resources. The ends of democracy and values are unimportant, even though he may be shouting them at public fora. The political tout is the hireling of the contractor and does his biding, even if it involves maximum dispensation of violence. For the tout, democracy means 'democratization of violence' and democratic access to the instruments of violence—and at times these undercut the state's ability to maintain law and order. Incidents of violence in most states of the federation, especially during the elections and after, illustrates this point. Anambra and Oyo States illustrate the dangerous dimensions of the activities of political contractors. The Ngige-Ubah and the Ladoja-Adedibu crises also illustrate these. It is our hope that in the next twenty years, political contractors and touts would have transformed themselves into legitimate politicians.

b) *Political Tolerance*

The tolerance of the opinion of others and the extension of the democratic space is another challenge. In Nigeria, the present actors seem not to understand democracy or have not learnt from the politicians of the past Republics. There is so much political intolerance among politicians, it is amazing and yet disgusting. Intra-party squabbles have led to deaths. How, for example, does one explain the show of force demonstrated by the Nigeria Police in Kano at the ANPP rally on 23rd of September 2003? Dr. Chuba Okadigbo allegedly died as a result of the rough handling of this rally. What good excuse did the police have for denying ANPP the permit to hold the rally— beyond the usual 'security reasons'? How does one explain government's use of force during the Nigeria Labour Congress (NLC) demonstration against its hike in fuel prize? How can one explain the abuse of court process by the Federal Government- after having its case against the NLC thrown out in Abuja, and yet taking it to a court of coordinate jurisdiction in Lagos? The Lagos court granted the injunction, which became popularly known as *black market* or *bolekaja* injunction. Political leaders must not only be responsive to the yearnings of the people, they must demonstrate a high sense of constitutionalism in their actions. They must tolerate the opposition because this country belongs to all of us. We must nurture the democratic plant of freedom with demonstrable understanding and mutual respect for one another.

The excessive dependence of the Obasanjo regime on coercion was anti-democratic, and even dangerous for the political class.

c) *The Electoral Process*

While winners would call the 2003 elections free and fair, some losers would call it fraudulent. On balance, as a political observer, the 2003 elections in many parts of Nigeria were very fraudulent. The 2007 elections were perhaps the most fraudulent in Nigeria's history. Politicians, because of insecurity, put their rigging machines on overdrive and ended with overkill. The elections were disastrous exercises—detracting from our democratic learning process and potentially challenging our process of national integration. Given the cynicism in the polity, I humbly suggest that:

i)   all members of the current Independent National Electoral Commission (INEC) be relieved of their duties, while consultations be undertaken for a new and more neutral INEC comprising members of all political parties, NGOs and CSOs. Currently, INEC does not have any credibility.
ii) There is a need to revisit the voters register by the new INEC,
iii) Laws governing contributions to party and individual campaign funds be established, and there should be a one-term Chief Executive for all levels of government, starting from 2007.

We need to sanitize our electoral process to help restore electoral legitimacy to INEC and restore people's confidence in electoral democracy. Rigged elections disenfranchise the people and set a false agenda for governance.

d) *Attacking the problem of poverty*

The so-called *dividends of democracy* are only visible in a few states, and the Governors of these states must be commended. No one cares for democracy on an empty stomach. We must not forget that a democratic culture and stability cannot thrive in a society where there is abject poverty. Our poverty alleviation/eradication programmes have so far failed to tackle the problem. We need to work seriously on these in order to save our democracy. With our abundant human and natural resources, we strongly believe that our poverty is related to the ineptitude and inefficiency in the governance of the polity. Our governments, at federal, state and local levels must summon the courage and will to fight this menace, which from all available indicators, is increasing. The army of the unemployed poses great threat to the security of life and property of individuals, and the political stability of the polity.

e) *Security to Life and Property*

Since 1999, an atmosphere of insecurity has enveloped the polity. Initially, one thought that the removal of the tight lid under military rule had led to a new sense of freedom in which freedom had been transformed into license. Over the years, there have been at least, two hundred cases of violence – communal and others. Armed robbery has become part of our normal life. Political and other homicides have become rampant in the system— no different from the situation under the military. The assassinations of the late Minister of Justice, Chief Bola Ige, Marshall Harry, the PDP Chairman in Kogi State and Chairman Anambra Bar Association and his wife, among others, show how life has become really unsafe. The entourage of the former Governors of Niger, Lagos and Benue States were attacked on the road. Democracy presupposes responsibility. It presupposes that politicians will be responsible enough, to be crisis dampners rather crisis than escalators. It also means that government should effectively maintain law and order to encourage the 'rule of law' and prevent the aggrieved from taking laws into his/her hand. Unfortunately, the Nigeria Police seems overwhelmed, while the constant use of the military for police duties is dangerous for everyone. Government must also stop the intimidatory technique of using the Nigeria Police to enable it get away with illegalities as practiced under Obasanjo. Government must demonstrate civility, decency and caution in the use of its security services, which are paid from our tax funds. They are paid to maintain the system for all of us and not for a few incumbents in government.

3. The Challenge of Attitudinal Re-Orientation and Leadership

a. The challenge of Patriotism, Discipline and Social Conscience

Candidly, it is my belief that with 50% patriotism and discipline among leaders and followers, we would be able to transform this country into an industrialized power – given our human and natural resources. Our aggressive self-interest – both among leaders and followers – has blocked our chances to develop. It is not enough for leaders to call for patriotism, when their words and actions do not demonstrate such. Nor is it important for leaders to call for discipline and sacrifice when their lives indicate the opposite. We must all develop a social conscience – which is sensitive to the rights of others. Our road users, as an illustration, hardly care who else uses the road. When their vehicles have engine problems, they leave it in the middle of the street, instead of pushing it to the kerbside. The whole system is like that. We must accommodate others and accept one another as we experience our bitter and sweet moments. We must remember that our destinies are interwoven, whether we like it or not. In the process of globalization, nations get together to face common challenges because they find themselves individually too small for their individual challenges. We cannot be different. A smaller Nigeria only renders us less efficient. In addition, it will expose Africa to new forms of recolonization. We must therefore abandon the loose talk of secession, which easily come to our tongues, and embark on more effective ways of making this Nigeria work well. We must build a Nation.

b) *Political Leadership and Statesmanship*

It is clear that since 1999, the political class had not learnt that leadership entails listening to your followers, persuading them when necessary, and providing guidance and foresight. At the Federal level, General Obasanjo, as President, still exhibited *messianic arrogance* and *residual militarism*. Many Chief Executives in the states share this trait of residual militarism with him. These leaders, at all levels, have not learnt that once elected, they must transform themselves into statesmen. Our experience has shown that many of our leaders are still politicians – there is no principle they cannot mortgage, there is no value they cannot adulterate, and there is no law or rule they can not bastardize. From the election of the Senate President in 1999 through attempts to remove the former Speaker of the House of Representatives (Alhaji Ghali Na'abba) and those of states, the abortive 'coup' in Anambra, to fraudulent actions by leaders in the process of passing electoral act, and the election of Senator Wabara as Senator and President of the Senate, the politics of self-interest, not statesmanship dominated the polity. The political class must wake-up, demonstrate better understanding of the kind of leadership required in a multinational Nigeria, otherwise they would be committing a class suicide.

The way our political leaders respect the rules of the game of politics, their ability to imbibe the democratic values of accommodation, tolerance of opposition and participation; and their ability to demonstrate gallantry in defeat and grace in victory, will determine the extent of harmony in the Fourth Republic. Reconciliation is a basic component of this process and the leadership must be so inclined. The task of nation-building is complex and the dynamics of reconciliation are infinite. The leadership must therefore build the confidence of its citizens as it strives to balance conflicting claims. In the final analysis, structures and institutions alone cannot build understanding and cooperation in the polity. The attendant human values of tolerance, fairness, justice and honesty are essential ingredients, which the leadership must imbibe and promote.

Conclusion

We have tried to argue that the Twenty-First Century poses many challenges of nation-building in Nigeria. We have also argued that Western models of nation - building are really not this available to Nigeria as options at this point in time. In addition, we suggested that the problems of nation-building in Nigeria are historical and multidimensional.

We have also argued that Nigerians have made significant efforts to transform the country from a "mere geographical expression" to "an organic state". They now need to transform the organic state into an organic nation. However, in this process, echoes of the past are still very much around, even if these are heard within different structures; which often detract from efforts directed to achieving national unity. Finally, we suggested that unless we substantially overhaul the ship of the nation-state, we shall find ourselves as inept cripples in the Twenty-First Century of globalization and high speed information technology and services.

We have moved from the stage of *coexistence,* through *contact* to the middle phase of *compromise.* Currently, not only have Nigerian groups developed "sufficiently complex diverse and interdependent" relationships requiring peaceful reconciliation, the civil war had forced Nigerians to discover many areas of compatibility, amidst their diversity of identities and interest.

Candidly, our identities have not coalesced yet–in fact, they take on aggressive dimensions which simmer to the surface quite often. These occasional upwelling may jolt the system from time to time. There are many waves to be encountered in Nigeria's process of nation-building. At times, the ship may be badly rocked, but not destroyed. From such catastrophic experiences, Nigeria may find new arenas for compromises and reconciliation.

Federalism still provides a conducive grid for our nation-building efforts. The reasons for the adoption of federalism are still very much around. The mutual fears and suspicions of one another by Nigerian groups are likely to continue, over different issues, using new competitive techniques. But it is hoped that as groups interact and establish mutual confidence in one another and in the federal system, necessary compromises will be effected and conflicts managed. I do not believe that Nigeria will break-up in the foreseeable future.

Paradoxically, Nigeria's complexity has been its saviour. It has made it more difficult for groups to easily pull out of the federation. The current complaints are, in a way, good for the system. They are part of the processes of adjustment of the federal pendulum as it swings between centripetalism and centrifugalism in the nation-building process. These adjustments can be painful and, at times, may put heavy strains and stresses on the nation.

We require political leaders with skills in effecting appropriate compromises and conflict resolution. The challenges of nation-building now, call for our collective sense of patience, accommodation and tolerance. These are not the cheapest commodities to be purchased in the political market place where people operate under stress, yet they are indispensable. Important too, for nation-building are leadership qualities such as Justice, Fairness inclusiveness and Equity which are cardinal to the survival of our nation. We have done well, we can still do better. Nation-building, is after all, an infinite process, because the process of national integration are infinite— always requiring refinement.

NOTES

1. Michael Batty and Bob Barr, "The Electronic Frontier: Exploring and Mapping Cyberspace" in *Futures*, 26(7): 699-712.
2. John Herz, *International Politics in the Atomic Age*, (1969); and "The Territorial State Revisited: Reflections on the Future of the Nation-State" in James N. Rosenau, (ed.) *International Politics and Foreign Policy: A Reader in Research and Theory* (New York: The Free Press, 1969) p. 257.
3. Alvin Toffler, *Power Shift: Knowledge, Wealth and Violence at the Edge of the 21st Century* (Great Britain: Bantam Free Press, 1990)
4. Dennis Goulet, *The Uncertain Promise: Value Conflicts in Technology Transfer* (New York: 1Doc/ North American Inc., 1977) for a very interesting analysis of this topic.
5. United Nations Development Programme, *Human Development Report 1997* (New York: Oxford University Press, 1997) p. 82.
6. UNDP, *Human Development Report 1997*, p. 91.
7. *Ibid.,*
8. *Ibid.,*
9. Boutros Boutros-Ghali, "Global Prospects for The United Nations" in *Law and State*, Vol. 53/54, 1996,p. 150.
10. See G. Almond and B Powell, *Comparative Politics: A Development Approach* (Boston: Little Brown, 1962) and L. Binder, *Political Development in Changing Society* (Berkeley: University of California Press, 1962)

11. David B. Guralnik (ed.), *Webster's New World Dictionary* Vol. II (New York: The World Publishing Company, 1970) p. 946.
12. M. G. Smith, "Institutional and Political Conditions of Pluralism" in L. Kuper and M. G. Smith (eds.), *Pluralism in Africa* (Los Angeles: University of California Press, 1971) p.32.
13. Ali A. Mazrui "Violent Congruity and the Politics of Retribalization in Africa" International, Vol. III No. 1 (1969) P. 105
14. Lewis Coser, *The Functions of Social Conflicts* (New York: The Free Press 1956) P. 88.
15. This does not make sense in developing or Third World States. For a good discussion of this, see Stein Rokkan, "Centre-formation, Nation-Building and Cultural Diversity: report on UNESCO Programme" in S. N. Eisenstadt and Stein Rokkan (eds.) *Building States and Nations,* Vol. I and II (Beverley Hills: Sage, 1973)
16 Ali A. Mazrui and Michael Tidy, *Nationalism and New States in Africa* (London: Heinemann, 19784) p. 373.
17 Thus writing to the Nigerian Head of State for the creation of separate state (from Benue-Plateau State) within Nigeria, the Plateau Student Association stated:
    The Tiv and Idoma social set up is completely different from that shared by groups on the Plateau. There has been no cultural tie between our people of Southern Benue. History has it that we in fact we never knew of their existence until recently.
    Plateau Student Association, "Our Stand for A Plateau State" letter to His Excellency, General Yakubu Gowon, HFMG, dated 13 June 1974 (unpublished mimeographed letter, p.2.)
18. J. Coleman, Nigeria: *A Background to Nationalism* (Berkeley: University of California Press, 1958)
19. See Nelson Kasfir, "Cultural Sub-Nationalism in Uganda" in Victor Olorunsola (ed.) *The Politics of Cultural sub-Nationalism* (New York: Doubleday, 1972); also see similar cases in Pierre Alexander, "Social Pluralism in French African Colonies and in State Issuing Therefrom: An Impressionistic Approach" in Leo Kuper and Smith (eds.) *op. cit.;* and C. Turner "Congo-Kinshasha" in V. Olorunsola *op. cit.*

20. *Ethno-regionalism* is used to refer to the crystallization of the identity of the major ethnic groups with the regional administrative boundaries. In Nigeria, there were three major ethno-regional groups: the Hausa-Fulani in the Northern Region; the Ibo in the Eastern Region; and the Yoruba in the Western Region. In such situation the desire to protect regional interest implicitly involves the desire to protect the interests of the major group in that region in competition with those from other regions. The region as an administrative unit becomes the base for competition with other ethnic groups.

21. Oluwole Alajina, *Egbe Omo Oduduwa Monthly Bulletin* quoted in Coleman, *op. cit.* p. 346.

22. Minutes of the First Inaugural Conference of the Egbe Omo Oduduwa, June 1948, in Coleman, *op. cit.* p. 346.

23. *West African Pilot* (Lagos), July 6, 1949, in Coleman, *op. cit* p. 347.

24. Chief Obafemi Awolowo, *Path* to *Nigeria Freedom* (London: Faber and Faber, 1947) pp. 47-48.

25. *Legislative Council Debate,* Nigeria, 4 march, 1948, p. 227, quoted in Coleman, *op. cit.* p. 320.

26. Note that while Nigeria was technically unitary, it was very much decentralized—in fact the center virtually preformed the functions of a confederal unit.

27. T. N. Tamuno, "Separatist Agitations in Nigeria Since 1914" *Journal of Modern African Studies* 8, 4, (1970).

28. See Kalu Ezra, *Constitutional Development in Nigeria,* 2nd Ed. (London: Cambridge university Press, 1964) pp. 187-188.

29. These associations included the Middle Zone League (MZL) and Middle Belt Peoples' Party (MBPP). These two fused to form the United Middle Belt Congress (UMBC).

30. Nigeria, *Report of the Commission Appointed to Enquire into the Fear of Minorities and the Means of Allaying Them* (London: HMSO, (n.d. 505, 1958).

31. General Gowon, Address to the Conference of the Public Service Commission in Nigeria, Lagos, November 5, 1968.

32. In 1963, the Midwest Region was created out of the Western region—thus making 3 regions in the south.

33. The population (in millions) as announced by that office in 1963 is as follows;

North	29.8
East	12.4
West	10.3
Midwest	2.5
Lagos	0.7

34. In Ahmadu Bell, *My Life, op. cit. p. 110*

35. General Gowon observed:

    Under the Old Constitution, the regions were so large and powerful as to consider themselves self-sufficient and almost entirely independent. The Federal government which ought to give lead to the whole country was relegated to the background. The people were made to realize that the federal government was real government of Nigeria. (Broadcast to the Nation, 26 May, 1968).

36. The Eastern region accused the Northern region of misusing the "little power we surrendered to them to preserve a unity which does not exist" by locating the Kainji Dam and a host of other things in the North. It added, "Now they have refused to allow the building of an iron and steel industry in the East and paid experts to produce a distorted report. "J.P. Mackintosh, *Nigerian Government and Politics* (London: Allen and Unwin, 1966) pp. 557-558. On the other hand, the *Nigerian Citizen* owned by the Northern government, pointed to the two loan agreements totaling over $7.5 million… to be divided for two projects in the East and Western Regions… We believe deeply now that there is an ORGANISED CONSPIRACY IN HIGH PLACES AGAINST THE NORTH". (Mackintosh, *op, cit.* p.551).

37. Azikiwe's State House Diary' had accused Okpara and his Eastern colleagues of threatening to secede on 26 December 1964 (See *Daily Times,* 13th January 1965). However, Mackintosh (p.604) reported UPGA leaders as accusing only the President (Azikiwe) of having "contemplated breaking up the federation because he had felt that attacks on him and on the Ibos were becoming intolerable". Yet, Okpara was quoted on the same day as having said that "if this is

how the NPC wants to run the election then this country is finished", and that "disintegration was inevitable if the NPC continued to act in ways that would undermine unity of Nigeria". (*Daily Express,* 22 December,1984). It was reported that Ahmadu Bello welcomed the idea of Eastern Region's secession, if given the time to "divide our assets" (*Daily Express,*30 December 1984). See Mackintosh, *op. cit.* p. 604 for discussion.

38. An illustration of this was the acceptance by Western and Easter Regions for Israeli aid and relations with Nigeria, and the Northern Region's refusal to recognize the existence of Israel and partake in the sharing of such aid, see C.S. Philip, Jr. *The Development of Nigerian Foreign Policy* (Evaluation: North Western University Press, 1964).

39. It may be important to note some of those who describe the relationship in these terms also have at the back of their mind the fact that Tafawa Balewa (The Prime Minister) was the second in command in NPC and was seen as one who took orders from his senior, the Sardauna of Sokoto, Sir Ahmadu Bello. The impression is contradicted by Mr. Muffet's accounts in his volume, *Let the Truth Be Told:* The Coups of Nineteen Sixty Six, Vol. 1, (Zaria: Haudahuda Publishing Company, 1982).

40. By 1965, the NPC (the Northern People's Congress) controlled political power in the North. The Eastern and Midwestern Regions were under effective control of the NCNC (the National Council for Nigerian Citizens); and the Western Region was effective under the AG (the Action Group).

41. In the context of political violence in the old Western Region, this was a process in which political enemies were burnt alive, using vehicle tyres and petrol.

42. See Federal Republic of Nigeria, *Memoranda Submitted the Ad Hoc Conference on Constitutional Proposals for Nigeria.*
(Lagos: Government Printer, 1966). This document has the memoranda submitted by various delegations. The contributions demonstrate very clearly that Nigeria was a fragile state and that she could not lay claims to nationhood.

43. General Ankrah was the then military Head of Ghana's

Government.

44. Federal Republic of Nigeria, "The Constitution" (Suspension and Modification) (No. 9) Decree 1966. Decree No. 59.

45. The Federal Republic of Nigeria, Decree No. 18, 1967. Also see Federal Republic of Nigeria, *The Meeting of Military Leaders held at Peduase* Lodge Aburi, Ghana, 4 and 5 January 1967 (Lagos: Federal Ministry of Information, 1967).

46. In his broadcast of the above date Gowon assumed full powers as Commander-in-Chief of the Armed Forces, and declared state of emergency in the country. See *Sunday Daily Times* 28th May, 1967.p.1 and *Sunday Post,* 28 May, 1968,pp. 8-9.

47. For the gradual process of centralization of authority by the Military, see. J. Isawa Elaigwu, "The Military and State-Building: Federal-State Relations in Nigeria's 'Military-Federalism,' 1966-1967" in the A. B. Akinyemi, P.O. Cole and W. Ofonagoro, (eds.) *Readings On Federalism* (Lagos NIIA, 1979), pp. 155-181.

48. Billy Dudley, *Instability and Political Order: Politics and Crisis in Nigeria* (Ibadan: Ibadan Press, 1963) pp. 176-177.

49. See Alh. Shehu Shagari, *Beckoned To Serve* (Ibadan: Heinemann, 2001) for a more detailed discussion of this period from his perspective.

50. See J. Isawa Elaigwu, "Military Rule and Federalism, *loc. cit.,* pp 166-193;.

51. *Report of the Constitutional Conference* Vol.2, p.61.

52. Ranjit Sarkaria, "Forward" in S. C. Arora (ed.) *Current Issues and Trends in Centre-State Relations:* A Global view (New Delhi: Mittal Publication, 1991) p. 3.

These political zones are-

North-West	North-Central	North-East	South – South	South-East	South -West
Sokoto	Benue	Borno	Delta	Abia	Lagos
Kano	Plateau	Adamawa	Edo	Anambara	Ogun
Jigawa	Kogi	Yobe	Rivers	Enugu	Oyo
Zamfara	Niger	Taraba	Bayelsa	Imo	Osun
Kebbi	Nasarawa	Bauchi	Akwa-Ibom	Ebonyi	Ondo
Kaduna	Kwara	Gombe	Cross-Rivers		Ekiti
Katsina					

53. See *The News,* 15, November 1999; *The Punch,* February 23, 2000 pages 1 and 2; *This Day,* February 29, 2000, pages 1 and 2.
54. *Vanguard,* March 27, 2000, p.1.
55. *Vanguard,* May 9, p.1. Also see *This Day,* July 19, 2003,p. 13. Zamfara Governor supported the call for confederation- *This Day,* July 12, 2000, p.1.
56. *Sunday Vanguard,* March 19, 2000, p. 1.
57. *The Source,* Vol. 6. No. 25 April 3, 2000, p.12.
58. *Ibid.,*
59. As an illustration the tragic death of hundreds of people in Jesse; and the petrol fire between Ifie and Ijala in Warri south Local Government in which about 150 people were feared to have died.
60. *Vanguard,* September 26, 2000, pp. 31 and 33. Also see *This Day,* August 16, 2000p. 10; July 28, 2000,p.7 July 24, 2000 p.13; July 17, 2000, p.1.
61. *The Punch,* September 4, 2000, p.2.
62. *Vanguard,* September 15, 2000, p6.
63. *Vanguard,* July 27, 2000. p.5.
64. The nearest Nigeria went to a Confederal Constitution was crisis period 1966-1967, when the Federal Military Government issued Decree No. 8, 1976, of March 17, 1967, in response to the Aburi peace accord in Ghana.
65. *Vanguard,* April 17, 2000 p.1; Also see *The Nigeria Standard,* August 17, 2000, p.7; *Abuja Today,* August 9-15, 2000, pp 1and 2.
66. *Vanguard,* April 17, 2000p.2.
67. *Vanguard,* August 19, 200, p.6. As Dan Suleiman of the Middle Belt Forum put it,
    … our position is not new now it has become necessary for he Middle Belt and the Union of the Niger-Delta to meet because of the extreme positions that are being taken (by) other regions in the federation which are not in the best interest of Nigeria.(The Nigeria Standard, August 17, 200, p.10)
68. *Vanguard,* August 17, 2000,p.10).
69. *Ibid.*

70. *Tell,* (Lagos) No. 38, September 18, 2000. According to Chief Ojukwu:
    I certainly still believe that whatever it is, our struggle will be infinitely easier and more successful if East and west can re-accommodate each other… So if Ohaneze meets with Afenifere it is a good thing. If we go further and continue meeting, it is a better thing. If they even go further and create Ohanifere, it will even better… (p.29)

71. *Daily Champion,* September 10, 2001, p.1.

72. *Newswatch,* October 29, 2001, p.39.)

73. *Vanguard,* July 19, 2002, p2.

74. K. C. Wheare, *Federal Government* (London: Oxford University Press, 1964)

75. See Ranjit Sarkaria, "Forward", *loc. cit.*

---

* *The original version was delivered as the IPPA* Annual Distinguished Lecture, 2004 – *at the Institute of Public Policy and Administration (IPPA) University of Calabar, Calabar. February 22, 2004*

CHAPTER 4

DEMOCRACY AND GOOD GOVERNANCE

Conflict is an inevitable aspect of human interaction, and unavoidable concomitant of choices and decision... The problem, then, is not to count the frustration of seeking to remove inevitability but rather of trying to keep conflicts in bounds. [1]

Introduction

In this chapter, we shall deal with three related issues – Democracy, Peace and Good Governance. What is Democracy? What is our understanding of the word — Peace? What is good governance? To what extent are peace and good governance imperative for a durable democratic polity? What are the challenges of democracy in Nigeria? What are the prospects for peace and good governance?

We do not claim to have the answers to these big questions, but we shall make a few suggestions to guide our discussion. We suggest that:

1. the concepts of 'democracy' and 'good governance' are essentially alien to Africa. These concepts need to be domesticated to Nigeria's (indeed Africa's) local conditions and targeted to her peculiar problems;while democracy provides a conducive medium for peace and good governance, peace and good governance are also imperatives for a sustainable democratic polity;

2. the majority of the members of the Nigerian political class and their followers have little commitment to constitutionalism, but are ironically more concerned about constitution-making;

3. the greatest threat to peace and democratic good governance in Nigeria is the political class (in government and in the political arena) who see democracy only in instrumental terms; they are not committed to democracy as an end, and have little sensitivity to the extent of "democratic deficit" created by their actions and activities;

4. Nigeria needs institutional, processual, and attitudinal changes in order to meet the challenges of peace and democratic governance; and

5. for a sustainable democratic polity and national development, we must imbibe a democratic culture of tolerance, accommodation, and hard work; and enshrine the values of *justice, fairness* and *equity*, as guides for all actions/ activities.

Let us now turn to our first suggestion on the concept of *democracy, peace* and *good governance.*

Democracy, Peace and Good Governance: A Definational note.

The term *democracy* is perhaps one of most polemical words in the political dictionary. It has been subjected to so many interpretations and adaptations in various parts of the world, that over time, it has become value-ridden.[2] In the context of the globalization of the world, the impression is often given that 'democracy' is *good*; to be 'undemocratic' is *bad*. The Greek originators of the concept must be very confused about it today, given the problems of Western democracy in Greece in the recent past. Nonetheless, it is possible to identify some universal characteristics or principles of democracy, which are adaptable to local situations in various parts of the world, depending on their peculiar conditions.

For us, *democracy* is a system of government based on the acquisition of *authority* from the people; the institutionalization of the *rule of law;* the emphasis on the *legitimacy* of rulers; the availability of *choices* and cherished values (including freedoms), and accountability in governance.

This definition brings out the principles of democracy. For us, these principles include the locus of authority in a democratic polity. *Authority* emanates from the people. Any authority which does not emerge from the consent of the people is not democratic. How consent is operationlised may vary from one system to the other. Secondly, a democratic polity must be based on *the rule of law*. Law cannot be arbitrary in a democracy. There are specified limits to power and how

142

it can be used. In addition, there should be an acceptance of the "rules of the game" of politics by all the players, if arbitrariness is not to creep in at a later stage. There are no sacred cows before the law, and no individual takes the law into his hands because the system provides opportunity of redress for the aggrieved.

The third characteristic of a democratic polity is that it must be *legitimate.* Legitimacy involves two processes. One of these is that the leader has the *right to rule* - that is to say - that given the law or the rules for accession to power he is the right person to be there. The institutional mechanism for his accession to power would depend on the particular country and people. The other is that he is *ruling rightly.* This is to say that he is performing well, given the ends for which he has been elected or chosen.

In addition to these, is the fourth, the element of *choice.* The people should have the right to effect changes in the leadership or the government of their country, given available alternative leadership. In some countries the plebiscetarian system is used. In some others, other mechanisms for providing choice are used. Choice also includes all basic human freedoms of thought, movement, association, worship and others, in relative terms. Fifthly, there must be *accountability.* Leaders must be held responsible for their actions as representatives of the people who are trusted with power to achieve particular ends, and must also account for such actions periodically.

These five points may be seen as the minimum characteristics of democracy. However, the institutional framework for their operation may differ from one country to the other. Does democracy mean Western democracy? No! It is also important to note that *democracy is not necessarily the most efficient and inexpensive system.* In fact, it is very expensive. It will really be wishful thinking to assume that democracy is the *elixir* to all problems of development. It is not. It *provides for relative peace and a conducive medium for development to take place.* In fact, it generates its own problems, to which solutions must constantly be found.

Let us expand a little on the principle of accountability and transparency because it shall come up later. The principles of *Transparency* and *Accountability* are intertwined. Basically, transparency refers to the ability to see clearly through objects. As an illustration, some of us would like to see clearly through a drinking glass to make sure that it is clean before we use them. Transparency refers to our ability to exhibit clearness in action, which puts such actions above question. A transparent process or system is one that is open, very clear and very easily recognized. If a process is not clearly understood, open or recognized, it is not transparent. How transparent, for example, is our electoral process? How transparent is the privatization exercise? We shall get back to this point later.

Accountability refers to the ability of a public functionary to give satisfactory explanation for his or her action. If sovereignty resides with the people, then government should be responsible and accountable to the people. Accountability therefore goes beyond the use or misuse of public funds. The actions of leaders should be subject to constant analytic x-ray. After all, a Constitution merely provides for a "basis of expression of harmony and a foundation of conduct." It accepts that discipline is important and that necessary limitations on incumbents are essential. Thus, in the 1999 Nigerian Constitution, there are many provisions which are aimed at making public officers responsive to the public pulse, disciplined in their activities and dedicated to the *service* of the people - not as masters, but as servants.

In essence, accountability is the *heart* of democracy. Since power rests with the people who delegate such powers to representatives to carry out specified functions on their behalf, such representatives have the responsibility to account for their service. Similarly, transparency is the *blood* of democracy. Its purity and cleanliness gives life to the heart and the democratic body. It embellishes the functioning of the polity and reinforces legitimacy of representatives or political leaders. Candidly, democracy exhorts a high level of accountability and transparency for the system to operate relatively smoothly, thereby ensuring political stability and the security and welfare of its citizens.

Governance is another concept that has increasingly attracted international attention. The African tradition of communalism in which each one is brother's keeper is a symbolism of governance. From the extended family system to the centralized forms of human organization, interactions among individuals and communities have been guided by cherished norms that are in our modern world reconceptualized as governance. Although, the concept is as old as human development, it has only been recently employed in development circles by international development agencies. It is promoted by these agencies in various ways. Underdevelopment is tied to the absence of 'good' governance. 'Good governance' has become a condition for accessing international funds. Again, this makes 'good governance' to assume a Western outlook. 'Good' governance is therefore a value-laden term, and needs to be demystified. Indices of good governance need to be clearly spelt out.

Governance, according to UNDP, is "the exercise of economic, political and administrative authority to manage a country's affairs at all levels. It comprises mechanisms, processes and institutions through which citizens and groups articulate their interests, exercise their legal rights, meet their obligations and mediate differences".[3] The nature of governance depends on: i) "the form of political regime", ii) "the process by which authority is exercised in the management of a country's economic and social resources for development' and iii) "the capacity of governments to design, formulate, and implement policies and discharge functions".[4]

In essence, 'good' governance deals with how those who have the authority of the state make efforts to achieve the goals or the ends of the state— *the maintenance of law and order;* the *provision of welfare for its citizens* and *the pursuit of national interest in the global arena.* Governments therefore exist to achieve these ends. It refers to the process and quality of governance and the role of the civil society and the private sector. Western democracy insists that 'good governance' entails the existence of democratic institutions and values.

'Good' governance depicts an ideal. However, to work towards this ideal, individuals, groups, corporate entities and governments must be guided by certain values, norms or principles in their dealings. These principles include participation, equity, the rule of law, transparency and accountability, as well as the effectiveness and efficiency in the delivery of public services.

Participation is the fundamental principle of good governance. It is an indication of the inclusive nature of the system of decision-making. Are the interests of both men and women, young and old, the minorities and the vulnerable in the society considered in decision-making? In essence, high premium is put on such democratic values such as equality and freedom (of association and expression). This means that apart from governmental institutions typical in representative democracy, there should be avenues for the civil society organizations to feed input into the decision-making unit. There should also be avenues for the reconciliation of the various interests in the society in order to reach a broad consensus. Yet the nature of relations between the elected officials and the electorate determines the impact of the constituency on policy decisions. This input by the people is regarded as an important feedback dimension of 'good governance'.

Equity and *inclusiveness* are also indicators of 'good governance'. To what extent is government fair to all – majority and minority groups, male and female citizens? Government must be seem to treat all as equal citizens and this must be reflected in the distribution of resources. Government must be inclusive and should not treat any group as *pariah*.

'Good governance' presupposes the *rule of law*. This means there must be a constitutional/legal framework, and a system of enforcement of laws, the administration of justice, and the promotion of equity, justice and fairness. Are fundamental human rights guaranteed and protected? How impartial is the judicial system? How civil and incorruptible is the law enforcement system? How dedicated to constitutionalism are public officials and servants? These are some indicators of the quality of governance in a country.

Transparency and Accountability are the cornerstones of 'good governance'. These have political/administrative and financial aspects. Are decisions taken and enforced according to rules, procedures and regulations? What is the nature of information flow? How accessible are decision-makers? How effective is the system of checks and balances among the various arms of government and across the ranks of the public service? Are decision-makers accountable to the people for their decisions? A transparent and accountable system of decision-making and administration leaves little or no room for financial irregularities. The level of corruption indicates the level of 'good' or 'bad' governance in a society, precisely because it diverts desirable public funds to private pockets. It must be noted that corruption goes beyond issues related to money and material things. Processes of governance could also be corrupted. Thus when the Economic and Financial Crimes Commission (EFCC) *'whitemails'* legislators and prods them to impeach their governors, EFCC was engaged in a corrupt activity. It is indicative of the maturity of the nation that the judiciary reversed all cases of impeachment through corrupt practices.

'Good' governance entails the *effective and efficient delivery of services*. This requires governments to be responsive and responsible in order to meet the needs of the citizens. It requires decision-makers to be resourceful and innovative in the management of scarce resources in order to reduce poverty and poverty-related problems (such as illiteracy, endemic and pervasive diseases). Good governance also entails the utilization of natural resources for sustainable development. *Subsidiary* emerged from European political vocabulary (in the 1990s) as another principle of good governance. It addresses the issue of *decentralization* in a political system. Subsidiary implies that the lower levels of government which are closer to the people and are better placed to deliver services more efficiently should be given the responsibilities of providing such public goods and services. This may require devolving powers to lower levels of governments, and constitutionally guaranteeing these powers as well as providing adequate resources for them to accomplish their constitutional responsibilities. It also involves giving special attention to the rural areas and urban slums.

Finally, it is important to note for that many Africans, unless the *human being* is used as the basis of development, there is no good governance. There must be visible changes in the quality of life of the individual and groups. Cold statistics of good governance make no sense to most Africans.

Peace is not the absence of conflicts. There shall always be conflicts where more than one person lives. Interests often clash, thus resulting in conflicts. It is not the conflicts but how they are managed that is important. Peace is about how conflicts are managed to ensure relative stability, law and order in order to enable human beings carry out their daily activities. Peace is a societal condition which ensures relative social stability and order through the dispensation of justice, fairness and opportunities for accommodation by formal and informal institutions, practices and norms.[5]

The concepts of democracy and good governance are not only interlinked, both demand accountability as a principle. Democracy is a means of achieving 'good governance'. After all, military regimes have in-built seeds of instability as the Nigerian experience has shown. Authoritarian regimes depend on coercion, which is not a durable or sustainable political commodity. Accountability is very central to democratic governance. For a government to be democratic and for governance to be qualified as 'good', the repositories of power and managers of resources must be accountable to the governed, responsive to the demands of the people, and be guided by the principles of the rule of law.

There can be no viable democracy without relative peace. Yet relative peace is often assured by 'good' governance. Both 'good' governance and peace are therefore imperatives for a durable democratic polity. Members of the political class and leaders, (at all levels) should note this. When political leaders become violent conflict/crises generators, they threaten the basic foundations of democracy; they may be committing class suicide.

Between May 1999 and July 2009, the research conducted by the Institute of Governance and Social Research (IGSR), Jos, Plateau State, Nigeria, shows that there have been 343 cases of violent electoral and communal conflicts[6]. These are only violent conflicts in which one or more persons lost their lives and property destroyed. Electoral violence accounts for 176 of these cases, while ethno-religious and land issues account for the rest. In almost all cases, fingers of accusation point to political leaders, government officials, traditional leaders and religious leaders. Thus ten years of our sojourn in the path of democracy have been watered by blood, littered by wanton destruction, and seen our impatience, intolerance, irresponsibility, disenfranchisement of the people, disregard for the rule of law; low level of legitimacy, the violation of the principles of choice and freedom, and highly demonstrable lack of accountability.

We must tell ourselves the home truths. Only truth based on facts can enable us to 'exorcise' the spirit of violence, indiscipline and lack of patriotism. We must correctly evaluate our past, boldly assess the present, so that we can make useful contributions to a glorious tomorrow for generations yet unborn. Pretence, hypocrisy and sycophancy are not therapeutic in Nigeria's current condition.

How have we operated our democratic polity so far? What lessons emerge from our past?

Democracy, Peace and Good Governance In Nigeria: 1960 – 2009

Democracy between the military and civilian elites

Alfred Stephan makes an interesting distinction between *Liberalization* and *democratization*. According to him, liberalization refers to "a mix of policy and social changes" such as reduced "censorship of the press, safeguards for individual rights, release of political prisoners and toleration of political opposition." On the other hand, democratization "entails liberalization but is a wider and more specifically political concept." Democratization "requires open contestation for the right to win control of government, and this in turn requires free elections, the results of which determine who governs."[7]

Nigeria's history of democratization began in the terminal colonial period partly as a result of nationalist activities. Her independence on October 1, 1960, marked an important threshold- a transition from colonial dyarchy in the late 1950s to Nigerian civilian rule in 1960, with democratic institutions modeled on the British Westminster Parliamentary system. The new political elites had the duty of not only institutionalizing the democratic process, but for developing a political culture which would buttress the inherited institutions. There were high hopes of Nigeria emerging as a fertile and large field for the growth of democracy in Africa.

By 1965, however, it had become very clear that the *ballot box* and the future of plebiscetarian democracy had become very bleak. A number of factors in the system gave this indication: the

1. break-down of the rules of the game of politics which profusely polluted the political stadium (and in absence of avenues for

political ventilation) made politics as dangerous for players as well as spectators;

2. gross misuse of political power;
3. misappropriation of public funds and widespread corruption among public officers;
4. imprudent political and economic decisions in allocation of scarce but allocatable resources;
5. erosion of the rights of individuals;
6. disenfranchisement of the Nigerian populace through blatant rigging of elections;
7. conspicuous consumption of politicians, amidst the abject poverty of the masses; and
8. excessively powerful regional governments which threatened the relatively weak federal centre with wanton abandon.

Candidly, with the benefit of hindsight, these offences were by far less in proportion than those committed by their successors, except for the centre-region relations.

In fact, the nature of federal-region relations was such that Nigeria's federal-centre relations had become very tense. As a Nigerian Head of State once put it:

> ...the regions were so large and powerful as to consider themselves self-sufficient and almost entirely independent. The federal government which ought to give lead to the whole country was relegated to the background. The people were not made to realize that the Federal Government was the real government of Nigeria.[8]

By 1965, the first attempt at the use of the *ballot box* had been punctuated by crisis. Our federal experience had been chequered by the centrifugal pulls in all directions.[9] And in no time, the *bullet box* (soldiers) relegated the *ballot box* (democratic polity) to obscurity, and the parliamentary system was kicked brutally to a fatal future.

The military intervened in politics. But the *political physicians* soon became political patients in need of medication. Not used to the politics of compromise, disagreements among the military, in the context of Nigeria's loose federation and ethno-regional politics, escalated to the level of a civil war which lasted till January 1970.

The military elite engaged in elite instability through coups and abortive coups till October 1979 when another attempt at the democratization of the polity led to the expansion of the parameters of the ballot box and the shrinking of the boundaries of the barracks. This Second Republic lasted from October 1979 to December 1983, when the military imploded into the political arena, thus shrinking the parameters of the ballot box once again and extending the boundaries of the barracks. The reasons for the failure of the Second Republic were no different from the reasons for the failure of the First Republic, except in variants and contexts.

If the political intolerance which trailed attempts at political succession in 1964 and 1965 had led to blatant rigging of elections and the crises arising there from, the elections of 1983 were reputedly profusely rigged, and the crises arising there from led to a military coup. In fact, by 1982 opposition political parties had begun to join students and labour unionists to call for military intervention in politics. Politicians in the opposition to those at the central government probably forgot that military intervention meant class suicide for the political class.

It is instructive that in 1964/65 as well as in 1983, the issue of political succession had unduly overheated the polity and eventually provided the excuse for military intervention. We shall return to this issue later.

Again, not learning from the past, just like politicians, the military came back again into the political arena with an aggressive puritanic fervour. Many politicians and public officers received jail terms ranging from 30-60 years and more. The military soon found itself a victim of the same ailments they had set out to cure. Military coups and abortive coups and conspiracies continued through the 1990s. In fact, there was a brief period of the Third Republic in which there were hopes that the transition to civil rule, would lead to a democratic polity. But this was aborted after the crisis which trailed June 12, 1993 Presidential elections.

A stop gap was found in an interim government set up to organize the Presidential election. It was overthrown by the military on

November 17, 1993. Thus, again, Nigeria reverted to a military regime. This time, inspite of the report of the constitutional conference, there was a transition programme tailored to a self-succession agenda of the military leader. As part of Nigeria's contribution to political innovation in democratic history, there was plan that the five political parties adopt one Presidential candidate. The death of this military leader, General Sani Abacha, led to the initiation of a new transition programme by the new military leader – General Abdulsalami Abubakar. This transition which ended on May 29, 1999, ushered in the current civilian regime.

By 1999 therefore, of Nigeria's thirty-nine years of existence, the military had ruled Nigeria for twenty-nine years. In essence, the military had become a political power contestant in Nigeria's political stadium. It can be argued that the "bullet box" held a far superior sway in the polity than the ballot box. Some members of the political elite have called the military, the "alternate political party." Of Nigeria's fifty years of her existence, Nigeria has had eleven military coups and abortive coups. Of these, only three military coups have been against civilian regimes - in January 1966, December 1983 and November 1993. Three of these coups have been against military regimes - July 1966; July 1975; and August 1985.

Similarly, there have been five abortive coups and conspiracies – all against military regimes - February 1976; December 1985 conspiracy; April 1990 putsch; March 1995 and December 1997 conspiracies. There were numerous other conspiracies which never came to public knowledge. But it is instructive that all the abortive coups were against military regimes - probably a sign that it is more difficult to overthrow military governments. Or does it simply indicate that the propensity to coup is greater under military regimes? After all, as Jean-Jacques Rousseau once observed, "where might is right, any might that is greater than the first succeeds to its rights."[10]

From our political development, it is clear that the military has been part of the solution to some problems but it has also been part of some of the problems. The military fought and maintained a single Nigeria, thus transforming her from "a mere geographical expression" to an organic state, struggling to weld itself into a nation. Yet, if the military had come in as political physicians, they had been transformed into political patients by Nigeria's murky political terrain. The military almost lost its soul and its institutional integrity through its misadventure into politics.

Dividends of Democracy Versus Democratic Deficit

Since May 29, 1999, politicians in government have continued to use the phrase "dividends of democracy". Often, they use this phrase to refer to the provision of material welfare to the people. Among such "dividends of democracy" are - roads, rural electricity, potable water, improved educational and health facilities, housing, sports infrastructure, support for greater agricultural output, employment and the like. In fact, the former Minister of information, Prof. Jerry Gana, led a team of pressmen to visit the thirty-six states to showcase "dividends of democracy" in Nigeria in the first two years of civilian rule. Awards were given to State Governors who excelled in delivering these dividends.

In fifteen years of military rule (before the inauguration of the Fourth Republic) there were many actions which violated the basic freedom and rights of individuals and groups. Throughout these years, the people of Nigeria lost their right to choose their leaders, and lacked institutions that would enable them to associate politically with one another, aggregate and articulate the group interests. In fact, the basic right, in plebiscetarian setting, to vote or make inputs into decisions which would affect one's life was denied. Participation under military rule was *political mobilization* of the masses for social or political action by government from the top. Participation as *political access* from below was hardly available.

In addition, democracy provides rights to individuals and groups. It presupposes the right or freedom of expression by the individual. Under military rule, the expression of such rights had the consequences of incarceration and inhuman treatment. Critics of military governments easily found themselves brutalized physically and psychologically. Often, their fundamental human rights were profusely violated.

Our understanding is that the *dividends of democracy*, since May 29, 1999, include: the freedom of expression and other freedoms (with due respect to the fact that each freedom bears with it an obligation), not license. We utilized our rights to vote (even if these were dented by the rigging of elections). We elected our leaders (even if some of the leaders manipulated that process). Our governments at different levels must now be accountable for their actions and we can demand such. They will not be accountable to a Commander-in-Chief of the Armed Forces. In addition, we can insist on transparency in government business. Leaders in government can no longer violate our human rights with impunity and get away with it, unless we let them. I did not hear the Federal Ministry of Information give awards for these categories— the expansion of the frontiers of freedom or liberty and respect for human and individual rights.

As a Social Scientist, one is aware that in the history of development material welfare—roads, jobs, food, power, education, health and others—are easier to provide under authoritarian rule. In Britain, issues of economic distribution were handled before political rights. The success of the 'Asian Tigers' lies in their utilization of authoritarian political structures for aggressive economic development. Democratization followed later. Singapore is an illustration. You do not need a democratic government to achieve an economically buoyant and material welfare state. If this is our understanding of democracy, then let us pause and think again. These economic and other benefits encourage us to ask for our political rights.

One agrees with Dr. Tony Momoh when he observed that:

> food and jobs and safety are what people expect of those who govern. Communism and other dictatorial routes to governance have been immensely more successful in providing foods and clothing and safety and jobs. But how free have the people been to enjoy these so-called good things of life? ....In democracies, therefore, there is entrenched a most satisfactory way of ensuring that freedom or fundamental rights are not only guaranteed but protected too...[11]

Interestingly those who shout *dividends of democracy* are often not very sensitive to the *democratic deficit* created by their behaviour or actions. For our purposes (in simple terms) any action or behaviour of actors which detracts from, or erodes the bases of democracy is "democratic deficit." Thus when the President or a legislator violates the constitution; or by-passes due process; or takes actions which challenge the rule of law; or erodes the basis of authority by going dictatorial, or refuses to be transparent and accountable for his actions, he is consciously or unconsciously engaging in a process, the result of which would be *democratic deficit* - an action, detrimental to the democratic process. Is it not time for all Nigerians to watch out for democratic deficits in their polity? This challenge also goes to the media.

The Challenges of Peace and Democratic Governance

Since May 29, 1999 we have tried to make a rough transition from military rule through civil rule towards a democratic polity. This has been very difficult. However, we have made some progress since May 1999 and there are some positive signs on the political horizon. There has been greater freedom of speech, thought, worship, movement and association since 1999. Similarly, the parameters of political contestation through political parties have witnessed positive changes even if political parties are not necessarily democratic in their internal structures. In the past nine years, the military has been in the barracks and has embarked on a reprofessionalization programme. Under Obasanjo, there were attempts at economic reforms (even if only on paper) in the form of National Economic Empowerment and Development Strategy (NEEDS), which intrigued Western countries. In addition, from almost a *pariah* state, Nigeria began to operate as a proud actor in the comity of nations.

Yet our tortuous and inchoate democratic journey has experienced major challenges. These challenges may be classified under: 1) democratic deficits 2) the political economy of development; 3) the dynamic of our socio-political setting; 4) the foundation and dynamics of the Nigerian Federation; and 5) security, law and order.

Let us start with threats posed by the democratic deficit in the actions/activities of the operations of the polity.

1. Democracy and Democratic Deficits

Nigeria has had a long history of military rule. The vicissitudes of Nigeria's political history have had negative impact on the process of democratization. The transition from a military to civilian rule has become only a stepping stone in our journey to democratic governance. Though from May 1999 we have made some progress, our democratic structures are fragile and the processes are fluid.

Civil rule may have all the laws and institutions of democracy without these necessarily being underpinned by democratic values. In other words, there may be democratic institutions operated undemocratically, as the absence of a minimum level of democratic political culture and the lack of adherence to the rules of the *game of politics* lead to conflicts and crises. Most of the conflicts and crises which have characterized Nigeria's path to democracy, are associated with undemocratic values which underpin our national life – that is, building supposedly democratic structures on undemocratic foundations and values. Let us illustrate this point.

The Electoral Process

Democracy is not all about elections. Elections are vehicles for the establishment of representative government. While winners called the 2003 elections free and fair, some losers and observers called it fraudulent. On balance, for those of us as political observers, the 2003 elections in many parts of Nigeria were very fraudulent. The April 2007 elections were even more fraudulent than the 2003 elections. Domestic and international observers confirmed this.

The Yar'Adua government began its rule in the throes of crisis of legitimacy. Many Nigerians believed that he did not have the "right to rule" because he did not have the people's mandate. The Supreme Court later legally confirmed that he was duly elected. As an indication of personal courage and decency, Yar'adua accepted that the elections which brought him to power were flawed, even if the ultimate result would has been the same. He set up the Electoral Reform Committee and the committee later submitted its report. Government subsequently issued its *White Paper* on the Report and even sent some bills to the National Assembly on this matter. However, some Nigerians are skeptical about the willingness and the ability of President Jonathan and the PDP to implement the report. Others wondered why the Iwu-led election commission still conducted bye-elections despite the commission's records. The volume of exhibits displayed at the tribunals and in the media, and Prof. Iwu's numerous public statements made the commission look complicit in the alleged rigging of the 2007 elections. The courts seem to be unraveling these issues, and in some cases, did come down heavily on INEC.

The judiciary exposed the irregularities of the 2007 general elections. It reversed some governorship elections and some cases of elections into the legislature at federal and state levels. We witnessed the installation of Governors Peter Obi of Anambra State, Rotimi Amaechi of Rivers State, Adams Oshiomhole of Edo State and Olusegun Mimiko of Ondo State. We also saw the re-run elections in Sokoto, Bayelsa, Kogi, Cross River and Ekiti States. By and large, Nigerians are developing more confidence in the judiciary than in the past. This is a good omen for democracy and good governance.

Of equal importance to good governance is what transpires at the local government level. Good governance requires responsible and responsive political leaders at the grassroots. These leaders must not only be elected but also held accountable for their actions by the electorate. Unfortunately, State Independent Electoral Commissions (SIEC) are alleged to be mere instruments for legitimatizing the imposition of candidates of the ruling party and the State Governor. Elections at the local government level are generally believed to be hardly free and fair. In most of the states which had conducted local government elections, one noticed that the element of choice by the people had been eroded in the electoral process. They were cases of assured-victory for political parties controlling state governments irrespective of which political party is in power at the state level. This rigging of elections poses a great challenge of restoring the confidence of the electorate. It is a major evidence of *democratic deficit* in Nigeria.

Electoral Malpractices

Given the perception that the control of state power is important, groups often decide which political platform is the best for the pursuit and the promotion of their interests. Thus, politics in Nigeria is not a game but a battle. Nothing succeeds as much as success and nothing fails as much as failure. The exclusion of political failures has been a major source of conflict.

In addition, the blatant rigging of elections creates a reservoir of ill-will for the so-called winners. Seeing no prospects of peaceful change, the aggrieved often take the violent route. Even the judiciary could not, in such circumstances be trusted. Similarly, the political intolerance of members of political parties generates intra-party and inter-party conflicts. At times, ethno-religious sentiments get mobilized to achieve targets. . The Jos crises of 2001 and 2008 are a good examples of violent conflicts which started because of perceived rigged elections but which later took on ethno-religious colouration. In addition, the *Tazarcemania* (self-succession complex) of political incumbents generates conflicts as there are often zones or groups which are opposed to the self-succession agenda of the incumbents. Thus, electoral malpractices often offend the sensibility of those already dissatisfied with the incumbent. As Senator Salisu Matori of Bauchi observed:

> ...If we can all be honest to one another, especially our leaders, by demonstrating transparency and accountability, Nigeria will begin to enjoy peace. But as far as we still have elite, people with selfish motives, Nigeria may not witness any meaningful development; so the earlier we bury our selfish and political motives the better. We should come together and start seeing ourselves as One Nigeria, because whether Christians or Muslims, we belong to one God. No religion preaches that you should kill or destroy properties...so politicians should desist from using innocent youths to ferment trouble because these youths are powerless, but it is politicians that supply them arms and money for Indian hemp and after taking such drugs they begin to kill because they have lost control of their memory.[12]

The emergence of militants in the Niger-Delta who could neither be controlled by politicians nor government is allegedly traceable to politicians who had armed young people to influence the 2003 elections. It is understood that these youth groups then became 'monsters' and defied any control by their political mentors. This situation is also found in other parts of the country.

Political Tolerance

While our electoral laws, institutions and processes need reforms, the greater part of the problem has to do with the operators of the electoral system and players. Perhaps, no amount of reform can change the Nigerian electoral system and politics in general. Political tolerance of the opinion of others and the extension of the democratic space is therefore another challenge. In Nigeria, the political actors seem not to understand democracy or have not learnt from the politicians of the past Republics. In the Fourth Republic there have been so much intolerance among politicians, it is amazing and yet disgusting. Intra-party squabbles have led to deaths. Even since May 2009 many politicians have been assassinated by their opponents while political violence still takes place in some parts of the country.

In order to avoid the development of one-party state, General Buhari, Alhaji Atiku Abubakar, Alhaji Shekarau, Alhaji Tinubu, Olu Falae and others made an attempt to create a National Democratic Movement. This attempt seemed to have failed before it actually was operational. There is nothing wrong in a party ruling for one century, if this is done legitimately and without the forced subjugation of opposition parties. Thus the disposition of some politicians who find solace in the corridor of power to make (by hook or crook) Nigeria a default one-party state is not good for democratic development. We believe that a strong opposition will make our democracy more vibrant, while an authoritarian dominant one-party state only grooms the military as an alternative political party. Coopting or buying members of the opposition to join one's political party is cheap and short-lived in its consequences. It is counterproductive to democracy. While inclusiveness is acceptable, a virile opposition is the hope of our democratic polity.

Political Parties

Nigeria has over fifty political parties. Essentially, political parties are expected to aggregate and articulate interests of their members and provide alternative governments based on their programmes or platforms. Unfortunately, many of these political parties exist only by name or surface at the crucial point in the distribution of funds to political parties by the Independent National Electoral Commission (INEC). These parties are essentially undemocratic in their internal structure, and really neither aggregate nor articulate the interests of their members.

More important for democratic governance is that there should be a political culture of tolerance of the opposition. Nigerian political elites have not learnt this important democratic value. As an illustration, the Speaker of Kaduna State House of Assembly threatened that his party would ensure the re-election (or is it selection?) of Governor Sambo whether or not the people liked it, even it meant using sticks, machetes and others.

While receiving Governor Mahmud Shinkafi of Zamfara into the People's Democratic Party (PDP) from the All Nigeria People's Party (ANPP), Governor Lamido (PDP) of Jigawa said:

> The only job we know is to destroy opposition and we are here to do everything possible to dismantle the opposition.[13]

He went further to declare that PDP had no apologies for "being a big and strong party with strategies to muzzle any opposition".[14] In reaction, General Buhari of the ANPP protested loudly about the PDP attempt to crush the opposition.[15] Politicians must learn that opposition oils the democratic process. The destruction of the opposition in the past had always left the military as the viable opposition. This situation cannot help usher in the political stability needed for Nigeria's Vision 20:2020. Divergent viewpoints are necessary for creating a virile society which is active in developmental process.

The future of democracy in this country depends on our ability to institutionalize political parties, thus making them to accommodate our various ethnic and religious differences. Our parties must be effective institutions for aggregating our interests, articulating them and pursuing the achievement of the same. They can only do this if they are democratic in their internal structures and processes.

Leadership and Statesmanship

Since we started our journey in democratization in May 1999, three major political groups have emerged in the political arena. These are the *politicians,* the *political contractors* and the *political thugs.* The *genuine politicians* know how to acquire and use political power for the ends of the state—the maintenance of law and order, the achievement of the welfare of the people, and the pursuit of national interest in interaction with other nations. These are few and have become endangered specie.

The *political contractor* is a businessman for whom democracy is a tolerable nuisance in the calculus of profits. The electoral process is a commercial process in which deals can be made in the form of investments in politics. Thus, from the Ngige-Ubah saga in Anambra State to the Ladoja-Adedibu showdown is Oyo State, the political contractors insisted on their pounds of flesh. There are more political contractors than politicians. It is hoped that the political contractors in 20 years, may transform themselves into genuine politicians.

The *political thugs*, often brazen and rough, are usually hirelings of the political contractor. The only value of this group is the maximum dispensation of violence and/or threats of violence as may be requested by the political contractor. The political thug democratizes violence— thanks to the big unemployment market which swells up their rank.

Good governance and accountability entail the tolerance of divergent views, the accommodation of political opponents and the widening of the frontiers of politics through inclusiveness but not alienation and exclusion. Our leaders, once in the State House must accept that they have become *statesmen* and no longer soap box politicians. They must accept that they are no longer ethnic and religious champions or parochial opinion leaders. They have become the *fathers* of all irrespective of the ethnic group, language, geopolitical unit, or religion to which they belong. They now transcend all these and must respect the country's "unity in diversity" and "diversity in unity".

In essence, our leaders have not learned that once elected, they must transform themselves into statesmen. Often many of them remain politicians in State Houses. There is no principle they cannot mortgage, no value they cannot adulterate, and there is no law they cannot bastardize. Genuine critics of their actions are dubbed 'saboteurs' and reactionaries, as if this country does not belong to Nigerians. Many politicians and political leaders have learnt nothing from the past. They behave as if Nigeria belongs to them to milk and exploit, while the rest of us are mere tolerable nuisance. It is no wonder that there is a big disconnect between leadership and followership, and between government and the people.

We must, as members of the elite, remember that we are a privileged few. We must use our blessings from GOD to impact positively on the lives of people around us. In position of public trust, we must render selfless service because the pangs of justice will catch up with us someday and demand that we account for our stewardship.

Leadership thus remains a vital factor in effecting desirable compromises in our democratic federation. The way our political leaders respect the rules of the games of politics; their ability to imbibe the democratic value of accommodation, tolerance of opposition and participation; and their ability to demonstrate gallantry in defeat and grace in victory, will determine the extent of harmony in the future.

I am convinced that, given Nigeria's enormous human and material resources, a visionary and patriotic leadership with exemplary traits and high sense of discipline, and patriotism and determination among her people, this country will be transformed into a land of envy for many African and other countries. As Nigerians, we know our problems. We know the solutions to these problems. Let us have the courage to stand up together to solve these problems with a collective sense of purpose, discipline and patriotism.

Autonomy of Public Institutions

One evidence of democratic deficit is the personalization or politicization of public institutions, paid for by public funds. These public institutions include Radio Houses, newspapers, parastatals and others. Public media houses at state and federal levels exhibited nauseating biases in the electoral process. Public media houses became megaphones for the party or the individual in power. All Nigerians, through their tax, pay for the operation of these public institutions which do not belong to political leaders in government but to the people.

Government officials use government property recklessly and often for private purposes. No public agency should contribute to the campaign of any political candidate. Election tribunals have dossiers of allegations on how the military, the police and other security forces were compromised as agents or officials of the party in government, to rig elections and intimidate the people. This is clear misuse of public institutions. It is a dangerous pattern of democratic deficit. The use of the armed forces and other security agencies for domestic politically partisan purposes can be very dangerous, even to those in government.

All public institutions should be autonomous and neutral to all political actors and activities in the state. We must strive to protect the integrity of public institutions which will serve different leaders and political parties in government.

Executive-Legislative Relations

Our 1999 Constitution provides a presidential system along the United States model. This means that the three arms of government are relatively autonomous of one another in the spirit of desirable checks and balances in the system. Since 1999, at all tiers of government, there have been attempts by the executive to engulf the legislature. At the federal level, former President Obasanjo's use of state machinery to incite changes of leadership in the first Senate of 1999 – 2003, is all too well known to be repeated. But Obasanjo met his match in Hon. Ghali Na'abba, who not only resisted Obasanjo's destabilization attempts, but also launched his counter-offensive by getting the House of Representatives to embark on the impeachment of Obasanjo. The intervention of General Yakubu Gowon and Alhaji Shehu Shagari saved Obasanjo from the clutches of Na'abba and Pius Anyim (then the Senate President).

President Yar'Adua respected the autonomy of the National Assembly. Even when he was encouraged to intervene in the case of Hon. Etteh, (the former speaker of the House of the Representatives) he refused. He felt it was a matter for the National Assembly to resolve. Unfortunately, most Houses of Assembly seem to be in the pockets of the State Governors. In any case, many members of the State Houses were sponsored by these Governors in their election. In fact, in the 2003 elections, many pliant candidates were sponsored by various incumbents of executive branches at the Federal and State levels. The autonomy of the legislative branch is important in carrying out its constitutional mandates of law-making, over-sight and representation. While cordial working relations among arms of government is desirable, the honourable members of the legislature should not betray the trust of their constituencies.

The Judiciary, Institutional Hygiene and Political Rectitude

Over the years, the judiciary has been castigated by Nigerians for being corrupt and inefficient in the delivery of justice and in carrying out its adjudication functions in the federation. There were clear cases of ineptitude on the part of some judicial officers in highly visible cases such as the Anambra governorship and Akwa-Ibom election tribunal scandals.

The Supreme Court has given landmark judgements in a number of cases since 1999. These are illustrated by its judgements on the revenue allocation formula; the electoral law; the local government law; the Lagos state statutory allocation for local government; and the deduction of debts owed by tiers of government from the Federation Account by the Federal Government. However, the lower judiciary has been found wanting in many instances. Similarly, the lack of confidence in the electoral tribunals and the frivolous use of injunctions, have shaken the very foundations of confidence in the judiciary.

However, the judiciary embarked on institutional hygiene and self-purification. The National Judiciary Council (NJC) took drastic actions against erring judges. The sacking of Justices Kusherki, Egbo-Egbo, Adamu, Nnaji and others, gives us hope for an unbiased judiciary — not contained and tucked under the ambit of the executive branch. If the NJC in its self-purification crusade succeeds, it may restore the people's confidence in the judiciary.

The judicial process is gradually being reformed to make the process of dispensation of justice faster, but it is still not good enough for the 21st Century. Cases still take long. Access to justice by the common man is hardly existent, and cases are often prolonged for too long for the financial and psychological staying power of the average Nigerian.

The ineptitude of the politician and INEC has transferred to the judiciary, political functions not designed for it. The numerous cases of electoral fraud and malpractices in elections especially 2003 and 2007, loaded the judiciary with petitions. The judiciary has shown great courage in carrying out political rectitude by reversing many of the declared results. The judiciary reversed six governorship elections; ordered that two governors be sworn-in, while run-off elections were to be held in four cases. It also annulled some elections into the legislature at all tiers of government. On February 5, 2007, the election of the Anambra State Governor was nullified by the Appeal Court and the incumbent was asked to vacate his office.

In a demonstration of courage, the judiciary reversed the cases of illegal impeachment of governors of states encouraged by President Obasanjo, with the active assistance of the Economic and Financial Crime Commission (EFCC) under the leadership of Nuhu Ribadu. Thus, the impeachments of Governor Ladoja of Oyo, Dariye of Plateau, Peter Obi of Anambra States were reversed by the Appeal Court. On balance, most objective observers would agree that the judiciary has courageously carried out political rectitude as a result of the failure of politicians and INEC. If the judiciary had been accused for being partly responsible for the failure of the Third Republic, it has contributed immensely to the survival of the Fourth Republic.

2. The Political Economy of Development

Economic Empowerment and Poverty Eradication

There can be no durable democracy nor can governance be qualified as 'good', without a viable economic base. No one cares for democracy on an empty stomach. We must not forget that democratic culture and political stability cannot thrive in a society where there is abject poverty. Our poverty alleviation/eradication programmes have so far failed to tackle the problem. Our economy is still in bad shape: the exchange rate is about **₦150.00** to one USA dollar; inflation still haunts our hopes for a good take home pay; some banks are still tilting towards collapse; the manufacturing sector has experienced closures in spite of our privatization process (the latest being the textile factories); there seems to be greater invasion of our market by external forces than investment; our infrastructure are dilapidated; our educational system is collapsing and the health sector is severely in pains. Perhaps, the financial sector has remarkably been transformed. In my lecture at the National Institute of Policy and Strategic Studies (NIPSS) Kuru, on February 18, 2008, I said "our banks have grown so big that they advertise on CNN. Sadly and ironically, the real sector of our economy is starved of reasonable business capital and factories are closing down. There is still need for more regulation of the banking industry". I was vindicated by the *tsunami* which swept through the banking sector which was managed by the Central Bank Governor, Lamido Sanusi. In spite of all these, the private sector is still small and heavily tied to the apron-strings of the public sector.

Generally, while reforms are welcome, the human being should be the object of reforms. It is not enough to mention that there are poverty alleviation programmes. The truth neither is that our experience since 1999 shows that these programmes are not well thought-out nor coordinated. At state and local government levels, we all know how the poverty alleviation money is thrown down the drain-pipe. When programmes tend to contribute to poverty escalation rather than alleviation, government should stop and review its activities. The Yar'adua/Jonathan's administration has its Seven-Point Agenda. But it is sad to note that very few Nigerians (including public officials and servants) understand or feel committed to the seven-point agenda. Even the Vision 20: 2020 appears to be less understood by Nigerians. How then can we launch the economy to the desired position with poverty still ravaging our people; with power supply still very epileptic, and our factories are closing one after the other? How can we become one of the 20 largest economies at the rate we are going, by 2020?

The global economic meltdown has hit both industrialized and developing economies very hard. For an economy that largely relies on *petronaira,* it cannot be any harder. We seem sentenced to budget deficits as our foreign reserve dwindles. We can however turn around the current situation to fortune. We can make it a blessing in disguise. We need to diversify our monocultural economy. We must not forget that rural communities are the 'engine' of growth. They are the greens of the country, rich in land and labour even though they may have scarce capital and infrastructure. We must diversify our economy and produce more than we are doing. Our consumption pattern must be regulated, if we are to become a developed economic power by 2020. It is important, as part of our extractive and productive mechanism, that government funds agriculture, solid minerals and small and medium manufacturing sectors. Now is the time for the Government to wade into the crisis-ridden sectors of the economy as the erstwhile champions *of the free market* in the West are now investing money into their productive economic activities. From deregulation, the apostles of the free market in the west have opted for guided regulation. What lessons does this experience have for us?

With our abundant human and natural resources, we strongly believe that our poverty is related to the ineptitude and inefficiency in the governance of the country. Our governments at federal, state and local levels must summon the courage and will to fight this menace, which from all available indicators, is on the increase. Our deregulation and privatization policies must be pursued with all sense of patriotism and sincerity, transparency and accountability. From available evidence (even in the media) the privatization exercise had been transformed into the personalization of our national assets. Some cases of privatization must be revisited for justice and equity.

Given our federal system of governance, it is imperative that the Federal Government should carry state and local governments along in development planning, without necessarily robbing them of their constitutional autonomies and developmental priorities. The pursuit of national economic development in a globalizing economy has increasingly made intergovernmental relations in federal systems a necessity. Structures and institutions of inter-governmental policy coordination should be re-aligned for this purpose.

In Nigeria, we have very good structures and institutions of inter-governmental policy coordination. Part of our problem has been the lack of political will, the neglect of due process and/or our apparent inability to respond to development challenges in our federal setting. The NEEDS-SEEDS-LEEDS (and now CEEDS) case is a good example of how a federal fiat occasioned by the former President Obasanjo's authoritarian style made mockery of institutions and structures of intergovernmental relations. We must begin to see a revitalized relationship between federal, state and local government planning commissions or departments. The Constitution provides for the National Economic Council as a useful intergovernmental agency. It should be strengthened with a viable secretariat and made more functional. The federal government must assist in developing the capacity of agencies/commissions/departments saddled with the responsibility of initiating, formulating, analyzing, implementing and monitoring development policies at all tiers of government.

Unemployment

Given the economic hardship and high level of unemployment, 'armed youths for hire' are available at cheap price. While the Federal Government 'deregulates' the economy, politicians 'deregulate' violence and the control of the instrument of violence, which is supposed to be the cardinal duty of government. The armies of the unemployed are always willing to find new jobs as body guards, assassins, and canon-fodders in communal violence. The conspicuous consumption of political office holders (whose backgrounds were well known before they assumed offices) amidst the abject poverty of the people, not only alienate, but generate hatred. Candidly our level of unemployment is directly related to our security. Government should review or scrap the *National Poverty Eradication Programme* (NAPEP) and replace it with an inter-governmental agency which partners with the private sector for urgent actions in this area. We may want to learn fast from other countries how they are tackling the unemployment problem.

The Corruption Conundrum

Some Nigerians have no doubt earned their only country a bad reputation in terms of corruption. No nation is free from the corruption cancer. But the fact that we are always, rightly or unfairly, rated among the most corrupt nations is devastatingly irritating. We do not need to be told that our roof is leaking. Corruption is real in our society. It is a menace to our individual, societal and national life. It happens in the open and in the dark. We need not belabour the fact that corruption is the bane of our progress. How can we fight it?

Nobody should be seen to be above the law. While leadership is important, our values of leadership must change. Leaders should not be seen as those who dispense largesse from the public treasury for our personal use. Leaders should be seen as those who prudently use our resources for public good. In addition, the hands that cuff others must be clean to send clear messages to all. The President Yar'adua and Jonathan expressed their determination to fight corruption. On a personal level, President Yar'Adua was not accused of corruption. However, many Nigerians complain that there are many people with unclean hands in and around Yar'adua/Jonathan administration, thus casting shadows of corruption over his administration. Is the President a victim of his political context in which he rose to office? Have our Governors, Ministers, Legislators, Permanent Secretaries, Chairmen and Councilors also gotten the message? Are the Policemen on the streets, the Messengers in the office, the Classroom Teachers, Businessmen and Contractors alike conscious of the desirability for change? Herein lies the need for aggressive advocacy.

Unfortunately, as some Nigerians feel, the withdrawal of cases against Ribadu and Nasir El-Rufai by the Jonathan administration gives wrong signals about government determination to fight corruption. Some people feel that government should have allowed the law to take its course, and only pardon them if it came to that.

The wind of change against corruption has been sweeping from Peru, Chile and Argentina through Italy, Japan, France, Thailand to Taiwan, Italy and Costa Rica.[16] — witnessing how former Presidents and leaders have been brought to trials with some convicted and jailed for corruption. What is happening in this country? Can we amend the laws of our anti-corruption agencies to give them enough teeth to bite? The lesson in anti-corruption crusade must start from the top.

Importantly, our anti-corruption agencies must be seen to be ready for the task. The past experience, in which they were used as instruments of political victimization and vendetta, cannot be tolerated. These agencies should be guided strictly by law. Most importantly, the civil society should be involved in the fight against corruption. They should not only serve as whistle-blowers but also as the eagle eyes of the society. Corruption is multi-dimensional. Corruption does not only involve money. It also involves the abuse of trust, processes and institutions. It is our suggestion that we should concentrate on the prevention of corruption by establishing appropriate mechanism for checking it. This will reduce the number and cost of cases prosecuted. If we must rebrand Nigeria, we must start from within government, and its determination to be exemplary should not be in doubt.

3. The Dynamics of Nigeria's Socio-Political Setting

There are many factors in our socio-cultural setting which have impact our peace and democratic governance in Nigeria. Let us briefly look at a few of these.

Migration and the Indigene/Settler Problems

In some parts of the country, especially in the Middle-Belt area, there has been substantial influx of migrants in the last 20 years. In the context of competition for scarce resources and the importance of the control of the state for the distribution of these resources, new lines of cleavages develop among groups. As indigenes organize for the control of their polity and economy, so do the *settlers* press for their rights of participation in these processes. Beyond a threshold, *settler* communities threaten the indigenes' position of hegemony and control. While the 'settler' gets *defensively aggressive* in its relations with the indigenes, the indigenes get *aggressively defensive,* often resulting in violence with the full mobilization of ethno-religious loyalty and commitments.

Traditional Social Stratification and Ethnocentrism

Very often some citizens of ethnic and religious groups consider themselves as hailing from aristocratic traditional backgrounds, and arrogantly exhibit ethnocentrism in relations with other groups. At times, these people relate to other groups (that is when they care to) with disdain, extending their ethno-religious status recklessly to domains of the socio-cultural preferences of others. Politicians do this with nauseating efficiency. It is no wonder that traditional leaders 'sell' or 'award' titles more under democratic politics than under military regimes in Nigeria. This often offends the sensibilities of other people who find other platforms for checkmating the nuisance of these leaders. Our history has witnessed violent conflicts as a result of this behaviour.

Deliberate Manipulation of Ethnic and Religious identities

There are instances when politicians, traditional and religious leaders deliberately manipulate ethnic and religious identities of groups. There are enough evidences to show that quite a number of ethno-religious conflicts are caused by politicians and political leaders. The level of hypocrisy among our political leaders is nauseating. Some of these politicians have no constituencies from which to demonstrate their relevance except through their narrow ethnic and religious groups. Without being religiously judgemental, they are not genuinely religious in their actions and faith—whether they claim to be 'born again' or is it 'born against' God. Their personal lives do not show that

God has a place in them. They exude religious bigotry and ethnocentrism with demonstrable arrogance. They symbolically use churches and mosques as their theatres of operation in the day time, while consulting *babalawos* or the *juju priest* or even ritualists at night. It is important that they maintain this semblance of *churchianity* and *mosquianity*, bereft as these may be of the core values of Christianity and Islam. This is because it is their lifeline for survival. They pollute young children with their bigotry and copiously exhibit ethnocentric arrogance. Ethno-religious conflicts in Nigeria are mostly generated or exacerbated by the political class. Since no commission of inquiry ever punishes them, they hide behind their ethno-religious curtains as untouchables—constantly brewing and dispensing new forms of violence. Genuinely religious people respect the ways of life of others and treat human lives with dignity. They know that since they did not create, they could not take the lives of others.

The Challenge of Patriotism, Discipline and Social Conscience

Candidly, it is my belief that with 50% patriotism and discipline among leaders and followers, we would be able to transform this country into an industrialized power – given our human and natural resources. Our aggressive self-interest – both among leaders and followers – has blocked our chances to develop. It is not enough for leaders to call for patriotism, when their words and actions do not demonstrate such. Nor is it important for leaders to call for discipline and sacrifice when their lives indicate the opposite. We must all develop a social conscience – which is sensitive to the rights of others. Our road users, as an illustration, hardly care who else uses the road. When their vehicles have engine problem, they leave it in the middle of the street, instead of pushing them to the kerbside. The whole system is like that. No society grows or develops without some appreciable level of patriotism and discipline. We all must exhibit these qualities and let our younger ones copy these. What message do we pass to our younger ones if we give traditional titles to people with questionable character? Are we celebrating corruption, immorality and indiscipline? Are we promoting materialism over traditional values of hardwork, dedication, honesty, and humility?

We have embarked on a project of re-branding this country. Many Nigerians are skeptical about it. This is partly because previous efforts failed to bring positive results. But should we stop trying because of past failures? Should we condemn ourselves, our children and children's children to a destiny that we can change? I strongly believe with patriotism, discipline and social conscience, we can change that bad image some of our compatriots here and abroad have created for our country. We should try to encourage those aspects of our value system that promote patriotism and discipline—at family and community levels. We should not give room for those vices—laziness, indiscipline, immorality, corruption and others, which make us ashamed.

Constitutional Change

In the life of every nation, its constitution undergoes amendments, given new exigencies. In Nigeria, we have had the 1960, 1963, 1979, 1989 and 1995 (draft) Constitutions before the present 1999 Constitution came into being. Many observers of Nigeria have suggested that perhaps the problem with Nigeria is not with the quality of its constitution but with the operators of the constitution. Thus one may be tempted to ask, if constitutionalism rather than constitution-making has been Nigeria's main problem, why is there a demand for mega-constitutional change? More importantly, can we manage the constitutional change we are rather desperately yearning for? Since 1996, South Africa has effected at least 15 amendments to her constitution and the process continues. Why can we not take an evolutionary approach to constitutional change?

History shows that very often, countries which engage in mega (huge or major) constitutional changes suffer from one form or the other of mega political hemorrhage. Often such major constitutional changes have negative impact on political stability. It is often preferable to engage in evolutionary and piecemeal constitutional changes. A few clauses can be taken at any point in time and amended, without unduly stressing the polity.

In fact, our experience since 1999 illustrates the difficulty in the implementation of the constitution, with clear cases of *democratic deficit*. There is therefore the need for a more determined effort on our part to implement the constitution, and then embark on subsequent piecemeal amendments to avoid the destabilizing impact of mega-constitutional changes.

4. The Foundation and Dynamics of Nigerian Federalism

At the terminal period of transition from military to civilian rule in 1998-1999, there were signs of the resurgence of aggressive subnationalism which had been suppressed under the regime of General Abacha. After May 29, 1999, when the military handed over power to civilians, latent aggressive subnationalism exploded into violence. One reaction to the over-centralization of power by various military regimes was the emergence of strong centrifugal forces especially among groups which felt disadvantaged in the system. Many subnational groups believe that if the Nigerian federation were not as centralized as it was, they would have had a fairer deal in the federation.

Under this "democratic" polity, the suppressed "angst" of various groups with the Nigerian federation found expressions in many ways. The emergence of a fiscally and politically titanic center had questioned the basic sense of security of groups. Some groups have begun to wonder aloud if the federal association was meeting their objectives, and if desirable adjustments should not be made in the federation to give everyone a sense of belonging. We suggest some areas/issues that require attention of political leaders.

Challenges of Extraction (Production) and Distribution[17]

There is too much emphasis on the distribution of resources in this country. This has made the distribution of scarce but allocatable resources a very contentious affair. At the Political Reform Conference (2005), one of the hottest moot-points was the issue of resource distribution. The Niger-Delta had pressed for the control of their

174

resources from 25% but gradually evolving up to fifty percent on the basis of derivation. A number of reactions to this suggestion prompted the withdrawal of the South-South delegation from the conference. The Niger-Delta insurrections and the Yar'Adua Amnesty Programmes were directly related to the issues of distribution and welfare. The Niger-Delta people felt neglected amidst Nigeria's oil boom. The oil which is being extracted from their communities, seem to have little impact on their welfare. This led to violent militancy in the area. President Yar'adua in 2009 offered amnesty to the militants, if they laid down their arms and registered in a rehabilitation programme. Many militants did, and joined rehabilitation programme. Yar'adua's sickness and subsequent death probably has some effects on the quality of implementation of the programme.

Structural Adjustments of the Nigerian Federation and Minority/Majority Divide

The creation of states (from 12 in 1967 to 36 in 1996) from the original 3 (later 4) regions in the country, created new sets of problems among the various groups in the federation. The creation of states had its own political rashes. The first is the emergence of boundary problems. While these intra-communal boundary problems were intra-regional and intra-state, they suddenly became inter-state, and therefore took on higher saliency. The Tiv-Jukun conflict over boundary and land, for example, was transformed from an intra-state to inter-state conflict, after the creation of Benue and Taraba States.

Also the history and the sense of cultural identity of groups, amidst the identity explosion all over the globe, has been partly responsible for the ethno-religious conflicts as groups resist perceived threats to their identities. In the Nigeria case, the reduction of the original big regions and later states created newer problems along the majority-minority divides. In the old Northern Region, for instance, the creation of states dealt a big blow to whatever remained of northern identity. The new states, especially from the old minority areas, buttressed by new and separate administrative and political identities, often opposed the resurgence of the old Northern identity. They clung to their new found identity jealously, until some of these states started suffering from an implosion arising from the internal competition among groups.

In each new state, following the creation of additional States, there emerged *new majorities* and *new minorities*. Often, many of the *new majorities* (who were old minorities), are even more vicious than the old majorities, thus creating new bases for conflicts in the new setting. In essence, only a state leadership which demonstrates fairness, justice and equity in governance will reduce the intensity of conflict appreciably.

5. Security, Law and Order, and Conflict Management

Since 1999, an atmosphere of insecurity has enveloped the polity. Initially, one had thought that the removal of the tight lid under military rule had led to new sense of freedom which were transformed into license. As mentioned above, over the last ten years, there have been at least, 343 selected cases of violence – communal and others. Armed robbery has become part of our normal life. Political and other homicides as well as kidnapping of people for ransom have become rampant in the system.

Clearly the greatest problem in the country is the security of lives and property. This is not unrelated to the lack of good governance which has alienated people from government. The first step towards stability is to restore mutual confidence between the government and the citizens, as citizens become part of the security collective. Democracy presupposes responsibility. It presupposes that politicians will be responsible enough to be crises-dampners rather crises-escalators. It also means that government should effectively maintain law and order to encourage the 'rule of law' and prevent the aggrieved from taking laws into his/her hand. Unfortunately, the Nigeria Police Force seems to be overwhelmed, while the constant use of the military to perform police duties is dangerous for everyone. The emergence of vigilante groups and ethnic militias is a demonstration of the failure of the Nigeria Police Force and other security agencies.

Apart from the problems of capacity and discipline, the neutrality and indispensability of the Nigeria Police is seriously questioned. The impeachment cases in Ekiti, Oyo, Plateau, Anambra and Bayelsa under Obasanjo, were easily carried out because of the centre's control of the police and security agencies. We had argued in the past that the time was not ripe for state police, based on our experience of the misuse of local government police before 1966. The Persistently brazen misuse of the Nigeria Police by the presidency, under President Obasanjo, has however made one to revisit this argument. We now strongly suggest that the Nigeria Police Force should be decentralized such that it can operate efficiently in each state. The Governor of the state should have some delegated powers from the President such that within certain limits, he can operate effectively in collaboration with the Commissioner of Police in the state, referring only very serious matters to the President and the Inspector-general of Police. There should be State Police Service operating under special conditions, for states which so desire. This should be constitutionally delineated. Police, should become a concurrent matter.

Politicians should not politicize and destroy the credibility of the Nigeria Police. Nor should the Police Force allow itself to be destroyed. The Police Force is an important source of hope of the ordinary man in his or her desire for the rule of law. Political leaders must be careful that they do not politicize the police to the extent of committing class suicide. Our President Yar'Adua provided succour for the polity with his civility and policy of the rule of law. President Jonathan has promised to continue in this path. Government's intimidatory technique of using the Nigeria Police to enable it get away with illegalities as under Obasanjo is unconstitutional. Government must demonstrate civility, decency and caution in the use of its security services, which are paid from the people's tax funds. They are paid to maintain the system for all and not for a few incumbents in government.

The spate of violent conflicts since 1999 is partly a reflection of how our skills in the management of conflicts have been demonstrably poor. Government is always caught unawares. There is hardly any serious effort at establishing a data bank of conflicts and funding relevant institutions to carry out analyses. Often our responses are therefore *ad hoc* and stereotypical. A functional early warning system, properly funded and managed would have helped us to prevent conflicts or, at least, manage emerging conflicts and crises, effectively and efficiently. One is aware that there are efforts in this regard by the Institute for Peace and Conflict Resolution (IPCR). As mentioned earlier, most of the conflicts in the country are caused by the elites – political, religious, traditional, ethnic and others. These elites must stop playing the role of conflict generators, and move forward to help Nigerians to re-establish mutual confidence among themselves as they struggle to build a strong and viable political community.

Prospects for Peace and Democratic Governance: Towards a Prosperous Future

Nigerians have cause to be optimistic about the future inspite of certain negative signals on the political horizon. That we have been able to stay together as a nation-state for about fifty years is an achievement. We have been able to establish some salient compromises in our integrative process. From a virtual *pariah* state, we have joined the comity of nations as active participants in global activities.

Since 1999, we have gradually widened the frontiers of our democracy. Inspite of infractions, there is greater respect for human and individual rights. Nigerians have experienced greater freedom of the press, of thought, of religion, and of association. The civil society (though still largely dependent on donor agency support) are more proactive and interventionist than in the past. The Nigerian electorate (inspite of the pangs of poverty) is becoming more enlightened and has begun (in some states) to stand up for its rights. Generally, the greatest *dividend of democracy* has been the opportunity for the people to take decisions which affect their lives. Yes, we are not really there yet, in terms of achieving our best in all the areas mentioned above, but we have started, and God willing, with our collective determination, we shall get there.

We have not done what we should have done to transform us from a poverty-stricken Third-World country to an industrialized one, given our human and natural resources. Many Nigerians are angry about how we have wasted opportunities, talents and material resources. They are disappointed with leaders and their followers who are still using 18th Century technique to govern our country in the 21st Century, drowned in the vortex of primitive accumulation, consumption and vanity.

We cannot allow our failures in the past to be obstacles to our success today and in the future. We should collectively and sincerely learn from our past; see these failures as challenges, and determine - with hardwork, discipline and patriotism - to chart a new and positive course in our national development.

The prospects of peace and democratic good governance in Nigeria are good, even in the context of our murky present. But we must collectively determine to take our destiny in our hands, by taking appropriate actions to correct the shaky foundations of the past and lay concrete bases for the future today, to enable our successors achieve their aspirations. In this regard, we humbly make the following recommendations.

1. **The Democratic Polity**

Our leaders must stop seeing democracy in instrumental terms. All of us must work hard to make democracy work. The alternative is an authoritarian regime (probably military regime). Democracy is expensive and perhaps, even slow and not very effective. But it provides a peaceful and conducive environment within which development can take place, and within which individuals and groups can determine their future. We must seek democracy as an end.

a) *One-Term Chief Executive* — we recommend one-term chief executives at all tiers of government, given the aggressive politics of fraud and corruption which goes with political succession in multiple-term Chief Executives. We recommend a single term of five years, as an interim provision for the next thirty years when our politicians would have become more experienced in electoral politics and the politics of succession

b) *Strengthening the Electoral Process*
    i) *Enhancing the Neutrality of Electoral Bodies.* The polity gets tense over the issue of electoral reforms wherever this comes

up for discussion. These are not sentimental matters. INEC should be seen to be independent and neutral. Perhaps, Nigerians are spending too much precious time quibbling over who appoints the Chairman of INEC, because of the importance of personalities rather than institutions in the country. Let us concentrate on how to make the Chairman and commissioners *independent* and *neutral*. It is therefore recommended that the constitution be amended to make

-   INEC responsible to the National Assembly;
-   The Chairman and members cannot be sacked by the President, without the votes of ⅔ rds of the members of the Senate and the House of Representatives;
-   The Chairman of INEC shall submit a quarterly report of the National Assembly, copying the President of the Federation;
-   INEC funds shall come from the Consolidated Revenue Fund, (or first charge from the Federation Account) and INEC shall be an independent financially accounting body, subject to the usual auditing rules;
-   All cases of gross misconduct against members shall be duly investigated and such reports submitted to the National Assembly, without prejudice to other actions by other agencies of government.
-   No members of INEC shall belong to any political party, but NGOs, civil society and other relevant sectors of the society shall be duly represented.
-   The National Assembly shall make laws determining what constitutes 'gross misconduct' by members of the Commission, and the punishment for these.
-   While the imperatives of our federation and democracy desire it, I believe the State Electoral Commission should not be allowed to exist for an interim period of 20 years, when the system would have been more used to electoral process. This is because of our experiences in the last nine years in local government elections. If state electoral bodies should

continue to operate, we must clearly spell out their functions
and guides for action.

ii) *Strengthen the Political Parties*
  - We need to revert to the issues of formation, registration and
  funding of political parties not only to open the democratic
  space to all, but also ensure internal democracy in these
  parties, while ensuring that all registered political parties are
  strong enough to carry out their functions—aggregation of
  interests, interest articulation, and serving as alternative
  governments.

iii) *Political socialization*
  There is need for political socialization of the youth in
  schools and the *political education* of the adults, to understand
  the negative consequences of electoral fraud and violence;

iv) *Courts and tribunals*
  - *It is desirable to establish credible institutions for dealing
  promptly with grievances.* The election tribunals should have
  a limit on their operations. No public officers should be
  sworn in until his/her case has been disposed of at the
  tribunals and Appeals Courts. Election petitions cannot
  continue throughout the expected tenure of incumbents as
  we have had since 2003. All election cases must be
  concluded within six months from the date of election. We
  had done this in 1979 and 1998. We should revert to this old
  order. Candidates can have fair hearing within three
  months. In any case, those who have been in court over
  elections for over these years, still complain about fair
  hearing. There must be a time limit on electoral litigations.

v) Enable the mobilization of genuine civil society organizations
  and the media to monitor and observe elections;

vi) *Sequence of Elections:* if all elections cannot be held on the
  same day, the sequence of the elections must be such as

would prevent a bandwagon effect. We suggest the following sequence as the country had practiced in 1998:

√ Local government Elections
√ State Houses of Assembly Elections
√ Governorship Elections
√ National Assembly Elections
√ Presidential Elections

c) *Change in the Attitude of Politicians*

*   *Promoting the Culture of Tolerance and Moderation*
    Politicians must imbibe the democratic values of accommodation, tolerance of opposition and participation. It is in the interest of politicians that they are *gracious in victory* and *gallant in defeat.* They must leave the door open for erstwhile failures to enter otherwise they will find it difficult to make graceful exits when they want to do so. In office, they must transform themselves from *soap box politicians to statesmen* who also have responsibility for all, including those who did not vote for them. Finally, they must distinguish clearly between national interests which transcend politics, and issues which can be politicized. They must learn that politics is a *game,* not *a battle.* In this process, people give and take. A 'winner takes all' position only creates unnecessary tension in the polity.

*   *The Rule of Law*
    Let us allow our institutions to grow. Let processes get routinized in such a way that the personality of and individual is not overwhelmingly important. This is essential for the entrenchment of the rule of law which assures—freedom and equality and the dignity of man. Democracy and the rule of law are inextricably linked, as shown earlier. All citizens are equal before the law, and the poor has a right to fight for his/her rights against the rich and powerful. Our *constitution* must be accepted as a supreme document which guides our actions.

- *Constitution and Constitutionalism*

It is our contention that there is too much emphasis on *constitution-making* for our own good. No constitution is perfect and for all times. This is why there are amendment provisions. No constitution can implement itself. We, as human operators, are responsible for the operations of the constitution. However, our compliance with constitutional provisions leaves much to be desired. Our record in constitutionalism (ie constitution in practice) is poor. Let us gradually amend the 1999 Constitution to meet our needs, as we experience problems with it. Let us abandon this notion of a wholesale constitutional review. After all, we must remember that *mega-constitutional* change may lead to mega political instability. We should opt for an evolutionary approach by amending sequentially the various necessary clauses, rather than constantly re-inventing the wheel. Political stability is important for democratic governance.

Let us suggest few possible areas of urgent but sequential amendments over time.

The various clauses related to electoral reforms.

- *The Immunity Clause:* The Chief Executive of any of the governments in the three tiers of government should be immune against all civil cases while in office. Nothing should preclude these cases from being resuscitated when he/she vacates office. The law can be amended to take care of this. This is to prevent the Chief Executive from spending most of his valuable time in court over issues which would never have amounted to gross misconduct in any case. However, these Chief Executives should have no immunity in criminal matters. If investigated, found guilty, and subsequently impeached, such a Chief Executive should be tried in a court of law. Criminal matters may amount to gross misconduct and cannot be left till the end of such executive's tenure of office.
- The *tenure of Chief Executives* – should be limited to one term of five years; for the next 30 years and;
- A Review of the powers and responsibilities including the movement of the Nigeria Police provision from Exclusive to Concurrent list.

-   Amend the process of fiscal federalism, including the appointment of an Accountant-General for the Federation (as separate from that of the Federal Government) as a custodian of the Federation Account.

d) **Security, Law and Order** - Most people would prefer peace without democracy than democracy in war.

-   *Reprofessionalization of the Military*: our military should be transformed into a modern military with increased professionalization with up-to-date hard and software and fire-power in order to meet our regional and subregional requirements. The military should also be encouraged to become part of our development efforts as done in other countries such as Egypt, Britain, US, Indonesia and others.

-   The Nigerian Police must be over-hauled to meet current challenges:-
-   Training and re-training of police is very essential in effective policing of democracy.
-   Provision of sufficient equipment and logistics.
-   The Nigeria Police should be decentralized to provide for zonal operational autonomy. Occasionally, it may be extremely necessary, for the military to be called to support the restoration of order, but the rules of engagement must be very clear.

e) **Socio-Economic Setting.** Candidly, no one cares for democracy on an empty stomach. Let us mention a few factors which attract our attention.

-   *Diversifying the Economy:* The economy is a very urgent matter if it is not to feverishly continue to respond to the vagaries of international setting. We need an Economic Emergency Fund – to help us invest these resources in areas which will diversify the economy. We have placed less emphasis on production, and more on sharing. Can we reverse this trend before we cut our noses to spite our faces? Also, I believe foreign investment is important, but I also believe that foreign invasion of the economy is dangerous. Where do we strike the appropriate balance?

- *Deregulation and Privatization*: I believe that most Nigerians want deregulation. But they want deregulation in a deregulated context—that is, a context in which, for example, the oil refineries are working and we are not exporting crude in order to import refined petroleum; the smuggling of petroleum across borders is stopped; petroleum products are available locally, and one in which there are visible evidences of acquired resources being used for particular welfare services such as attempted by Directorate of Food, Roads, and Rural Infrastructure (DFRRI) and Petroleum Trust Fund (PTF). In addition, privatization within reasonable limits and guidelines is essential, but privatization as an excuse for acquiring our national assets is really *personalization* of our assets. We need to tread carefully and transparently in this area.

- *Our infrastructure*: power, roads railways and others, need immediate attention since many other forms of development depend on them. We must not be oblivious of the fact that without adequate infrastructure, no foreign investor will put his capital in our economy—no matter the number of foreign trips our President makes. Even the local investors are going out of business, partly due to unstable power supply, non-availability and/or high cost of industrial fuel. Instead of flying around the world to seek investors like President Obasanjo did, let us stay home and create the enabling environment for investment, as Malaysia did.

- *Poverty*: Democratic culture and stability cannot thrive in a society where there is abject poverty. Our poverty alleviation/eradication programmes have so far failed to tackle the problem. We need to work seriously on these in order to save our democracy. With our abundant human and natural resources, we strongly believe that our poverty is related to the dysfunctional governance in the polity. Our governments at federal, state and local levels must summon the courage and will to fight this menace, which from all available indicators is increasing. The army of the unemployed poses great threat to the security of life and property of individuals, and the political stability of the polity. The post-amnesty period for the Niger-Delta militants is crucial. The former militants must be properly rehabilitated in order to avoid a new security problem.

- *Education*: is the motive force of any society. Development in the 21st Century hangs on it. Perhaps we have bitten much more than we can chew in this area, especially with the proliferation of universities. A situation in which ten chemistry students share a microscope, and universities produce chemistry students without adequate chemicals for their laboratory work, is appalling. I believe that we should start by rationalizing our universities. Universities should continue to be in the concurrent list for now. But federal universities should be rationalized and some merged. There is no reason why seven good and big Medical Schools, Six Faculties of Law, Six or Seven Faculties of Engineering, Seven Faculties of Information and Computer Technology, as well as Architecture, and others– spread out across the country and properly staffed and appropriately funded – should not serve as centres of excellence for the country. No single state can handle these problems. It lies squarely at the door of the Federal Government. Even then, the federal government alone cannot cope with the burden. The private sector should be aggressively co-opted into this exercise which should be coordinated by the federal government. Universities should find new ways of also generating badly needed funds, without necessarily passing the burden to poor students. Cooperation with other institutions and the private sector, as well as getting research grants and endowed chairs from outside the universities, are some options. We cannot move forward in the 21st Century by turning out half- baked citizens. This is not a good foundation for achieving our vision 20:20-20.

- *Literacy and Public Enlightenment*: For a new democratic culture and stability, there has to be a literate and reasonably well-educated citizenry. Only where there is a high degree of literacy, a public reasonably well informed on civic matters, and adequate and open channels of communication, can democratic culture develop successfully. There should be a deliberate literacy programme aimed at producing civic interest and awareness on the part of the citizenry. Part of the literacy programme should be the encouragement of a vigorous public discussion and facilitated by means of institutional arrangements and constitutional safeguards that assure full opportunity for associations, meeting, communication, and for orderly protest. The National Orientation Agency (NOA) should be the arrowhead of this programme. No politician should be appointed as the Head of NOA. It should liaise with Ministries of Education to ensure the schools have civic education programme. Political parties and civil society groups should be involved in this programme. There should also be a conscious public enlightenment programme on the constitution. We need the Constitution to be translated into various local languages.

f) **The Challenges of Federalism:**

Under this "democratic" polity, some groups have wondered if desirable adjustments should not be made in the federation to give everyone a sense of belonging. We suggest some areas/issues that require attention of political leaders.
• *Distribution of Resources.*

All federations have this problem of distribution of resources. It is also imperative for federations to review their fiscal relations at regular intervals.

It is therefore recommended that the *Revenue Mobilization, Allocation and Fiscal Commission* (RMAFC), should collate available data and embark on vertical and horizontal fiscal equalization among the component units of the Federation. This should be an annual event, without prejudice to their role of recommending the revenue sharing formula. Fiscal equalization would transfer funds to less well-to-do states in some sectors for purposes of national development. At the same time, it retains funds in the states from where resources are extracted.

Anyone who has been to the Niger-Delta area knows that there is the need for greater resources to be pumped into this area for development. One wonders whether it may not be useful to recall the on-shore/off-shore dichotomy. Every state should be entitled to at least 50% of resources extracted from its base (i.e. on-shore) on the basis of derivation. This is with regard to on-shore oil and other resources. The other 50% should go into the DPA for sharing.

However, with regard to off-shore oil, 50% of accruals should go to an *Economic Stabilization Fund* (to be operated by the Revenue Mobilization, Allocation and Fiscal Commission), for purposes of fiscal equalization among tiers of government and this fund can thus be used to close the gap between oil and non-oil producing states. Of the remaining fifty percent, 10% percent should be allocated to the rehabilitation of mining areas (oil and non-oil); 10% for social development of oil mineral producing areas; and 30% to the Federation Account for the usual sharing. .

In addition, it is recommended that our excess crude proceeds should no longer be shared but 'stored' as Endowment Fund for the future generation. This Fund should have its Board of Trustees. The Board should have powers to invest this fund within and outside the country. A clean procedure of withdrawing funds after appropriation by the National Assembly for national issues of urgency should be provided.

One argument is that many oil companies are moving off-shore because of disagreements with oil communities. This arrangement should assist in ensuring that oil communities and companies reach agreement on harmonious co-existence. Democracy involves accommodation, negotiation and compromises. It presupposes that in doing so, we bear in mind our ultimate responsibility to be accountable to the people. The post-amnesty period in Niger-Delta provides a good time for a change in rhetoric, strategies and performance.

- *Citizenship (and naturalization) correctly belongs to the Exclusive* Legislative List. However, one aspect of citizenship is controversial in most federations. Given the demands for resolving the *indigene/settler* crisis, it is necessary to have the local aspect of *citizenship* in the concurrent list. The states can decide the residency requirement for one to become a *citizen* or indigene of a state, even though one is a citizen of Nigeria. One would then be entitled to all benefits of a state indigene, such as fees in schools and others. Residency requirements are not unusual in federations. Citizenship is Item 9 in the Exclusive List. It should be made clear that nothing in this section precludes a state from establishing its laws with regard to indigeneship.

- *The Nigeria Police Force*:   Given the nature of the Nigerian Federation, the Nigeria Police as a centralized instrument for the maintenance of law and order is inadequate. The powerlessness of State Governors in situations of violent conflicts is a clear testimony to the need for State Police. Police, should be removed from Item 45 and moved to the Concurrent List, Part II of the Second Schedule. This permits any state which so desires, to establish a State Police Service under approved guidelines. Those who are worried about State Governors misusing the state police should remember how Obasanjo misused the police and other security agencies between 1999 – 2007. A guideline should be clearly given so as to make the misuse of Police (state or federal) a matter for litigation by citizens who feel that their rights have been violated. State Governors, as Chief Security Officers of states are held responsible for the breakdown of law and order in their states, but have no powers or even security agencies to deal with such situations. This is an anomaly in federations.

- *The Creation of Local Governments*: Section 7 (1) of the 1999 Constitution provides that local government councils are guaranteed, and that every state shall, subject to section 8, provide for "the establishment, structure, composition, finance and functions of such councils". Section 8 (3-4) clearly stated the processes for the creation of Local Governments. However section 8 (5) states that the NA "shall make consequential provisions with respect to the names and headquarters of states and Local Government Areas provided in section 3 of this Constitution and in Parts I & II of the First Schedule to this constitution".

    Perhaps, we have at least two options to deal with this issue which has created confrontations between states and the Federal

Government. One option may be to remove the list of local governments from the Constitution. The question then is, what is the implication for statutory allocations to local governments? This brings us to the second option, which accepts local governments as guaranteed tier of government, but operational under state government. By this logic, the states are directly responsible for funding local governments. However, statutory allocation from the Federal Account will still go into the States Joint Local Government Account, on the basis of a flat rate as was the case before the amendment. Alternatively, all allocations meant for Local Governments in the FA can be sent directly for sharing among as many local governments as are created by states. This matter should not be a basis for quarrel between the federal and state governments. In essence the clauses 8 (5-6) would become unnecessary and states can create as many local governments as they want, without additional funds from the FA.

There is one problem outstanding. In some states the number of local governments was deliberately created to balance the imbalance in the relations among component ethnic groups in the state, would this equation be maintained by states creating local governments without any federal counter-check? The creation of states in such areas may be justifiable

- *Taxation*: - Item 59 of the Exclusive Legislative List is identified as a federal matter – "Taxation of incomes, profits and capital gains, except otherwise prescribed by this constitution". States complain that the Federal Government has all the lucrative taxes, thus robbing the states of sources of revenue. The onus is on the states to prove that they have been robbed of sources of lucrative taxes. One thing is clear though, that all tiers of government have been very complacent about revenue generation. They are all dependent on funds derived from the Federation Account, which are dominantly derived from petronaira.

- *The Structure and Process of Fiscal Federalism*

The policies of homogenization and centralization of military regimes have affected the structure of fiscal federalism – and these should be reviewed. Let us illustrate these:

- Split of the Office of the Accountant-General of the Federation and the Accountant-General of the Federal Government:
Given the distrust of the States and local government for the Federal Government in the handling of the Federation Account (especially under President Obasanjo), there have been demands for an office of the Accountant-General of the Federation as separate from that of the Federal Government. For relatively peaceful intergovernmental relations, we believe this split of offices should be effected. The Accountant-General of the Federation shall be the custodian of the Federation Account and account for all the contents of the Federation Account, while the Accountant-General of the Federal Government shall account for only Federal Government funds.

- *The Role of the Revenue Mobilization, Allocation and Fiscal Commission*
The Constitution of 1999, Third Schedule, Part I, Item N clearly states the functions of the Revenue Mobilization Allocation and Fiscal Commission (RMAFC). These functions include monitoring accruals into the FA and their disbursement. It also makes recommendations on the Allocation formula. In addition, the Commission has the function of determining.

The remuneration appropriate for political office holders, including the President, Vice-President, Governors, Deputy Governors, Ministers, Commissioners, Special Advisers, Legislators and the Holders of the offices mentioned in sections 84 and 124 of this constitution;...[18]

How can the RMAFC which does not know the revenue profile of states and local governments, fix salaries and remunerations of their political office holders? While the State House of Assembly (Section 124 (1)) can make laws to authorize the payment of such remunerations and salaries, these should not exceed the amount as "shall have been determined by the" RMAFC.

Candidly, each state should pay remunerations and salaries based on its revenue profile. There is nothing that stops the Chairman of Eti-osa Local Government Council from earning more than the Governor of Nasarawa State. This is one carpet of homogeneity under the military which must be rolled back so that some states do not collapse under recurrent expenditure. State Planning Commissions should be responsible for fixing the remunerations and salaries of state political office-holders. While

RMAFC is an intergovernmental agency, there are other more important functions for it to carry out as stated below.

In addition, the RMAFC cannot and does not mobilize funds. Its functions of making recommendations on allocation formula can be done without its current name. This commission should be renamed the FISCAL COMMISSION, performing similar functions as the Fiscal Commission in India and the Grants Commission in Australia. RMAFC should be managed by experts and not politicians who will carry out the functions of monitoring the fiscal relations among the three tiers of government. It should carry out an annual exercise in fiscal equalization among the three tiers, and horizontally within each tier of government.

- *Uniformity of Salary Structure*

While the Federal Government has the power to fix the minimum wage for its public servants, the states also have the power to fix the salaries of its Public Servants. Since the 1974 Udoji Commission Report Recommendations were accepted by the Gowon government, all salaries of Public Servants were harmonized. This was why the country witnessed many strikes over minimum wage in many states of the Federation between 2000 – 2003. As an illustration, the payment of Teacher Salaries Scale (TSS) generated tension because there were demands for paying same benefits across states. A state or local government should pay only the salaries it can afford, given its resources and other demands of development on the same resources.

Again, this is another carpet of homogenization which needs to be rolled back to give Nigeria back its federal credentials and identity – 'unity in diversity'.

- *The Concurrent Legislative List*

Perhaps a greater source of centralization than the Exclusive Legislative List is the *Concurrent Legislative List* (Second Schedules Part 11). Here are areas in which states and the Federal Government have concurrent jurisdictions. However, section 4 (5) clearly states that:

> If any law enacted by the House of Assembly of a state is inconsistent with any validly made by the National Assembly, the law made by the National Assembly shall prevail, and that other law shall to the extent of the inconsistency be void.[19]

The concurrent list has been an area of Federal Government's predatory incursion into the areas for which states should, ideally be responsible. How does one explain federal ministries in the areas of agriculture, rural development, water, tourism and culture? In fact, all the Federal Government needs to do in these areas, is to have policy units which would coordinate national policies on these matters. Similarly, the Universal Basic Education Commission, as an intergovernmental agency, is improperly located as a Federal outfit. This agency should be owned by states and local governments, while Federal Government intervention should be in the form of annual grants. States and local governments should appoint the head of this institution and pay for their staff. Can we reduce areas of federal adventures using the Concurrent List, so that states and local governments can take on more functions? This also means that states and local governments will be given more tax powers and funds to carry out their additional responsibilities. Candidly, the Federal Government is directly intervening in too many areas for effective and efficient delivery of services. The Federal Government can make interventions through grants-in-aid in specific areas of its concerns to states and local governments. It can be a very useful actor in the process of fiscal equalization.

g) *Leadership and Followership*

It is my belief that the problem of this country partly emanates from the quality of leadership and followership. However, since leaders are expected to lead their followers, let us remind them of some simple but important functions which they owe the society.
It is recommended that

- *Religious Leaders should*

- Encourage ecumenicalism—religious tolerance among their followers. Their followers should be encouraged to respect the faith and/or beliefs of others;
- be neutral facilitators in mediation for peace (if and when conflicts emerge among religious groups);
- rise in defence of peace, social stability and sustainable development in all circumstances;
- encourage the development of curricula of education for youth, which include prospects for job creation and self-employment, and peace studies;
- work with government and civil society organizations to prevent religious conflicts; and
- Demonstrate high moral values in their lives, speeches and actions.

- *Politicians*

As political leaders, politicians must rise above parochial and sectarian divides. They must:
- respect the "rules of the game" of politics
- respect the electoral process—play gallant losers and gracious victors;
- respect the constitution and be bound by it in their utterances and actions;

- operate within the law to seek redress and should not take law into their hands— they are not above the law;
- shun corruption and the looting of public treasury;
- not be crises-generators but crises-dampners — must build "bridges of - understanding" among groups;
- genuinely determine to serve the people and provide for their welfare;
- encourage the youth into paths of gainful employment and not sponsor them in acts of thuggery and violence;
- not politicize or manipulate ethnic and religious allegiances, and conflicts; and
- Never feel that they are indispensable because it leads to authoritarian propensities; moreover those who feel they are indispensable easily become disposable — as some have found out.

- *Governments*

Governments at all levels should:
- develop early warning signals to prevent violent conflicts;
- be sensitive in their decisions and policies so as not to provoke inter-communal conflicts;
- grow the economy and manage unemployment, and ensure good governance;
- control the level of electoral malpractices and political intolerance, and defend democratic processes;
- ensure the non-partisanship of security agencies;
- encourage and establish frameworks for constant dialogue and mutual understanding among ethnic and religious groups;
- lead and coordinate efforts towards resolving the problem of 'settler' and 'indigene' communities;
- provide relevant infrastructure in order to encourage economic development; and
- Train our youth and equip them with new skills, new perspectives and analytico-causal attitudes; with the determination to probe deep into their environment, to seek some synthesis between the material and the metaphysical universe, and provide new opportunities for mankind, without necessarily defying GOD.

Conclusion

In this chapter, we suggested that the concepts of democracy and good governance are essentially alien to Africa. These concepts need to be domesticated to Nigeria's (indeed Africa's local conditions, and targeted to her peculiar problems. We also argued that while democracy provides a conducive medium for peace and good governance, peace and good governance are also imperatives for a sustainable democratic polity.

It is our contention that the majority of members of the Nigerian political class and their followers show more commitment to constitution-making than constitutionalism. This is probably responsible for the extent of unconstitutional activities we have seen since 1999.

Similarly, we argued that the greatest challenge to peace and democratic good governance in Nigeria is the political class (in government and in the larger political arena). The members of this class see democracy only in instrumental terms; they are not committed to democracy as an end, and have little sensitivity to the extent of *democratic deficit* created by their actions and activities.

We contended that the country needs institutional, processual and attitudinal changes in order to meet the challenges of peace and good governance. To this end, we made a number of recommendations for the correction of our mistakes of the past, lay the foundation for our efforts today as we build the blocks of our nation and its development in the future.

Finally, it is my belief that for a sustainable democratic polity and national development, we must imbibe a democratic culture of tolerance and accommodation, hardwork, and enshrine the values of *justice, fairness* and *equity,* as guides for all our actions and activities. It is therefore our argument that our politicians must see politics as a 'game' and play it according to its rules. Prospects for future elections are clouded by the negative performance of INEC in the past, by the determination of some politicians (across political parties) that rigging elections is more important than winning them. Let me warn that politicians should learn from the past in order not to commit political suicide.

There is no single solution to our myriads of problems of national development. But we must be honest in our appreciation of the past, courageous in our contributions to the civilization of today, as we give hope to the future generation that their lives would be much better than ours.

NOTES

1. William Zartman (ed.) *Governance as Management: Politics and Violence in West Africa* (Washington DC: Brookings Institute Press, 1997), p.197.

2. John A. Wiseman, *Democracy in Black Africa: Survival and Renewal* (New York: Paragon House, 1990), p.6.

3. Edgar Pieterse, *Participatory Urban Governance: Practical Approaches, Regional Trend and UMP Experiences* (Nairobi: UNCHS, 2000), p.4.

4. The World Bank, *Governance: the World Bank's Experience* (Washington DC: The World Bank, 1994).

5. Christopher A. Miller and Mary E. King, *A Glossary of Terms and Concepts in Peace and Conflict Studies,* (University of Peace, Africa Programme Coordinating Office, Geneva, Switzerland) p.29

6. Institute of Governance and Social Research, (IGSR), *Selected cases of Ethno-religious conflict in Nigeria since 1980* (Jos: IGSR 2009)

7. Alfred Stepan (ed.) *Democratizing Brazil,* (New York: Oxford University Press, 1989) p. 349.

8. General Gowon, Broadcast by the Head of the Federal Military Government and Commander-in-Chief of the Armed Forces of Nigeria on 26 May, 1968. See Federal Republic of Nigeria, *Faith in Unity* (Lagos: Federal Ministry of Information, 1970) p. 108.

9. However it must be noted that there are many ways to centralize political authority. John Lewis, warned that "national programme, of Unification disrupt and undermine the existing patterns of authority of the local units", thus creating problems of authority which "impose restraints on politically induced change" from the

centre. He also observed that "unconscious reorganization of a society may aggravate or produce numerous impediments to the exercise of leadership". John Lewis, "The Social Limits of Politically Induced Change" in Morse *et. al.*, (eds.) *Modernization by Design* (Ithaca: Cornell University Press, 1965), p. 24.

10. Jean-Jacques Rousseau, *The Socail Contract or Principles of Political Right* (edited by Charles Sherover) (Cleveland: Meridian Books, n.d.), p.11.

11. *Sunday Vanguard,* January 27, 2002, p. 11.

12. *Vanguard,* (Lagos) March 22, 209, p. 22. Interview with Isa Matori.

13. *Daily Trust,* January 9, 2009, p.6.

14. *op. cit. Daily Trust,* January 9, 2009, p.6.

15. *Vanguard,* February 19, 2009, p.1.

16. Taiwan's ex-president and his wife were sentenced to life imprisonment, while two of his children were sentenced to 2-year jail term. Members of the former first family were sentenced for embezzling public funds, accepting bribes, committing forgery and/or money laundering. [*This Day,* Sept. 13, 2009, p. 21]. Former Costa Rican President, Rafael Angel Calderon, was convicted and sentenced to 5 years in prison for embezzling funds from Finish loan intended for medical equipment for public hospitals in 2004. The amount he embezzled was $520,000.00. [*Daily Trust,* October 7, 2009, p.22]. The Italian Prime Minister, Berlusconi, has had his immunity removed by Italian Constitutional Court.

17. See J Isawa Elaigwu (ed.) *Fiscal Federalism in Nigeria: Facing the Challenges of the Future* (London: Adonis and Abbey Publishers Limited, 2008).

18. Federal Republic of Nigeria, *Constitution of the Federal Republic of Nigeria 1999* (Lagos: Federal Government Press, 1999), p.147.

19. *op. cit.,* Federal Republic of Nigeria, p.2.

---

* The original version of this chapter was the text of a lecture delivered at the First Quarter Guest Lecture Series of the Institute for Peace and Conflict Resolution (ICPR), Abuja, Nigeria, October 12, 2009

CHAPTER 5

THE ARMED FORCES AND SOCIETY

Introduction

The late 1990s found Africa caught in the throes of another global frenzy - the democratic fever. Like the 1960s, the West is leading in this crusade for a 'democratic' world, and therefore a 'democratic' Africa. The hopes of a democratic Africa which came with independent African countries generally evaporated by 1965, giving way to the exhortation of the military as the sole institution best equipped for state and nation-building. The military then was regarded as political physicians capable of curing African states of their main ailment - political instability. Analysts claimed that the military was the most organized, cohesive, nationalistic, puritanic, self-abnegating and professional institution in the state.

Thus, there had been a retreat from a faddish democratic experiment to a line of institutional consolidation. Why did the first experiment in democracy fail? Have we transcended these issues? Have we established basic democratic institutions, nourished by essential democratic values? Are we making another false start by riding on the bandwagon of democracy, without adequate institutional base to suit our environment? Is every elected government democratic? Can we have a civilian elected government that is undemocratic?

Given the history of the very thin line between the *barracks* and the *ballot box* in Nigeria (and in other African States) how can we domesticate democracy and establish such institutions and processes as will ensure an enduring democratic polity? Has our political class learnt enough lessons from the past? If they have not, what arrangements can be made for them to begin by learning on the job without the military imploding into the arena as both umpires and political contestants? To what extent have we been able, in Africa, to routinize the management of defence in a democratic setting? What is the relationship between the armed forces and society in a democratic setting?

To what extent have we addressed the problem of a 'military tiger' on whose back we took a long ride? What are the conditions under which we can 'safely' get off its back and let the tiger co-exist with us in the same polity? To what extent is it realistic to expect a politicized military which has managed the country for about thirty years, calmly retreat to the barracks and play the apolitical, professional military? Are we learning from our past or are we reliving the past? Did General Abubakar's transition programme mark the beginning of the end of military rule in Nigeria?

Does the solution lie in total abolition of the military or its dissolution? What are the costs? To what extent do you engage in self-destruction when you destroy your military in the process of nation-building? Will Nigeria's problems of nation-building disappear after we have demilitarized the polity or do our problems transcend the military? Is the military just an additional "muddle" in our muddy waters of nation-building? We have more questions than answers and hope that our discussions here will help us to move forward. To answer some of these, we suggest that:

- the military is part and parcel of the process of state formation and is therefore a political institution;
- the military intervenes in the politics of every modern state - advanced industrial as well as non-industrial and developing;
- the traditional concept of an apolitical professional military is as alien to Africa as is the concept of civilian supremacy;
- the military in the modern Nigeria state is as much an imported institution as the political institutions in the state, and both the military and other political institutions (such as political parties, legislature and others) suffer from problems which accompany institutional transfers;
- While democracy is not alien to Africa, the current socio-political institutions of democracy are Western. Democracy in the modern African state needs to be domesticated or adapted to local conditions;
- arising from these is the emergence of the military as a *de facto*

political power contestant;

- the prospects for a stable democracy in Nigeria are intertwined with a number of socio-military and/or intra-military factors; and finally
- the demilitarization of the polity without adequate depoliticization of the military is an invitation to chaos; yet paradoxically that process of depoliticization involves the politicization of the military - herein lies the big question of the role of the military in politics, if a dark cloud is not to continue to hang over Nigeria's democratic horizon.

The Military, the State and Civilian Supremacy

The Military and the State

Traditionally, the formation of the state (especially the conquest state) has always intimately involved the military whether these were Greek and Roman city-states, imperial systems like the Chinese, Byzantine and Roman Empires, feudal states or societies like the Hausa-Fulani State in West Africa, or patrimonial states as found in Near-Eastern and Southeast Asian societies. In fact, "the growth of the polity in the direction of statehood was in part a process of militarization"[1].

This is abundantly illustrated in the definition of the state. Max Weber identifies the monopoly of the instruments of violence or coercion, as one of the most important attributes of the modern state. Similarly, Eugene Walter has defined the state in terms of the ability of its leader to claim "legitimate monopoly of force" and to command a "special body of men organized to use it."[2] In the same vein, anthropologists like Radcliffe-Brown, Fortes and Evans-Pritchard see political organizations as dealing basically with control and manipulation of force. As Fortes and Evans-Pritchard put it: "The political organization of a society is that aspect of the total organization which is concerned with the control and regulation of the use of physical force.[3] Thus the concept of force is crucial to the definition of the state; so also is the idea of a standing military to use this force.

Ali Mazrui therefore captured the point succinctly when he asserted that "Statehood... has so far been the final consummation of that marriage between politization and militarization,"[4] and that what we have now is a basic transition from "the warfare polity to the welfare polity".[5] This welfare polity has been marked by a paradoxical process of attempting to divorce the military (which contributed so much to the rise of the modern state) from politics in the state. Can the military really be kept out of politics? One cannot agree more with Welch Jr. and Smith that

> No nation's armed forces can remain apart from politics. Politics is concerned with the distribution of values and power within a society the military and can hardly be prevented from participating in that process in some manner.[6]

Like other political organizations in the state, the military participates in politics to protect its own interest. This point is even more pungently driven home by Uzoigwe when he contended and demonstrated (with cases) that

> In no state, traditional or modern, is the military totally divorced from the political structure. The degree of integration, however, of the military and politics varies from state to state.[7]

Our point so far is that the military has historically been part and parcel of the process of state formation and thus has been a crucial political institution within the state. Therefore, the military has never been totally divorced from politics as many people would like to believe. This brings us to our second proposition or suggestion that the military intervenes in the politics of all modern states - advanced industrial as well as non-industrial and developing.

Military Intervention in Politics

According to Finer, military intervention is "the armed forces' constrained substitution of their own policies and/or their persons, for those of the recognized civilian authorities.[8] The term 'constrained substitution' may refer either to 'influence', 'pressure or blackmail' or 'white mail', while the change in political incumbents would indicate 'replacement'. In fact, it can be argued that the processes of budgetary lobbying, expert advice on foreign policy and such others, are constrained pressures by the military to "substitute" their own policies, for legislative or executive policies. Many military institutions are known to have done this with great finesse using constitutional channels.

Our point becomes even clearer when one takes a look at Finer's 'levels of intervention'. These include (i) influence, (ii) pressures or blackmail, (iii) displacement, and (iv) supplantment. *Influence* involves (in a political culture where legitimacy is unobtainable by the military) the use of normal constitutional channels, or collusion or competition with civilian authorities - to alter the direction and content of policies. On the other hand, *blackmail* entails the use of intimidation or the threat of use of violence against civilian authorities in a political culture which resists overt military control. *Displacement and Supplantment* on the other hand , epitomize the failure of the military to defend civilian authorities against violence and/or the threat of the use of violence by the military to displace or supplant civilian incumbents, in a fluid political context in which the legitimacy of government is low or unimportant.

Given the above definitions and the distinctions among levels of intervention, it can be argued that the military in any modern state intervenes in politics, in one form or the other. For

"Any military has an impact on its political system, with its political roles being a 'question not of whether, but how much and of what kind'. No military, in short, can be short of political influence, save through the rape step of total abolition."[9]

It is the degree of intervention that primarily distinguishes between the United States military and the Nigerian military. While military intervention takes the form of budget lobbying, provision of relevant information and expert advice for strategic decision-making in the US, in Nigeria it takes the form of supplantment through a *coup d'etat.*

In the United States, General Eisenhower in his 1961 farewell address had warned Americans against the dangers of an 'immense military establishment'. According to President Eisenhower,

> "In the Councils of government, we must guard against the acquisition of unwarranted influence, whether sought or unsought, by the military industrial complex. The potential for disastrous rise of misplaced power exists and will persist."[10]

In Africa there have been more cases of military interventions at the levels of veiled pressure or blackmail, displacement and supplantment than there have been documented cases of intervention through influence. When the Ethiopian military put pressure on Emperor Haile Selassie to change his Prime Minister and Ministers in 1974, the military were intervening through pressures or blackmail. On the other hand when the Armies of Congo (Brazzaville, August 1963) and Hubert Maga in Dahomey (now Benin) (October 1963) intervened,[11] they were intervening at the level of displacement - displacing one civilian regime for the other. Outside Africa, an example of this would be the 'moderator' role of the Brazilian military between 1945-64 when it allied with sections of the political class and displaced incumbent civilian government, for new civilian governments. But when in 1964 the military took over political power in Brazil, it was effecting a supplantment of the regime.[12] The Nigerian coups in 1966, the Ghana coup in 1966, the Uganda coup of 1971, and the Sierra Leonean coup of 1997 are all examples of supplantment.

Many writers argue that in developing societies of Africa, Latin America, and Asia, military intervention through displacement and supplantment can be traced to the fact that in these areas the "norm of civilian control may not have entered the military ethic".[13] This argument contains some truth. But one may ask whether the idea of an apolitical, professional army is African. Is the concept of civilian supremacy not alien to Africa? To what extent are political and military institutions in post-independence African states indigenous?

Civilian Supremacy and Military Intervention

We argue that the idea of an apolitical professional military is alien to Africa. In fact, this idea was borrowed from Europe. In pre-colonial African states "the distinction between the military, economic, political, social and religious institutions of government were blurred.[14] In many cases, the average male citizen was a potential warrior – part of the "invisible" army. It is pertinent here to observe that the warrior in Africa is a political animal:

> The warrior, in a traditional society, was a political animal, more so than the rank and file of the citizenry. He saw politics as state power; he knew that the art of politics concerns how to acquire that power, how to wield it effectively, and how to preserve it. Most importantly, he knew the surest means of achieving state power is through the agency of the warrior.[15]

Military power was therefore an indispensable part of the political calculus in the traditional society. It was the life-blood of the state.

In pre-Shaka Nguni State, for example, the Chief and his Officials were also the Commanders of their people in war, and political leaders in peace and war. Thus, "the military and politics were dangerously fused.[16] The interlacustrine states of Bunyoro Kitara and Buganda provide another interesting set of illustrations. In these states, "the ideal king was the great warrior." As Uzoigwe clearly showed, here too, "the military was not distinct from the political structure: it followed closely the organization of the state". The 'Abakungu' (the territorial administrator) derived his power from the king, usually as a reward for military valour. In fact, Bunyoro tradition is known to have originally provided that only outstanding warriors be made Abakunga. [17]

On the West Coast, in Oyo State, the Alafin was required to be a great warrior who exhibited militant leadership. It is interesting that Alafin Ajaka was deposed by the 'Oyo Mesi' (Council of State) for his lack of militarism. On his rehabilitation or return to power, however, he was said to have been "more warlike than his predecessors." He had learned his lesson. While Oyo was not a military state, the military and political institutions were also fused. Even among the Kikuyu where kingship had been abolished, the "Kiama" or the council of elders which ruled usually comprised retired warriors. It is therefore interesting that the 'Anake' (young warriors who formed the council of war) not only represented the youth in government, but knew they could, through upward social mobility; attain the coveted position of 'Kiama'. Thus African warriors were "an indivisible element of the central government. But since "they were also military leaders as well as administrators, they played crucial roles in territorial administration. [18] The fusion of the state and the military made the African warrior a political animal. The apolitical professional military of the modern African state is therefore, not an indigenous institution.

Following our argument above, it is suggested that, just like the idea of an apolitical professional military, the concept of *civilian supremacy* is also alien to Africa. In a very interesting study, S.N. Eisenstadt demonstrated that the separation of civil and military authorities with the supervision of the military by civil powers, "lies in the modern European experience, and especially in the liberal ideology of the nation-state".[19] According to Eisenstadt, this concept derived from the historical experience of two types of societies - (i) the classical Greek and Roman city-states and (ii) the imperial system like the Chinese, Roman and Byzantine. In all these societies, "the military was seen as distinct from civil authority and control by the civil authority was deemed as a crucial problem."[20]

The failure to control the military had always caused disunity and disintegration for these societies. The Greek city-states fell because the warlords could not be controlled. Old Imperial Rome witnessed long periods of attempts by emperors to be independent of the military; and China had always had problems with its warlords in the periphery. Eisenstadt's argument, therefore, is that the concept of an apolitical professional military under civilian control is rooted in European attempts to centralize political authority. These attempts to control the periphery meant that autonomous but dangerous warlords had to be depoliticized and gradually turned into a professional institution. As he put it:

> "The greater the difference and distinction between the periphery and center and the greater the tendency of the center to mobilize and

control the periphery or the more that the center and periphery struggle over mutual control the more will the distinction between civil and military authorities tend to develop".[21]

This was the European experience. It was different from other types of societies where these elements of distrust between military and civil authorities were not as significant. Thus, the concept of an apolitical professional military under civilian control is European, not African. At independence colonial armies had become national armies. In many cases these colonial armies were seen as armies of conquest and suppression, rather than as symbols of these new nations.[22]

In essence, the problem of civil-military relations in African states is related to the problems of institutional transfer. Both political and military institutions in post-colonial African states were imported. But the values which underwrite these institutions had not been sufficiently internalized. Very often the rules governing these institutions in Europe were neither well understood nor accepted in Africa. Hence political institutions (parties, parliaments) inherited had difficulty in taking off. The colonial period was not a good schooling period. It was essentially autocratic, but bequeathed to Africans, European democratic institutions.

Democracy and the Politics of Governance

The term democracy is perhaps one of the most polemical words in the political dictionary. It has been subjected to so many interpretations and adaptations in various parts of the world that over time, it has become value-ridden.[23] The impression is often given that democracy is *good*; to be undemocratic is *bad*.

It is possible to identify some of the salient characteristics of democracy.[24] Among these characteristics is the locus of *authority* in a democratic polity. Authority emanates from the *people*. Any authority that does not emerge from the consent of the people is not democratic. How consent is operationalised may vary from one system to the other. Secondly, a democratic polity must be based on the *rule of law*. Law cannot be arbitrary in a democracy. There are specified limits to power and how power can be used. In addition, there should be an acceptance of the rules of the 'game' of politics by all the players, if arbitrariness is not to creep in at a later stage.

The third characteristic of a democratic polity is that it must be *legitimate*. For our purposes, legitimacy involves two processes. One of these is that the leader has the *right to rule* - that is to say, that given the law or the rules for accession to power he is the right person to be there. The institutional mechanism for this accession to power would depend on the particular country and people. The other is that he is *ruling rightly*. This is to say that he is performing well, given the ends for which he has been elected or chosen.

In addition to these, is the fourth, the element of *choice*. The people should have the right to effect changes in the leadership or the government of their country, given available alternate leadership. In some countries the plebiscetarian system is used. In some others, other mechanisms for providing choice are used. Fifthly, there must be *accountability*. Leaders must be held responsible for their actions as representatives of the people who are trusted with power to achieve particular ends.

These five points may be seen as the minimum characteristics of democracy. However, the institutional framework for their operation differs from one country to the other. Does democracy mean Western democracy? No! Very often some Western analysts equate democracy with their brand of democracy. They painstakingly count the characteristics of democracy in the United States or Britain, and pass judgements of 'guilty' or 'quasi'democratic' on other systems. Ironically, African (especially Nigerian) intellectuals who, critique the Western literature on this subject have also fallen prey to the same intellectual bias. Democracy is operated differently in various parts of the world, and often responds to its peculiar environment and its problems.

We contend that while democracy (given the characteristics spelt out earlier) is not alien to the country, the democratic institutions inherited at independence by Nigerian politicians were basically Western. Two major institutions of relevance to our discussion come to mind. These are - the *political party* and the *military*. Both institutions were borrowed from the West and have had problems of adaptation in the African political environment. The processes of institutional transfer at independence had implied the adoption of Western-type political parties and the military establishment.

Both were expected to perform the same functions as in Western countries from which they were borrowed. The political party was expected to aggregate and articulate the interests of the members, and provide alternate leadership and programmes of action. On the other hand, the military was expected, in the liberal Western culture of civil-military relations, to be professional, and apolitical, subject to civilian supremacy. The environment into which these institutions were being transferred was regarded as inconsequential. It was therefore, no surprise that many Western analysts were very disappointed in the 1960s when Africa did not turn out to be a major duplicate of Western democracy as it was expected.

They then lionized the military as the only modern, national, cohesive, puritanic and self-abnegating institution which could restore order and embark on modernization of their various countries.[25] From democracy, western analysts retreated to the importance of organization in the context of institutional fluidity in these 'praetorian' states. Again, as a new wave of demands for democratic polities sweeps across the country, it is not clear that many Western analysts (even though some of them are very sensitive) have learnt from the past; nor have their counterparts in the country.

A Western model of democracy cannot be transferred to Nigeria and be expected to succeed. Democratic institutions borrowed must be domesticated or adapted to local conditions, in the light of the country's experiences and problems. Let us illustrate this point. Political parties and military establishments were transferred to Nigeria in the terminal colonial period. As mentioned earlier, at independence colonial armies had become national armies. In many cases the colonial armies were seen as armies of conquest and suppression, rather than as symbols of these new nations.[26]

It was soon discovered that there was a major lag between these institutions and the values which were supposed to underwrite them. Both democratic and military institutions in post-colonial Nigeria were neither well understood nor accepted in the country. Furthermore, the military institutions as borrowed from Europe had not imbibed the professional values which created professional corporate identity and respect for civilian supremacy. This affected the development of professional values which should have buttressed the military establishment. By the time coups started punctuating the political process, the development of professional military values were only inchoate. It was therefore not surprising that the boundaries between the polity and the barracks were so blurred. Similarly, politicians schooled in the colonial authoritarian political culture, found it difficult to operate a Westminster parliamentary democracy with its emphasis on tolerance of opposition, accommodation of divergent viewpoints, and participation. The ethnoregional and geoethnic context in which they operated further complicated the problem. In addition, the concept of institutionalized opposition was not very common in Africa. Opposition emanated from within the main frame of the society and after due discussion, a consensus decision was usually taken. Thus the insitutionalized opposition of the new democratic setting had no culture to back it up, especially in terms of the accommodation of the views of the opposition and tolerance of dissent. Opposition was thus seen as personal animosity or enmity.

Many of the politicians had neither understood the rules of the game nor had they accepted them. For many of them politics was not a game, it was a battle. As the rules were blatantly violated, politics became a very dangerous 'game', for the atmosphere in the political arena became polluted, and in the absence of any form of ventilation, endangered the lives of the players as well as spectators. Yes, Nigeria had political parties (in fact, many of them) but lacked the values which would make them operate in a democratic setting. The exercise failed once; it failed the second time, failed the third time, and Nigeria is now back on the drawing board. We are not suggesting that these were the only reasons for the, failure of past attempts, but they were major reasons.

Did the politicians have the chance to reassess themselves and learn from their mistakes, albeit, in a hard way? No! The other borrowed institution, the military, had also been supposedly transferred 'successfully.' It had performed, creditably in the Congo (now the Democratic Republic of the Congo - DRC). In its role to kill and maim in the defence of the nation, it was no doubt relatively effective. But its functions were supposed to be essentially against

211

external enemies, not against its own nationals which it had a duty to defend. One of the cardinal values of the Western military, as pointed out earlier, was to respect the values of *civilian supremacy*. The Nigerian military was to be apolitical and professional, and only act on the orders of the civilian rulers. Had the Nigerian military adequately imbibed these values by 1966 when it was faced with political challenges?   No. Again, there was a lag between the borrowed institution and the values which were to make the institution operate smoothly in the imported Westminster model of government.

In January 1966, the military intervened in politics, contrary to the values which were to regulate its operations. This second institution had also failed. Since the 'disvirgination' of the military in 1966, it has engaged (like sex) in political promiscuity. It has become a predatory institution, imploding with reckless abandon into the political arena, thus rendering extremely fragile the boundaries between the ballot box and the barracks - an essential component of Western liberal democracy.

If there is any message this illustration has for us in this period of our new effort in democratic governance, it is that,

> To be successful, an African democracy must be sensitive to local conditions; the simple adoption of an institutional framework designed elsewhere is unlikely to be successful.[27]

If Nigeria had been bequeathed a British political model in 1960, in 1979 it made a trans-Atlantic trip to the United States in search of a new model. It failed. Nigeria's problem is not constitution-making. Nigeria's problem lies in constitutionalism (i.e. constitution in practice). Nigerian leaders seem not adequately concerned about the problems of institutional adaptation and domestication of democratic institutions and values. One of these is the role of the Armed Forces in Politics.

The Military as Political Power

One of our suggestions at the beginning of this paper is that the military is a political power contestant. Some members of the old political elite have called it 'the alternate political party'. Of Nigeria's almost fifty years of independence, the military has been in government for thirty years. Within this period, there have been nine military coups and abortive coups. Of these, only three military coups have been against civilian regimes - in January 1966 and in December, 1983, and in November 1993. Three of these coups have been against military regimes - July 1966 against the government of General Ironsi; July 1975 against General Gowon's administration; and August 1985 against the administration of General Buhari.

In the same vein, there have been six abortive coups and officially acknowledged conspiracies (all against military regimes) February 1976 against General Murtala Mohammed's government; December 1985 conspiracy and the April 1990 putsch against the administration of General Babangida; and the March 1995 conspiracy and December 1997 abortive coups against the General Abacha regime. There were numerous other conspiracies which never came to public ears. But it is instructive that all the abortive coups are against military regimes - a sign that it is more difficult to overthrow military governments. Or does it simply indicate that the propensity to coup is greater under military regimes, especially when might becomes right?

If the military had ruled Nigeria for about thirty years, is it correct to continue to use the Western political culture as an ideal for evaluating the Nigerian political system after all the experiences we have had? Or should Nigerians look inwards and create a democratic polity based on the realities of their experiences? Our contention is that the military is a political power contestant in the power equation in Nigeria. Therefore any discussion of power-sharing in the polity which ignores this, dooms the future of such democratic experiment to failure. The military has become a dark bogey hanging over Nigeria's democratic process. The prospects of democracy in Nigeria are intertwined with a number of socio-military and intra-military factors as well as issues arising from the dynamics of the Nigerian Federation. Civilian democratic rule, given Nigeria's experience, is probably an *aberration*. It was perhaps civilian politicians disturbing the military's political waters.

It is our suggestion therefore that the survival of a democratic polity in Nigeria goes beyond a well-crafted transition or electoral reform programme. We argue that there are a number of socio-military and intra-military problems which call for very serious attention at the same time. Let us briefly discuss each of these points.

First, over the years, the Nigerian military did not only become politicized, it came to manifest the socio-political and economic cleavages in the larger society.[28] If the military came in as political physicians, they became very sick patients in need of medical help. Setting out to solve political problems, the military became a problem itself. Its malaise had more tragic consequences for the system because of its control over the instruments of violence.

Second, by the nature of the Nigerian military administrations over the years, some military officers held decidedly political jobs. Often, having enjoyed the perquisites and paraphernalia of office, these officers often suffered from "re-entry shock" when they got back to the barracks. President Obasanjo's way of dealing with this was to retiring over 90 officers who had held political positions.

Third, military politicians, (i.e. those who have held decidedly political jobs) acquired certain perquisites of office. Their return to the barracks often had demonstration effect on their colleagues and their juniors who saw them as much "better off" materially because of the positions[29] they held in government. In addition, the issue of ego trip came into play as younger officers saw coups as the only route to engraving one's name in the nation's history and for becoming materially "better off".

Fourth, quite a number of military leaders (like their civilian predecessors) became corrupt while in office.[30]This had implications for the larger society in terms of essential values in: i) demonstrable leadership, and ii) political accountability, no matter how good the teaching process was in the transition period. It is also true that leadership corrupts followership as much as the followership corrupts leadership.

Fifth, related to the above point is the issue of a professional fighting force. To what extent can a military institution turn out courageous men, willing to lay down their lives for their country, if they have acquired so much material wealth and have too much stake for an effective effort to be made at the battle lines? What are the implications for institutional discipline, ethics and commitment?

Sixth, as the military remained in the political arena, so also did its level of discipline sag. Military discipline and respect for military hierarchy were some of the prices the military paid for being in politics. This is so obvious to good and professional military men that it needs no elaboration. Young military officers who joined the military to make a career out of it must be made to look forward to a bright professional and career future. Otherwise, their thoughts may derail into those areas which satisfy their sense of adventurism usually onto the political platform. If the military must retain its institutional discipline, ethics and professionalism, the time to salvage these is now. Since 1999, there have been training and retraining of the military – the reprofessionalization of the armed forces.

Seventh, there is the knotty problem of how to reorganize the military. Perhaps the attrition rate in the Nigerian military is about the highest in Africa. Because of its involvement in politics, many well-trained officers have left their chosen professional careers well before they had anticipated. One of the most disturbing aspects of the military today, is the level of insecurity. The old sense of security of tenure unless one grossly violated the rules of one's calling is gone. With this fading sense of security, the military not only lost *esprit de corps* of yesteryears, but also much of its professionalism and confidence. Since 1999, the military has been struggling to rebuild this sense of mutual confidence among members of the Armed Forces.

Eight, in a situation in which majority of retired military officers exude affluence outside the barracks and constitute themselves into a military bourgeoisie or a military commercial class, what signals are being sent to serving military officers and the civilian population?[31] Perhaps this will pose problem for the polity for a while, and probably fade away. It is probably a phase which Nigeria must go through given her experience in military rule.

Nine is the new balance of forces in the political arena. For many Nigerian observers, many retired and serving officers had acquired enormous wealth partly as a result of their sojourn in government. Not only do we now have a class of *bourgeois militariat* (the military as a commercial class) but the military which seeks to protect its interest as a class or as individuals, in or outside the barracks. As the new democratic polity takes its root, many Nigerians wonder the extent to which Nigerian politicians are in control of the political process. To what extent is the military as a commercial class transforming itself into the military as a political class in mufti? Or is this the beginning of new forms of cooperation between the ballot and the barracks?

These issues raised above are to demonstrate the complexity of establishing a democratic polity in a highly praetorian setting. Beyond the Nigerian transition programme these issues need to be adequately addressed. The role of the military also needs to be properly addressed: to what extent can the Nigerian military after thirty years in government be expected to become an apolitical professional military? Are Nigerians really not shying away from facing this problem when, inspite of their experiences in 1983, they opted for a Western liberal model of civil-military relations in the 1989 and 1995 constitutions? If the military had been quite innovative in crafting new political parties, why did Nigerian civilian leaders at the Constitutional Conference shy away from being innovative in delineating new roles for the military, given Nigeria's experiences?

Management of Defense

So far we have dwelt extensively on the problems of democratizing the Nigerian polity, particularly how the military fits into this process at the levels of both theory and practice. It is theory and practice necessary to identify the milieu in which our institutions operate. Even more important, our analysis attempted to throw up the problem areas which if not tackled early and adequately would pose serious difficulties for the future of Nigerian democracy, not to mention the management of defence in that setting. We will now turn our attention to the specific issue of managing defence.

Let us first identify patterns of civil-military relations. Nigerians often make the mistake that the Western liberal model to which they are accustomed is the only model for managing civil-military relations. We suggest that there are many other models of civil-military relations.

1. Models or Patterns of Civil-Military Relations

For our purposes, we may identify at least **nine** models of civil-military relations. These include: i) the Liberal Western Model; ii) the Socialist Model; iii) the Developmental Militia; iv) Conscious Civilianization; v) Peripheral Participation; vi) Civilian-Military Dyarchy; vii) Anarchist; viii) Militocratic; and ix) the Authoritarian One-Party State Model.

The Liberal Western Model

This model emphasizes the separation of politics and the military as in most Europe. This model of civil-military relations is predicated on the assumption that the military has no power of its own. Its legitimacy is based on the consent of the society. The supreme authority in the state is reposed in the elected government which then defines clearly the goals of the military. African states pretend that the military can withdraw to the barracks and stay there. Even the French experience does not attest to such a clean break immediately after withdrawal.[32] African military establishments have always staged a come-back as civilians prostituted political power, bastardized rules of the game of politics and adulterated the socio-political and economic processes. This is not necessarily evidence that the military is a more efficient achiever; but the military often symbolizes the nation amidst societal disunity.

We believe that African states, in which there have been military interventions in politics, usually have problems with this model, in the absence of adequate political education. If they want peace and stability, their dogged adherence to the liberal Western model, in the absence of the properties of such a model, may generate further instability. Ironically even African socialist intellectuals, in spite of all their rhetoric about the need for a socialist system, often ignore the pattern of civil-military relations or paradoxically, adhere to the Western liberal model. The military has never ruled the United States of America since its independence. General Eisenhower did not contest the Presidency as a military man or from the military constituency, even though his credibility acquired in military service gave him the necessary popularity at that point in time. Apart from the brief intervention by *Cromwell and the Roundheads,* Britain never had a military regime; therefore, the experiences of these countries may be useful but not necessarily models for emulation. If Nigeria must seek a democratic model to learn (not transplant) from, it is probably more rational to take a good look at India (which has never had a military coup, but is complex and diversified domestically as Nigeria). See what makes that democracy survive inspite of its complexity and political turmoils.

The Socialist Model

The socialist polity exhorts the supremacy of the State and state power in trust for the people. The underlying presumption is the ability of this system to maximize its distributive capability in order to reduce drastically inequalities among individuals and groups. If the liberal Western model exhorts the freedom of the individual, this model emphasizes the collective interest of members of the community. The mass Socialist Party is dominant and all-embracing. Even the military is part of this Socialist Party and has a stake in the government. The experiences of the old Soviet, the Chinese and the Tanzanian (under one-party system) illustrate this. Thus if Lin Piao, the late Chinese Army Chief of Staff was ambitious, he had to work within the party to manoeuvre his way to leadership, given his military support. He was said to have been quietly eased out in a helicopter crash.

This model is grafted on strong ideological commitment of the people. Where the ideological base is fragile, there may be coups and attempted coups. Thus, frightened to death by the 1964 mutiny, Julius Nyerere embarked on a new military establishment that would be part of the party, be subject to political education and have a stake in the government.[33] Yet Nyerere found later that there was an abortive attempt by some members of the military to unseat him. This was not surprising given the relatively weak ideological base in Tanzania then, and Nyerere's adventure into Uganda which gave his own soldiers a taste of what it is to oust a Head of State. With the fall of many socialist states, there has been a revision of this model.

The Developmental Militia

Yet, it is also possible to have a polity in which, while the military is either part of politics or out of it, its role is clearly defined in peace time. Here the military like all institutions in the state, is seen as an agent of development. Thus it participates in agriculture, builds direct roads, bailey bridges, offers paramedical health services in rural areas, engages in political socialization of youths, distributes food during natural disasters and contributes to the general developmental process.

If the military is part of a mass party, it does not pose as much problem as when it is outside the party. For as the military provides services to the populace in the face of the sagging legitimacy of the political leaders, it may be persuaded to implode into the political arena as managers of the polity. While the role of the military in developmental process could be defined, it is not clear how these roles in social services would detract from military professionalism and ethos. Even more important is the issue of the nature of relationship between the military and political elites. Increasingly, it has become imperative for the military in many states to find alternative sources of fund beyond the budget. A developmental militia model offers not only an opportunity for the military to contribute to national development but also reduces its dependence on the budget.

Conscious Civilianization[34]

Where the military have already intervened in politics, a number of options are open to the military leader. He can go Kemalist like Turkey's Ataturk did. Here the military hero pulls off his military uniform and becomes a full-fledged civilian. He is no longer in control of the armed forces. He then can subject himself to elections for the state's premier office. The dangers are that he may be overthrown or have his ambitions upset by his colleagues in the army unless he has support in the force and societal demands for civilian rule are great.

Nasser and Franco provide a good variant of this. Nasser's successors, Sadat, and Mubarak emerged from within the armed forces and their holds on the armed forces are reputedly strong. On the West

Coast of Africa, there are examples of civilianized soldiers - Idris Derby of The Chad; Compaore of Burkina Faso; Rawlings of Ghana; Mainasara of Niger; and Yahya Jameh of The Gambia. Rawlings has since served his term and exited Government House in Ghana.

Another variant of this model is where there is a conscious attempt by leaders to civilianize their political personality and at the same time create a verisimilitude of political parties as a means of mobilization of the masses. They retain their military constituencies. Late Mobutu Sese Seko of the Democratic Republic of the Congo (Zaire) and Eyadema of Togo tried these techniques. In Nigeria, General Sani Abacha tried to do the same when his government manipulated the existing political parties to nominate him as their consensus candidate. Since he died before the plot was dramatized it is still speculation on how he was going to manage this extra-ordinary demonstration of 'confidence' in him by essentially five political parties.

Yet a more humorous variant of this was the Central African Empire under former the late Emperor Jean Bedel -Bokassa. Bokassa civilianized himself into a civilian as the Emperor of the State. The way he was overthrown is a lesson to African leaders, if they ever care to learn.

Finally, an interesting variant of this model was the Union Government as suggested under Col. Acheampong's government in Ghana. The Union Government was to be formed without political parties and their electoral problems. As Ghana's former Transport Minister argued:

> The NRC rejected the academic view that 'democracy' is only secure and assured when the people are led like swine, once every five years, to vote in their rulers who proceed to ignore all their fears and aspirations.[35]

Unfortunately General Akuffo's coup prevented us from seeing what lessons this variant had for all. Museveni's Ugandan no-party democracy was an interesting variant of this. Museveni had to succumb to Western pressures for a multiparty democracy. Even with multiparty democracy he has retained his strong hold on the reigns of power.

Peripheral Participation Model

This model is a slight modification of a liberal Western model. It would require the Chiefs of Staff of each service of the Armed Forces or the Chief of Defence Staff to be ex-officio members of the Central Cabinet, without any veto powers in the decision-making process. The military's interest would be represented in the government while the Chiefs of Staff would have the responsibility of educating the military personnel on the necessity for maintaining civilian supremacy. The military chief could also advise the politicians when they transcend their constitutional limits. It assumes that the military elite would be politically conscious and articulate.

One of the flaws with this sort of political arrangement is that it assumes that the military chiefs always have the support of their younger colleagues . The chiefs could be classified with politicians by their colleagues especially, as the legitimacy of the regime sags. Secondly, it presupposes that these chiefs have no political ambitions of their own, especially after the military had just withdrawn from politics.

Civilian-Military Dyarchy

This is a model popularized by Nigeria's doyen of politics, late Nnamdi Azikiwe. Azikiwe's suggestion was that the military and civilians should share government for, at least, five years after the military has withdrawn to the barracks. The military would have the veto powers. The fear of many coups frightened Azikiwe to give the veto power to the military. After the first five years, the military should withdraw, leaving the civilians to run the government. Veto powers or none, the gun is enough veto power, and who can tell the military to go after five years?

A variant of this is to have an elected functional Head of Government while (during the interim period) there is a Military Council acting as the political umpire and performing the ceremonial roles of the Head of State. As Ghana's government under Busia found out, even this did not protect it against Acheampong's coup of 1972.

The Anarchist Model[36]

This model presumes that the greatest danger to the individual's power of expression is the state and organized government. It claims that the former "enslaves man's spirit, dictating every phase of his conduct. The latter is in essence ... tyranny, irrespective of whether it is government by divine right or majority rule. [37] Thus the military's legitimacy is also rejected. It "rejects the thesis that the complex social and political system of contemporary society necessitates the creation of a legitimate order in which the military as an institution or formal organization has a positive role to play as part of that system.[38] If all formal political structures and the armed forces are abolished, the danger to the individual would be eliminated.

Obviously, for developing countries groping for some semblance of order and political stability, the anarchist model seems too radical and irrelevant for any state. But it should be noted for its lessons for the building of nation-states.

'Militocratic Model[39]

In this model the whole polity becomes militarized. The military rulers entrench themselves in power, refuse to demilitarize and act as primary power contestants. Very often the military leader relies very heavily on coercive instruments of the police and the military to remain in power. The ruler tries to balance his two constituencies - civilian and military. The extent to which the whole society is militarized would depend on the personality of the military leader or group of leaders. As prime power contestants, these military leaders eliminate potential contestants.

Even, when in search of legitimacy they create institutions for civilianization, with their thumb on the gun to secure their ascendancy in both civilian and military constituencies as Zia Ul-Haque of Pakistan and Commander-General Samuel Doe of Liberia had demonstrated.

General Nimeiry, the former President of The Sudan and again, late Eyadema of Togo illustrate decidedly military regimes whose pretence to demilitarization disappeared over time. As power contestants, they relied on coercion. It was not surprising that Nimeiry was overthrown in a mass uprising in Khartoum.

Thus the dangers of bloody counter-coups are there in a decidedly a militarized model of the polity. In addition, as the military stays longer in politics, they lose their sense of direction and prove unable to adequately feel the political temperature of the system. A similar case was the military regime in Uganda under General Idi Amin. The regime may become insensitive and pose grave dangers to the citizens. If Idi Amin did anything to Uganda, it was that he united Ugandans against himself as he dispensed similar quantums of misery to each group. The danger of this model is that as the civilian populace forgets their misery under politicians, they switch their torchlights on the military successors in order to effect a political change. Thus, even if the military government exhorts the primacy of economics, it must live with the necessity to cope with the saliency of politics.

Authoritarian One – Party State Model

Does the history of Africa show that an all-embracing authoritarian one-party which subjects the army to civilian control is more successful in solidifying the boundaries between the barracks and the party? It is difficult to say. There are, however, indications that in some authoritarian one-party states, there had been fewer cases of military coups. Thus Ivory Coast, Kenya (despite attempted coup), Sekou Toure's Guinea, the military had over the years been subjected to civilian control. So far, after the introduction of multiparty democracy in these countries, these one-party dominant states have used their old firm grassroot network for the effective control of the military. Moreover, Ivory Coast has undergone gross forms of political instability since the death of Houphonet-Boigny. Kenya has avoided a military coup inspite of the massive electoral violence there; and Guinea has experienced military coups.

All these models and variants have deliberately been made to differ from traditional typologies of civil-military relations, in order to highlight our need to think of a model polity of our own which delineates the role for the military in politics.

2. **Military Withdrawal from Politics**

These patterns of civil-military relations show clearly that where the military has already intervened in politics, the nature of civil-military relations changes. In such situations, the ruling military elites have demonstrated basically four patterns in the process of democratization. First, the incumbent military elite may declare a self-induced democratic agenda for change, as happened in Nigeria (under Obasanjo, Babangida, Abacha and Abubakar), or under Rawlings' Ghana, and Strasser/Bio's Sierra Leone. Very often, it is similar to Indonesia's 'guided democracy'.

The second pattern may be described as arising out of a populist backlash. Here "democracy emerges as a result of a successful populist pressure" by the masses as happened in Benin and Gabon, but started and was aborted in Zaire (DRC) and Togo. This pattern of military disengagement may create a new basis for a democratic beginning.

There is, however, a third pattern – that of military recalcitrance such as in Togo and Zaire. Here the military resists popular pressures and digs in as rulers, even in the face of populist pressures, and depends largely on instruments of state coercion. Finally, there is a pattern of benevolent acceptance in which there is a tacit acceptance of military rule. It could include the civilianization of erstwhile ruling military elite. Uganda and Togo (under Col. Eyadema) are also examples. Uganda provides a revolutionary basis for a transition to democracy, while often, military recalcitrance may lead to a violent upheaval. In the Democratic Republic of The Congo, Laurent Kabila followed closely, Museveni's technique of launching the change of government from the bush. Like in Uganda, DRC (Zaire) witnessed the transformation of erstwhile 'terrorists' from the bush to the State House. Ironically the year 1998 witnessed the rise of erstwhile comrades against Kabila, and the internationalization of the rebellion among DRC's neigbhours. Col Eyadema died and power passed on to his son through a multiparty election. Similar situation took place in Gabon where Omar Bongo's son succeeded him in a multiparty election.

3. The Management of Defence in a Democratic Setting

The important issue is how DEFENCE is managed under any of the models above in civil-military relations under a democratic setting - irrespective of patterns of withdrawal. This is our next focus. Nigeria chose the Western – liberal model of civil – military relations

Constitutional Provisions[40]

Nigeria is "one indivisible and indissoluble sovereign state" which has established and equipped an Army, a Navy and an Air Force (collectively called the Armed Forces of the Federation) to
- defend it from external aggression;
- maintain its territorial integrity and secure its borders from violation on land, sea and air;
- suppress insurrection and act in aid of civil authorities when called to do so by the President (subject to the National Assembly);
- perform such other functions as may be prescribed by the National Assembly.[41] These form the purposes of the Armed Forces.

The 1995 Draft Constitution also enumerated the functions of the Armed Forces of Nigeria. "The Armed Forces may, subject to the Constitution, be employed for:-
a. Service in the defense of the Nation, for the protection of its sovereignty and territorial integrity;
b. Service in the preservation of life, health and property.
c. Service in the preservation and protection of the environment.
d. Service in compliance with international obligations of Nigeria with regard to other nations and international bodies.
e. Service in the provision or maintenance of essential services.
f. Service in support of National efforts for economic fulfillment.
g. Performing such other functions as may be prescribed by an Act of the National Assembly." (Vol. 1, p.123-4).

The 1999 Constitution, Section 217 states the necessity for the establishment of the Armed Forces and clearly delineates the exact functions of the Armed Forces as enumerated in the 1979 Constitution, as above.

In essence the Armed Forces are expected to defend the integrity of the state and its sovereignty against outsiders primarily, and not against its own citizens. The Armed Forces are trained to kill and maim in defence of the country and not to interfere in the country's internal socio-political structures and processes. The Armed Forces are therefore the repository of instruments of warfare monopolised by the State. Their use also has to be controlled by the State. It is the responsibility of the state to organise its Armed Forces and manage its use in the most efficient manner in a democratic setting. What provisions do Nigeria's Constitutions have for achieving this? What model of civil-military relations was adopted by Nigeria's various constitutions? Nigeria has always enshrined in her constitutions a western liberal model of civil-military relations which emphasize the principles of civilian supremacy.

The first thing to note is that the constitution declares itself supreme and binding over all authorities and persons throughout the Nigerian federation. It also states that the governance of Nigeria should only be undertaken by any person or group of persons according to the constitutional provisions made for that purpose. Any other law to this effect which is inconsistent with the Constitution is declared void. This is a diplomatic way of disallowing coups d'etat. The 1995 Constitution provides for the prosecution of anyone involved in the overthrow of government after that Constitution has been promulgated. [42] The 1999 Constitution, Section 1, subsection 2, clearly states that – " the Federal Republic of Nigeria shall not be governed, nor shall any person or group of persons take control of the Government of Nigeria or any part thereof ' except in accordance with the provisions of this Constitution."

The executive powers of the federation are vested in a democratically elected President who is also the Commander-in-Chief of the Armed Forces of the federation. He is also empowered to exercise his functions indirectly through his Vice-President, Ministers or other Officers in the Public Service of the Federation. However, as part of the checks and balances which a democratic set-up provides to guard against arbitrariness in the use of power, the exercise of these executive powers are in many cases, subject to the National Assembly. One of such is the power to deploy troops and to declare war. In the former case, the President requires a resolution of both Houses of the National Assembly sitting in joint session; while in the latter he requires approval only of the Senate. It is worth noting here as a reminder, that since defence matters are directly tied to the sovereignty of the State, legislation on defence is on the exclusive legislative list.

In the overall management of defence matters the President is assisted by other officers and institutions to whom/which he delegates certain powers. These are, for example, the Minister of Defence, the National Defence Council (NDC), the Chief of Defence Staff (CDS) and the various Service chiefs. The NDC and the National Security Council (NCS) are constitutional bodies. The President has the right to appoint Chairman and members to these two bodies without recourse to the National Assembly or any other body.[43] The NDC comprises the President as Chairman, the Vice-President as deputy Chairman, Minister of Defence; the CDS; the three service Chiefs; and other members as the President may decide. The NSC comprises the President and Vice-President as Chairman and deputy Chairman respectively; the CDS; ministers responsible for internal affairs, defence, and external affairs; the head of the National Security Agency as established by law; the Inspector-General of Police; and others as the President may appoint.

While the NDC has power to advice on matters relating to the defence of Nigeria's sovereignty and territorial integrity; the NSC advises on matters relating to public security to ensure the security of the nation. The powers of these bodies are advisory and they relate directly to the President. The powers to appoint the CDS and Service Chiefs lie with the President, so also is the power to determine the operational use of the Armed Forces. However, the use of the President's powers as Commander-in-Chief is subject to regulation by the National Assembly.

For the day-to-day military executive command, the functions of the President are carried out by the Service Chiefs subject to the supervision of the Minister for Defence. In the light of Nigeria's civil war experience, the office of the CDS was set up to facilitate the coordination of defence matters. The CDS (first appointed during the Second Republic), oversees the Joint Chiefs of Staff Committee (JCSC). The Committee is responsible for general coordination, joint operations and services like training establishments, medical services, reserves administration, defence industries, military intelligence, and others. In a state of national defence or state of emergency, however, operational executive command of the military is to be handled by the CDS through the Defence Minister, and subject to the overall directive of the President as Commander-in-Chief.[44]

While the President may not declare war without the sanction or a resolution of the National Assembly, he may publish the proclamation of a state of emergency before seeking approval from the National Assembly. A two-thirds majority of all members of each House is required to pass such a resolution. This is to be done within 2 days when the Houses are in session or within 10 days, when not in session, of publishing the proclamation. A state of emergency may be declared when the country is among others, at war or is in imminent danger of invasion or involvement in a state of war.[45] According to the federal system which Nigeria operates, each tier of government has its own legislative list and therefore sphere of influence. In a state of emergency, however, exceptions are made. The National Assembly may make laws for peace, order and good government with respect to any matters (whether on the exclusive list or not) as long as it appears expedient for the defence of the federation.

From the foregoing it is clear that Nigeria's Constitutions have gone to great lengths to ensure civilian control over defence matters. This control as we have seen is measured in terms of minimizing military power over defence matters. A few variations were made in the Draft 1995 Constitution[46] but the objective remains the same. The 1999 Constitution replicates the 1979 Constitution on this matter.

In the context of an inherited Western Liberal Model of civil-military relations, the management of defence in Nigeria's democratic setting has been carefully institutionalized. This also means that the military's influence in a democratic setting must use the offices of the Service Chiefs, Joint Defence Staff Office, the Minister of Defence, and the National Defence Council, and the National Security Council for purposes of influencing decisions. Lobbies, influence, veiled pressure or even 'whitemail' must be "exercised through regularized and accepted channels."[47]

The Armed Forces are expected to avoid any attempt to change policies through "displacement" or "supplantment" of its civilian masters. Nigeria had a civilian regime between 1979 - 83, and this professional, apolitical value did not prevent the military from intervening in politics again. What went wrong? Was it that the values had not been imbibed sufficiently, or that the concept of civilian supremacy was unacceptable to the military, or are Nigerians not learning enough from the past so as to revise the role of the military in the polity once it had lost its political innocence? Since May 1999, the military has remained in the barracks and has embarked on reprofessionalization through training and retraining. It is hoped that the politicians will not provide the military any excuses for imploding into the political arena again.

Depoliticization of the Military and Demilitarization of the Polity

Given Nigeria's own experience, can we realistically expect the well-laid-out constitutional provisions we have outlined to work successfully?

Elsewhere[48] we have argued that the Western liberal model has become dated in the light of Nigeria's experience. We believe that in Nigeria's blind adoption of 'democratic' models inadequately adapted to our politico-cultural environment, we may be storing greater legacies of instability for the future generation. Only a few concerned voices raised any alarm, and these were drowned in the frenzied voices of agitators of a pro-Western model of civil-military relations. Even socialists who recommended a socialist ideology for Nigeria seem oblivious of the contradictions in the Political Bureau Report which had recommended a socialist system of government and Western liberal civil-military relations. How, for example, can one recommend a socialist system of government and yet recommend a Western liberal model of civil-military relations? The military in a socialist system is 'politicized', not apolitical.

Some Nigerians have argued that the solution to the thin line between the *ballot box* and the *barracks* in Nigeria lies in running good government. What is good government? Who defines good government?[49] For our purposes, a good government must achieve the basic goals of a State - the maintenance of law and order, the provision for the welfare of the citizens, and interaction with other states on the basis of mutual respect and equality. Many Nigerian governments, civilian and military, have attained low marks on these.

The logic that good governance would prevent coups presupposes that the military have not yet intervened in politics, and that it is therefore apolitical and professional. It also presupposes that it would distance itself from politics as long as the civilian politicians perform creditably. But can the same thing be said of the military that has performed as political managers for over a score of years? Is it possible to demilitarize the polity without depoliticizing the military? Is it not true that, in order to depoliticize the military, we need to politically educate the military in order to share the values of the larger community? How easy will it be to inculcate the values of civilian supremacy in our military?

Our argument is that Nigerians must now deal with a role for the military in the Fourth Republic in order to reposition the military. So far, the political class seems to have accepted the Western liberal model of civil-military relations. While views may differ on this, it may be suggested that the Nigerian military should have some peripheral participatory role in politics. This has been done in Venezuela, Colombia, Mexico, Egypt and more centrally in Indonesia. Many countries are experimenting with ways of dealing with the political bogey called the military, in order to ensure the stability of the democratic polity. In Mexico, Brazil, Venezuela, Colombia, and Peru, the Minister of Defence often comes from within the military. It was rumoured that the military chaps were most displeased with the behaviour and the performance of Shagari's Minister of Defence. Did this contribute to the reasons for the 1983 coup?

Furthermore, how do you retain a large army such as Nigeria's in peace time? Thus, attempts were made to prune the military size and to increase its fire-power. Already there are concerns among Nigerians about the size of the military and the defence budget. We argue that the Nigerian military should play the role of a *developmental militia*. The military has some of the most sophisticated services in a developing country. These services can be used for developmental purposes. The military's engineering corp should be able to build bailey bridges in rural areas. The military in some western countries engages in civilian constructions. The argument that this will detract from professionalism of the forces is not really correct. The Egyptian military has an engineering liability company which bids for, and wins contracts for construction. They have demonstrated skills and completed jobs comparable to those done by the best companies in the world.

The military's paramedical units can help in the country's primary health care system. The military's *signal* or communication units can be deployed to help sustain civilian communication system. After all, when former President Reagan had problems with striking Air Traffic Controllers, he deployed military personnel to cope with the challenges on hand. The Navy believes that its dockyard can be re-oriented to service commercial boats and ships. The Nigerian Air Force has often asked for the opportunity to service commercial planes and to enable it train personnel for that purpose. These would lessen the dependence of the military on annual budgets. It is sad that while the country was privatizing, one heard little of the various military services buying shares and investing their resources in productive areas in order to expand their resource bases and strengthen their independence of the budgetary cycle, and the social flack it attracts from the elites. The time has come for striking a delicate balance between the demands for professionalism and the demands for active participation in development programmes. The military in the United States has been one of the most active participants in the industrial sector of that society. Infact, American technological revolution is just beginning to be demilitarized. The functions specified for the armed forces in the 1995 draft constitution clearly indicate that the drafters wanted the Nigerian military to be developmental in its performance. Can a new and professionalised Nigerian military take up that challenge?

Institutional arrangements must respond to the local conditions of Nigeria, her experiences, problems, and needs. Nigerians, particularly the political class, need to learn to be committed to democracy as an end. Otherwise, the military will continue to manage politics - setting the rules and the agenda.

An aggressive reprofessionalization of the military is a political imperative, if the military must regain its value, sense of pride, and *esprit de corps*. For its involvement in politics the military has paid a very heavy price - dilution of professionalism, while the nation paid the democratic price. New attempts at reprofessionalization should include more committed efforts towards coordination and greater harmony among the armed forces.

Paradoxically, the military requires an intensive politicisation or indoctrination programme. At one level, it needs to be politically educated in the Constitution it is supposed to defend, in order to know and respect its boundaries of operations. As an institution, the military must learn to be prudent with its finances. Accountability must be high on the agenda of our military elites. In civil-military relations it is also important that the military cultivate the art of linking up with essential sectors of the civilian community in order to resolve development problems or ease tensions that may arise in civil-military relations, in an atmosphere of mutual respect.

These suggestions are by no means exhaustive but they serve to underscore the point that urgent and drastic surgery needs to be performed in our civilian-military relations in order to save its soul. Since the military began to intervene in the politics of this country, it has been the greatest loser. It needs reprofessionalization, depoliticization, and proper investment in areas which would increase its fire-power, its self-confidence and shore-up its fragile institutional base.

Conclusion

We have argued that the Armed Forces (the military) have been part and parcel of the process of state formation and so it is a political institution. It therefore, intervenes in the politics of every modern state at one level or another. We then focused on the traditional African concept of the military and found that an apolitical professional military was alien as was the concept of civilian supremacy.

We then argued that the problems we face today stem from the institutions which we imported from the Western world, wholesale. Both the military and other political institutions which we imported, have failed us, particularly in our efforts at democratizing the polity. This is partly because the operators had not adequately imbibed the values which underpin these institutions from Britain where they inherited these institutions. We emphasized that democracy itself is not alien to us as Africans, but Western democratic institutions must be domesticated. Unless we do this, the military would continue to intervene as a *de facto* political power contestant. We also showed the institutional basis for the management of defence in a democratic Nigeria. We then concluded that unless we deal with crucial socio-military issues, the future of democracy in Nigeria is bleak.

We then discussed, even if briefly, a number of socio-military and intra-military factors which need to be addressed if our prospects for a stable democracy are to be any brighter than they are presently. It is therefore our conclusion that the solution lies not only in demilitarizing the polity but also depoliticizing the military. Paradoxically, this process of depoliticization, we argue, involves some form of politicization of the military.

NOTES

1. Ali Mazrui, *Soldiers and Kinsmen: The Making of a Military Ethnocracy* (Beverly Hills, Sage, 1975), p.76.
2. Eugene Walter, *Terror and Resistance: A Study of Political Violence, with Case Studies of Primitive African Communities*, (London: Oxford University Press, 1969), pp. 57-58; see Mazrui, *op. cit.* (1975), p.76.
3. Fortes and Evans Pritchard, *African Political Systems*, (London: Oxford University Press, 1950 ed.), p.79; also see Mazrui (1975), p.74.
4. Mazrui, *op. cit.*, p.75.
5. Mazrui, "Armed Kinsmen and the Origins of the State" in Mazrui (ed) *The Warrior Tradition in Modern Africa* (Leiden: D.J. Brill, 1977), p.9.
6. Claude Welch, Jr. and Arthur Smith, *Military Role and Rule* (North Scituate: Massachusetts, Duxbury Press, 1974), p.5.

7. Godfrey Uzoigwe, "The Warrior and the State in Precolonial Africa: Comparative Perspective", in Mazrui, ed. *The Warrior Tradition in Africa op.cit*, p.23.

8. S.E. Finer, *The Man on Horse-Back: The Role of the Military in Politics* (New York: Praeger, 1962), p.23.

9. Claude E. Welch, Jr. Civilian Control of the Military: Myth and Reality" in Welch Jr. (ed) *Ciyilian Control of the Military: Theory and Cases from Developing Countries* (Albany, New York: State University of New York Press, 1976), p.2.

10. Dwight D. Eisenhower, "From 'Farewell Address to the Nation', January 17, 1961 in Stephen E. Ambrose and James A. Barbar Jr. (eds) *The Military and American Society* (New York, Free Press, 1972), p.63.

11. Decalo uses the concept in this loose fashion. See Samuel Decalo, *Coups and Army Rule in Africa: Studies in Military Style* (New Haven, Yale University Press, 1976).

12. Alfred Stephen, *The Militarv in Politics: Changing Patterns in Brazil* (New Jersey: Princeton University Press, 1971).

13. Welch Jr. and Smith, *op.cit*, p.6.

14. Uzoigwe, *loc. cit.*, p.20.

15. *ibid.* p.23.

16. *ibid.* p.24.

17. *ibid.* p. 25.

18. *ibid.* p.28.

19. S.M. Eisenstadt, "Some Reflections on the Patterns of Regimes and the Place of the Military within Them: Towards a Revision of Accepted Assumptions in the Study of the Military" in Harold Z. Schiffrin (ed.) *The Militarv and State in Modern Asia* (Jerusalem, Jerusalem Academic Press, 1976), p.2.

20. *ibid.* p.4.

21. *ibid.* p.12.

22. N.J. Miners, *The Nigerian Military: 1956-1966* (London, Methuen and Co., Ltd., 1971) has very interesting quotations in this regard; for example in his autobiography, *My Life*, Sir Ahmadu Bello, the Premier of former Northern Nigeria reflected upon the role of the military in colonial period:

> "We did not like the soldiers; they were our own people and had
> conquered us for strangers and had defeated our people on the plains
> just before us. This feeling was common all over the North".

23. John A. Wiseman, *Democracy in Black Africa: Survival and Renewal*,
    (New York: Paragon House, 1990), p. 3.
24. See Patrick Chabal, (ed.) *Political Domination in Africa: Reflections on
    The Limits of Power*, (Cambridge University Press, 1986); J.A.
    Wiseman, *op.cit.*, Larry Diamond, J.J. Linz, and S.M. Lipset, (eds.)
    Africa, Vol.2. Democracv in Developing Countries (Boulder, Colorado:
    Lynne Reinner, 1988).
25. S.E. Finer, *The Man on Horseback*, (New York: Frederick A. Praegar,
    1962); Alfred Stepan, *The Military in Politics: Changing patterns In
    Brazil*, (New Jersey: Princeton University Press, 1971); Claude
    Welch Jr. and Arthur K. Smith, (eds.) *Military Role and Military
    Rule*, (North Scituate; Duxbury Press, 1974); Henry Bienen, *The
    Military and Modernization*, (Chicago: Aldine Atherton Press, 1971).
    J. Isawa Elaigwu, "Military Intervention In Politics: An African
    Perspective" *Geneva-Afrique: Journal of Swiss Societv of African
    Studies*, Vol. XIX, No. 1 (1981), pp. 17-38.
26. N.J. Miners, *The Nigerian Militarv: 1956-1966* (London: Methuen
    and Co., Ltd., 1971).
27. Wiseman, *op. cit.;* p.6.
28. See *Newswatch* (Lagos), May 7th, 1990, p.37-38.
29. Please read what the retired Major-General David Jemibewon had
    to say:

> It is unfortunate that people think that I am a millionaire... When people
> classify all retired generals as millionaires, they do not realise that those
> who are millionaires, if thev could be so described, probably occupied
> strategic position such that they stood a better chance of being
> economically well-off.@

> *(The Vanguard* (Lagos) August 1, 1989, pp.8-9). Underlining is
> mine for emphasis. The interesting point is that General
> Jemibewon, who was a former Military Governor believes that
> occupation of strategic post could embellish one's chances of

acquiring some benefits from office. Many would argue that he occupied a strategic post.

30. James Ogah, "Is Military regime the option?" in *The Nigeria Standard*, July 27th, 1988, p.7.
31. *Democrat.,* October 15th, 1988, p.8.
32. See the Chapter on "France: The Frustrations of a Colonial War", in Welch Jr. and Smith, *op.cit.,* pp.205-223.
33. As Nyerere put it –
   "There is always the risk about having an army at all in a developing country, but since you can't do without an army in these times the task is to ensure that officers and men are integrated into the government and party so that they become no more of risk, than, say, the civil service. "
34. C.E. Welch Jr. "Cincinatus in Africa", *loc, cit.,* pp.231-233.
35. *West Africa,* October 30, 1976, p. 1470, first colunm.
36. Gwyn Harries-Jenkins, "Legitimacy and the Problem of Order." in Harries-Jenkins and Van Doorn (eds) *The Militarv and the Problem of Legitimacy* (Beverley Hills: Sage, 1976), p.44.
37. *ibid.,* p.45
38. *ibid;*40. Harries-Jenkins, *loc, cit.,* p.41. I have borrowed the concept 'Militocratic' from this chapter but have changed the model drastically to meet our purposes.
39. Except otherwise stated, all references in this section are to Federal Government of Nigeria, *Constitution of Federal Republic of Nigeria, 1979,* (Lagos: Government Printer, 1979), hereinafter referred to as the 1979 Constitution. The 1995 Draft Constitution was never promulgated and thus never became operational.
40. 1979 Constitution, section 197 subsection l(a-d).
41. *Report of the Constitutional Conference Containing, the Draft Constitution Vol. 1. 1995* (Abuja: National Assembly Press, 1995), section I subsection 3. This Report is hereinafter referred to as 1995 Draft Constitution.
42. Other Federal Executive bodies require either Senate confirmation or consultation with the Council of State. See 1979 Constitution, Section 140-141. See Third Schedule, Part 1, item G, section 16, and item K, section 25 of the 1999 Constitution.

43. *Report of the Constitutional Conference Containing The Resolutions and Recommendations Vol. II 1995,* (Abuja: National Assembly Press, 1995), pp. 124-125.
44. Refer to 1979 Constitution, Section 265 subsections 1 - 5 for other conditions in which a state of emergency may be promulgated. See section 305 of the 1999 Constitution.
45. See for example, the following sections for a quick comparison of the 1979 and 1989 and 1999 Constitutions and the 1995 Draft Constitution.

Constitutional Provisions.

1979

-	Section 1 subsection (1) & (2) -	Modality of taking over government
-	Section 5 Subsection (3) (a-b) -	Power to deploy armed forces and to declare war
-	Section 1 1 (3)	- Public Order and Public Security
-	Section 122 subsections (2)	- Commander-in-Chief.
-	Section 140 (1) (e)	- National Defence Council (p.115) (h)
		- National Security Council (p. 116
-	Section 141 (2)	- Appointment of Chairman and members
-	Section 198 (3)-(4)	- Command and Operational Use
-	Section 265	- Declaration of State of Emergency

1989

-	Section 1 (2)	- Modality for taking over government
-	Section 5 (4-5)	- Powers to declare war and deploy forces
-	Section 128 (2)	- Commander-in-Chief

-	Section 151 (f)	-	National Defence Council (p.135)
	(1)	-	National Security Council (P.139)
-	Section 152	-	Appointment of Chairman and members
-	Section 216 (l)-(3)	-	Command and Operational Use
-	Section 317	-	Declaration of State of Emergency

1995

-	Section l(l)-(3)	-	Supremacy of the Constitution
-	Section 5(4)-(5)	-	Executive Powers to declare war and to deploy troops
-	Section 133 (2)	-	Commander-in-Chief
-	Section 154 (c)	-	National Defence Council p. 169
	(1)	-	National Security Council p. 176
-	Section 155 (2)	-	Appointment of Chairman and members
-	Section 218 (l)-(3)	-	Command and Operational Use.
-	Section 337	-	Declaration of State of Emergency

1999

-	Section 1 (1-3)	-	Supremacy of the Constitution.
-	Section 1(2)	-	Modality for taking control of government.
-	Section 5 (4-5)	-	The powers to declare war and deploy troops: the roles of National Assembly, and the Emergency powers of the president

-	Section 217(1-3)	-	Establishment and Composition of the Armed Forces of Nigeria
-	Section 218(1-3)	-	The powers of the president as Commander-in-Chief
-	Section 218 (4) &219	-	The powers of National Assembly.
-	Section 220 (1)	-	Provisions for compulsory military training or service.
-	Section 305 -	Procedure	for declaration of state of Emergency

48. Claude E. Welch, Jr. *loc. cit.* in *Civilian Control of the military, op.cit.*

49. See J. Isawa Elaigwu, "Military Intervention In African Politics: What Options for Nigeria?" Paper presented during the Arewa House Seminar, Ahmadu Bello University, Zaria, Silver Jubilee, 4th - 10th January, 1988.

50. As the African *Guardian* editorial put it,"the difference between the refusal or the inability of the military, to make all incursions into the political arena, and its reckless enthusiasm to break in, is a function of the appropriate political culture or lack of it. Those who hold strongly that good governance alone can prevent coups have not quite come to terms with the concept of inordinate ambition that is the hallmark of all pirates. "(May 21, 1990, p. 3.)

- Similarly, when General T.Y. Danjuma said - "The military never opposed coups because we never had a civilian government worth defending... I do not see any democracy in Nigeria during my life time" *(Newswatch,* May 21, 1990) he was pilloried in the press. May be Danjuma was referring to the inter-play of the ballot box and the barracks. If so, he had a point which many did not see at that point in time. Or was that the reason why he supported the return of a full General to the political arena? He supported General Obasanjo's desire to contest for Nigeria's Presidency, served as Minister of Defence even though he later fell out with Obasanjo because of the latter's style of administration.

The original version of this chapter was delivered to the Participants of the National Defence (old War) College, Abuja, January 6, 1999.

CHAPTER 6

TRADITIONAL INSTITUTIONS AND NATION BUILDING: THE DIALECTICS OF TRADITION AND MODERNITY

Introduction

This chapter identifies the role of Traditional Rulers (TR) in nation-building: the Dialectic of Tradition and Modernity.

For our purpose, traditional institutions are used narrowly to refer to the traditional ruler. By nation-building we refer to two dimensions of identity. One is closely linked to state-building. We refer to the progressive acceptance by members of the polity of the legitimacy of a central government, and identification with the central government as a symbol of the nation. This is the vertical dimension of nation-building that you not only have a state, but that people accept the authority of the state (and not merely its coercive power) and see its government as the symbol of their political community. Hence, secessionist bids in Nigeria, Ethiopia, the Sudan and Zaire were challenges to the authority of the central government and a denial of a shared sense of identity. The end of the civil war in Nigeria not only indicated the renewed acceptance of the Nigerian state by its citizens, but also an acceptance by Nigerians that the central government should be the symbol of an emerging Nigerian nation.

On the horizontal dimension, nation-building involves the acceptance of other members of the civic body as equal fellow members of a "corporate" nation—a recognition of the rights of other members to a share of common history, resources, values, and other aspects of the state—buttressed by a sense of belonging to one political community.

It involves the feeling that all members of the polity are entitled to a share of the *sweet* and the *bitter* in the process of political

241

development—not only the sweet. Nation-building, therefore, is the widespread acceptance of the process of state-building; it is the creation of a political community that gives a fuller meaning to the life of the state.

As experiments in state-building go on, so also have experiments in nation-building. These add to the strains on the capabilities of the political systems in all African states. Rajni Kothari was correct when he observed that in the Third World, "the concept of nation itself tends to draw less from cultural and linguistic notions which were the origins of national consciousness in Europe and more from a transcendent notion of statehood which coincides with nationhood".[1]

Furthermore, as Sheldon Gellar persuasively argued, the processes of state-and nation-building have witnessed the development of "state-nations" which recognizes the paradox of national integration, that is, "diversity in unity" and not only "unity in diversity". The process of nation-building could thus entail the creation of "state-nations" as well as "nation-states" as end-products.

> is not extinguished by... subordinate partiality... to be attached to the subdivision, to love the little platoon we belong to in society, is just the principle...of public affections.[2]

Perhaps it is the degree of attachment to the sub-national loyalties, which may threaten the whole. The process of nation-building consciously attempts to widen the horizons for sub-national loyalties to coincide with State boundaries, and ultimately partialized the level of commitment to the parochial groups.

Finally, we should hasten to argue that the processes of nation-building in African States have been punctuated by conflicts and crises. Given the diversity of the groups involved in this process, conflicts are inevitable. It is not just the conflicts, but the intensity of the conflicts without threatening the consensual values on which the association is grafted, that are important in the process of nation-building. As Ali Mazrui has suggested, "an accumulated experience of resolving conflicts between antithetical forces is, after all, one of the great indices of national integration".[3] After all Lewis Coser has argued that conflicts may be positively functional to group solidarity.[4]

In simple terms, while tradition refers to a patterned accommodation of practices over time, it has great impact on how societies respond to challenges. In some countries, such as Britain, there is no real written constitution but a compendium of traditional practices which govern the behaviour of incumbent leaders. In Nigeria, the TR symbolize tradition and its systematic sustainability.

Modernization, for us, refers to the process whereby man, in relation to other men, has changed his own environment through the use of a causal and inventive attitude, technology and organization. it also operates in a state by strengthening its functions of the maintenance of law and order, provision of welfare, and the pursuit of national interests in the global arena.

Let us ask a few questions at this point. What are the sources of legitimacy of the TR? Given our political system, what are the prospects of the survival of traditional institution? What is the role of the traditional ruler in the process of nation-building? To what extent can a traditional ruler traditionalize modernity and yet modernize tradition?

As an attempt to answer these questions, let us make the following suggestions:

a.   The term 'Traditional Ruler' is controversial and this Role has undergone changes over time since the Pre-colonial times.
b.   The dispositions of British and French Colonial rule influenced their colonial policies, and therefore their impact on the lot of Traditional Rulership.
c.   Traditional Rulership has come to stay and shall last for a long time, partly because of their highly adaptive capability and systematic penetration of the modern socio-economic and

political structure and the failure of modern state institutions.

d. We must create a plausible role for Traditional Rulers while strengthening institutions of the modern state in order to establish a democratic polity, partly based on Nigeria's history and tradition.

e. In the long-run, constitutionally guaranteed or not, Traditional Rulership is ultimately responsible for its survival and relevance in the Nigerian political system.

Traditional Rulers in Nigeria: From Transition to Transition

Nigeria's heterogeneity has also meant varying traditional political systems. What does the traditional ruler (TR) mean? It means, King, Chief, Emir, Oba, Eze, Obi, Tor, Oche, and others. Colonial rule had identified two types of societies in Nigeria—*centralized and non-centralized*. The *centralized* societies refer to those societies which have centralized leadership such as those under the Kwarrarafa Kingdoms, the Hausa-Fulani, Onitsha, Benin and many others. Yet there are *non-centralized* and more segmentary and egalitarian societies, which were prompted into centralization by colonial rule in the 1940s. These include the Berom, Tiv, Mumuyes, Nga, Mbula, Idoma and others. Controversial as the term TR is, the Political Bureau Report[5] adapted the operational definition used by the Dasuki Report—

> "A Traditional Ruler is a person who by virtue of his ancestry occupies the throne or stool of an area and who has been appointed to it in accordance with the custom and tradition of the area and has suzerainty over the people of the area."

1. Traditional Ruler in Pre-Colonial Societies

There were two basic types or forms of leaders in the traditional setting. First is the functional leader (who was often the TR). He was elected or selected according to tradition. The process of such selection could be by ancestral succession or heredity or by rotation among lineages and clans, qualified to produce the TR. The functions of the TR were sprawling and included legislative, judicial and executive (administrative) functions. In pre-colonial societies TRs were known to be very powerful, wielding power over life and death.

On the other hand, there were traditional leaders whose titles were basically *honorific*, for community services rendered. They have no legislative, executive and judicial functions.

The system demanded that the TR be a *political neutre*, who was father to all and who was accepted and deferred to, by all.

What were the sources of the legitimacy of TRs? In terms of *traditional legitimacy*, the 'right to rule' of the TR delineated through traditional processes over time. Often, these were hereditary, rotational and/or patriarchal. It is important to note that some societies in Nigeria and Ghana are matriarchal. The sovereignty of the TR resides in the people who 'elected' him through their accepted traditional processes. His authorities derived from tradition and are also so reutilized.

The tenure of the TR was usually for life, unless he engaged in what the traditional king-makers or 'elders' considered to be gross misconduct. In some cases, some traditional leaders were removed from office, as the *Alafin Ajaka* of the old Oyo Empire, found out. The TR occupied the apex of the social pyramid, and did not need to be promoted. As a matter of fact, in some pre-colonial societies, the fear of the TR was the beginning of wisdom. In addition, TRs were shrouded by a mystical aura of the supernatural, especially because of their link with their ancestors.

While the functions of the TRs differed from one community to the other, and from one region to the other, there were some general traits. Though often powerful, with powers of life and death, many societies provided checks and balances to prevent the emergence of despots and absolutism. As illustrations, Oyo had developed elaborate constitutional structure to check her TRs; in the Hausa-Fulani Emirates, the Waziri, the Madawaki and the Makama were good wedges to emirate authority; and the Oba of Benin often had his powers checked by his powerful chiefs.

Traditional rulers performed a number of roles in their societies. First, they often served as the symbol of ethnic/cultural identity of the society. Second, they carried out the role of uniting various groups within the society. Third, they were responsible for the security and the maintenance of law and order in their domains. Fourth, it was their function to promote and provide for the welfare of the people. Fifth, they served as religious symbols; and in some societies were actually the religious leaders, custodians and preservers of art, culture and traditions. Sixth, they carried out legislative, judicial and executive authority. Finally, the TRs were the ultimate and consummate mobilizers of the people for purposive actions.

Thus the TRs in pre-colonial Nigeria had all the accoutrements of power and wielded such in their respective societies.

2. Traditional Rulership under Colonial Rule: 1900-1960

The pattern of colonialism in Africa and the ideologies of colonial authorities also determined the autonomy of traditional institutions. While the French colonialism was *culturally arrogant but racially tolerant,* the British colonialism was *culturally tolerant and racially arrogant.*[7] Both had implications for the role of the TR under colonial rule.

Under the French colonial policy, the French were culturally arrogant. The French culture was the culture. You could be French if you worked had to be *assimilated* into the French culture. Race was not important. Thus 'Frenchified' and assimilated Leopold Sedar Seghor (of Senegal) and Houphonet Boigny (of Ivory Coast) could sit as Deputies in the French Parliament. The policy of assimilation was one of direct administration which provided very little autonomy at local level. However, the 2006 bush-fire violence in the inner-cities of Paris, showed clearly the failure of assimilation even in France.

British colonialism was racially arrogant. The British could not see how Africans could become black Brits. It was therefore better to set up an administration at their local level, to enable them operate the laws of 'civilized people' which were designed by British colonial officers. Thus, British cultural tolerance was also a product of its racial arrogance. The Lugard's *Dual Mandate* or the policy of *Indirect Rule* was applied to Nigeria, especially in Northern Nigeria.

Evidence abound about the changing dimension of British colonial rule. As historians and others have pointed out, one may identify some phases in British colonial rule in Nigeria, in its relations with TRs.

Phase I: 1900-1906: This period witnessed the deposition and humiliation of traditional leaders and it involved the conquest and direct administration of territories by colonial authorities. This period saw the humiliation, dismissal, exile and deposition of TRs. As British colonial authority extended its rule, it was hostile to traditional rulers because it saw them as opposed to British rule, and should be delegitimized.

Phase II: 1914-1960: This period saw the establishment of British colonial rule and the gradual incorporation of traditional rulers into the British colonial administration. It saw the emergence of Native Chiefs, with new and defined duties as part of the single British colonial administration. TRs were now paid by government. They were ranked into classes—1st, 2nd, 3rd, 4th, 5th and were subject to promotions. Their source of legitimacy under the Indirect Rule Policy derived from the British administration, which became their employers. In a way, TRs became public servants. The people lost the absolute control over the 'electoral' process and the ultimate selection of TRs. They were now responsible to a new employer, not the people. They received salaries and promotions from government. They now served as agents of government.

TRs had new accoutrements of power—police, prisons and courts. In essence, the people ceased to be the source of legitimacy of the TRs. Some of them enjoyed powers they never had before. Colonial rule thus strengthened the power of the TR.

It was therefore not surprising that many Nigerian nationalists were opposed to the inclusion of the TRs in the Richards Constitution as representatives of the people. Many nationalists believed that they represented the colonial government and not the people.

The functions of the TRs, under colonial rule, included executive (administrative), legislative and judicial:

a. Executive (Administrative)
i. Tax collection (including preparation of nominal rolls)
ii. Maintenance of law and order.
iii. General supervision of the administration of justice.
iv. The administration of police and prison.
v. Population count.
vi. Inter-communal peace.
vii. Settling quarrels in areas of personal law and heredity.
viii. Welfare functions–roads, health, transport, construction of buildings, and others;
ix. House of Chiefs together with the House of Assembly constituted the Executive Council of the Regions. Some Chiefs (especially in the North) were appointed Ministers without portfolio.
b. Legislative
i. By 1951 McPherson Constitution and the Lyttleton Constitution of 1954, there were established Houses of Chiefs which legislated with the Houses of Assembly on matters affecting the regions.
ii. Voted money for the expenditure of the regions.
iii. House of Chiefs discussed bills in conjunction with the House of Assembly and could recommend amendments to the central legislature.
iv. House of Chiefs could elect fellow members to the central legislature.
c. Judicial

Perhaps the greatest changes to the authority of the TR were to be found in his judicial powers. The **First phase** saw the establishment of 'Native Courts' in the Southern Protectorate (see Native Court Proclamations of 1900, 1901, 1903 and 1906) – which created new class of 'Chiefs' – e.g. 'Warrant chiefs' in Iboland and Chiefs in the Delta area.

- Chiefs at this stage in S/Protectorates – located and arrested criminals but could not try cases. The colonial commissioner and the Resident had this role.

249

- In the North and South – judicial role – drastically reduced just before the amalgamation and formal colonial rule.

During the **Second phase** from 1914:

o   Native Courts Ordinance–created Native Administrations with Native Courts of Appeal.

o   Created *'Paramount Chief'* who now inherited the judicial powers of the Resident.

o   *Paramount Chiefs* supervised District Heads.

o   Both in Yoruba land and in Emirate system, the *Paramount chiefs* now sat over criminal matters; appeals could move to the Divisional Native Courts and then to the Resident at the Provincial level.

Traditional leaders were very powerful and were strengthened by Colonial Administration – (i.e. Native Court Proclamation) which stated, that "where a Native Court is established in any district, the civil and criminal jurisdiction of such court shall as respects natives be exclusive of other native jurisdiction in such districts... by any other native authority whatever." This excludes any checks from the traditional society.

In essence, colonial authority enhanced the judicial powers of the TR. Though no longer at the apex of the social pyramid, traditional leaders found themselves strengthened by the new political authority – colonial rule. This was often antithetical to the position of the nationalists.

The wave of nationalism and anti-colonial rule after 1945 created a new platform. It saw the heightened tempo of Nigerian nationalism. Nigerian nationalists and politicians (and there were some such as Ahmadu Bello, who hailed from the Dan Fodio dynasty) generally saw TRs as pro-colonial rule and anti-nationalism. This formed the basis of their opposition to TRs in the 1946 Richards Constitution and the 1951 McPherson Constitution.

In the terminal colonial period, a number of changes took place in response to the anticipated folding of the colonial umbrella. In Northern and Western Regions emerged the Houses of Chiefs which legislated together with the Houses of Assembly. As more educated members of the elite got into the political arena, even in the North, there were greater hostilities between TRs and the colonial administration on the one hand, and these elites on the other.

3. Traditional Rulers and Politicians

Under politicians, local government laws put all chieftaincy matters under appropriate ministry. New regional government made laws taking over the control of traditional leaders. Government was now "to approve or set aside the appointment of, and to suspend, depose or exile a traditional ruler". Thus, Nigeria's new political elites became the employers of TRs and established laws for controlling them. Often, recognized TRs could appoint subordinate chiefs on behalf of the regional government.

At independence (1960) the judicial status of the TR was still high, even if there were more changes in structure than substance. However, TRs were no longer at the apex of the socio-political pyramids, educated Nigerians, especially the politicians had taken over. That these new political elites could bark and bite, was effectively illustrated by the deposition of Alh. Muhammed Sanusi (The Emir of Kano) and the one-penny-a-month Oba in the Western Region.

Yet, it was the various military regimes which gave TRs the death blow.

4. Traditional Rulers and the Military Political Avalanche

The military regime which imploded into the political arena in 1966, also imploded into the relatively safe cocoons of TRs. In 1966 federal and regional governments took over local police (Native

Authority Police in the North) and prisons. In 1967, twelve states were created in Nigeria, thus atomizing the old regions. As if this blow was not enough, native or local courts were taken over in 1968. These were big blows to the TR especially in the Northern Region.

In 1976, TRs were removed from local government administration, and were placed in a new Local Traditional Councils, which were essentially advisory in nature. The 1979, 1989, 1995 draft and 1999 Constitutions further constrained the role of TRs in the polity—to Local and State Councils of Traditional Rulers. The 1999 Constitution does not even give TRs representation in the Council of State.

Currently, there is a debate over the appropriate political role of the TR. While some people, including some traditional rulers opt for a National Council of Traditional Rulers, others are opposed to this. It does seem that it is not a question of whether or not; it is probably a question of how, where and how much.

Let us restate the point we made earlier in our list of suggestion—that traditional rulership has come to stay and shall last for a long time, partly because of their highly adaptive capability and systematic penetration of the modern socio-economic and political structures, and the failure of modern state institutions. In the long run, constitutionally guaranteed or not, the traditional rulership is ultimately responsible for its survival and relevance in the Nigerians political system.

Let us now turn to the dialectics of tradition and modernity. To what extent have TRs been able to modernize tradition and traditionalize modernity?

Traditionalization of Modernity and the Modernization of Tradition

To what extent have there been attempts to modernize traditional institutions (i.e. traditional rulership)? Has it been possible for TRs to adapt to the exigencies of the modern sector?

The Modernization of Tradition

Over the years, the concept of traditional rulers who are old, illiterate and versed in traditional practices seem to have faded away. Increasingly, enlightened, educated and accomplished public servants have become interested in the post of traditional rulership. Among traditional rulers who have had modernizing impact on the institution are military generals, academics, civil servants, police officers and others. These entrants into the corridors and inner rooms of traditional institutions have added lustre to these institutions.

Among such enlightened traditional rulers are Oba Akenzua of Benin, HRH Professor Edozien of Asaba, HRH Ikoi Obekpa, the Och'Idoma, HRH Sir Alfred Torkula, the Tor Tiv, HRM Mr. Jacob Buba, the Gbong Gwom; HRH the Shehu of Borno; Alh. Sa'ad Abubakar, the Sultan of Sokoto.

As if to illustrate the invasion of traditional institutions by elites of the modern sector, the National Institute for Policy and Strategic Studies (NIPSS) once published a list of traditional rulers who had gotten mni from the Institute.[8]

Since 1970s, there has been a push by most societies in Nigeria to have educated and experienced traditional rulers, inspite of the enormous erosion of the political power of these posts. Often the power of 'election' or selection witnesses many contenders. Why have traditional institutions attracted so much interest among the educated elite? Well, it may be because of the traditional legitimacy which these institutions offer, especially for retired public servants. But perhaps, the influence wielded informally by incumbents of traditional institutions, is the most attractive dimension of this elite influx into the traditional sector.

Thus, with new and enlightened members, especially since 1970s, there have been attempts to modernize traditional institutions, and make them more adaptable to the demands of the modern sector. Similarly, the values, customs (such as modes of rituals and sacrifices) have also been modernized by the Western educated elite, now in the traditional sector. This has enabled traditional institutions to adapt to new demands of the modern sector.

Perhaps, there are other factors which deserve mention here. With the excessive effusion of Western values through instruments of modern technology, there have been cultural nostalgia and glorification of some traditional values and customs by the elite. Modern technology including cameras, films, radio, television and others have become available tools for the expression and dissemination of tradition. These technological resources have helped to provide cultural continuity amidst the discontinuities of societal changes in Nigeria. They also provide for the inter-generational transfer of cultural values and traits.

For some Nigerians, traditional rulers (inspite of the abuse of office by some) still command respect among the people, who see them as less corrupt than politicians. Moreover, as political rulers visit states, they engage in the political legitimating of traditional rulers by paying courtesy calls on them. Some traditional rulers have shown greater empathy with their people than 'elected' politicians and have acquired greater legitimacy. Moreover, the failure of modern institutions for the maintenance of law and order (such as the police) has meant greater dependence on the traditional leaders for the restoration of peace and societal harmony.

In essence, the changing quality of leadership of traditional institutions and the demands of modernization for new adaptive capability have saved traditional institutions from going under.

The Traditionalization of Modernity

If the traditional sector had to respond to the demands of the modernity, it must also find a conducive network for penetrating it.

Traditional rulership has intricate networks in the public services, governments and even the private sector.

Over the years, there have been wild craving for traditional legitimacy among elites in the urban societies in Nigeria. This has led to requests for (and in some cases the purchase) of traditional titles among politicians, public servants and others. The result of this search/craze for traditional titles has been the opportunity for traditional rulers to establish networks for penetrating the modern sector. As modern elites seek traditional legitimacy, modern institutions also get traditionalized. The frontiers of influence of the traditional ruler expands with the number of new traditional title–holders strategically positioned in the modern sector. Thus the traditionalization of the modern sector is actually a network for the penetration of that sector.

In addition, beyond the negative dimension of unnecessary body exposure, the hosting of the Festival of Arts and Culture—is a process of traditionalization of modernity. Old values and customs are exhibited in the modern sector. Properly harnessed, some old values may help to curb the exuberance for materialism and negative aspects of imbibed Western cultural traits.

There are other symbolic forms of penetration of the modern sector by the traditional institutions. The appointment of TRs as Chancellors of Universities and as Chairmen of Boards of Parastatals, also enable TRs to make dentations into the modern sector. Very often, during crisis situations TRs acquire greater visibility and saliency as mediators and as agents for peace and harmony. Their credibility escalates during crisis situations, especially if these are crises among politicians.

TRs as symbols of identity and culture appeal to their subjects in the modern sector. Where these TRs have religious functions, their credibility and utility in the modern sector are embellished. Under military rule, in the absence of modes of popular participation, TRs served as links between the government and the people.

On balance, TRs have managed to survive because of their high adaptive capability, especially in response to the exigencies of modernity and time. Their utilization by the modern sector has also enhanced their durability.

Traditional Rulers and Nation-Building

From the above arguments, it is clear that traditional rulership cannot be wished away. They cannot perform decidedly political roles since these would clash with the dynamics of democratic politics. Yet, perhaps, their greatest role is in creating unity among their communities and serving as bridge-builders between their communities and others.

Among the challenges faced by TRs are:

ii. The challenge of unity – extending handshakes across ethnic divides as we build a new political community called the Nigerian Nation;

iii. The challenge of building bridges across religious divides,

iv. The challenge of modernising traditional institutions without losing the essentials of tradition: this includes crafting mechanisms for institutional adaptability; and

v. The challenge of elongating the life of the traditional institution through the penetration of the modern sector of the society.

This is why inter-communal and inter-state visits by TRs should be encouraged. One, therefore, wonders if it is really worth it, to limit the movement of TRs within Nigeria. We need to build a nation out of our state. The demands for our collective survival and need for national unity makes it imperative for us to utilize the services of TRs, especially for nation-building.

Even now, TRs still have other functions to perform, if these can be properly delineated. These functions include:

• Inter-communal peace (over land, religion, and others)

256

- Mobilization of the populace for purposive action
- Symbol of religion and cultural identity
- Communication with the masses
- Judicial functions, especially in matters of communal harmony, chieftaincy, personal laws etc
- Supervisory executive functions.

We can work out a mechanism for integrating TRs into carrying out these functions, to enable us build a peaceful and united nation, with a buoyant economy.

Recommendations

TRs will not, and cannot, be phased out by government regulations. They can only die natural death when they become irrelevant or cease to adapt to the exigencies of time. So far, traditional institutions have been subtle and relatively perceptive and efficient in handling the challenges of governance and nation-building.

Therefore we recommend that:

a. Restrictions placed on movement of TRs should be relaxed to enable them meet other obligations in nation-building. Safeguards should be put in put in place to ensure that this privilege is not abused;

b. TRs should be made the Chairmen of Development Committees of Local Government under their domain. The Local Government Chairman should be the Deputy Chairman and Executive Secretary. This committee should discuss and review capital development projects, in the interest of the masses;

c. TRs should still be represented in the National Council of States – (we are opposed to a National Council of Traditional Rulers);

d. Government should establish a more functional State Council of

Traditional Rulers, with clear terms of reference including:

- matters of Chieftaincy (which have reached crises proportion).
- conflicts over land and communal boundaries
- religious issues

e. State Traditional Council as State Court of Appeal on customary matters, especially issues of chieftaincy (this will require a second look at the structure of customary and Shari'a courts);

f. Government should continue to use their services in the modern sector – especially as Chairmen of parastatals and

g. TRs should serve to regenerate arts and culture.

h. TRs may form a National Association of Traditional Rulers, an NGO, which could become an advisory body to governments, but they must avoid an association that is seen as a government parastatal

Traditional Rulers as Their Own Enemy

TRs must protect their individual and collective interests by their actions. They:

- must play the 'father' to all and avoid party politics;
- must provide wide umbrage for religious practices and tolerance;
- should regularly review their skills and techniques for the penetration of the modern sector, without corrupting it;
- should do nothing in their speeches and actions to degrade the moral and cultural dignity of the throne;
- should be frank and yet serve as moderating influences among contending interests in their domains;
- should play the role of traditional statesmen and avoid being embroiled in petty little quarrels and living in corruption;
- must eschew traditional authoritarian propensities and embrace the values of democratic governance by carrying their people along;
- should constantly educate themselves to widen their horizon of perception; and

• should continue to learn new skills of diplomacy and negotiation. Failure to do these may render them irrelevant. Thus traditional Rulership is responsible for its survival and relevance in the Nigerian political system.

Conclusion

We have shown how the traditional institution of rulership has undergone many changes. We also illustrated how the British and French colonial rule influenced their colonial policies and their impact in the lot of traditional rulership.

It is our contention that traditional rulership has come to stay and shall last for a long time, partly because of their highly adaptive capability and systematic penetration of the modern socio-economic and political structure, and the failure of modern state institutions. We also argued that the Nigerian polity must create a plausible role for TRs while strengthening the institutions of a democratic polity, partly based on Nigeria's history and tradition. TRs have important roles in nation-building if properly integrated into the process.

Finally, we posited that in the long run, constitutionally guaranteed or not, traditional rulers are ultimately responsible for their survival and relevance in the Nigerian political system.

NOTES

1. Rajni Kothari, "The Confrontation of Theory with National Realities: Report on an International Conference" in S. N. Eisenstadt and Stein Rokkan (eds.) *Building States and Nations* Vol. I and II (Beverley Hill: Sage, 1973) P. 104.

ii. Edmund Burke, as quoted in S. Huntington, *Political Order in Changing Societies* (New York: Yale University Press, 1968) p. 30.

iii. Mazrui, A "Violent Congruity and the Politics of Retribalization in Africa" in *International Affairs*,Vol, XXIII, No, I (1969) p. 105;

Mazrui and Tidy *op. cit.* p. XII; Ade Ajayi, "The Congruity of African institutions Under Colonialism", in T.O. Ranger, *Emerging Themes of African History* (Nairobi: East African Publishing House, 1968) p. 194; also Irving Leonard Markovits, *Power and Class in Africa* (Englewood Cliff, New Jersey: Prentice Hall, 1977) p. 47. J. S. Coleman, *Nigeria: A Background to Nationalism* (Berkeley: University of California Press, 1971); H. S. Awe, "Traditional Rulers in Nigeria and their changing Judicial Status". *Development Studies Review* Vol. 2, No. 1, October 1978, Pg. 114–131, A. A. Olaspa, "The Role of Traditional Rulers in Local Government – Western Nigeria Experience in Historical Perspective" in Oladimeji Aborisade, (ed) *Local Government and the Traditional Rulers in Nigeria* (Ife: University of Ife Press 1985) Pg. 51–66; A. E. Afigbo, *The Warrant Chief: Indirect Ruler in Southern Nigeria* 1891 – 1929, (London: Longmans, 1972).

iv.   Lewis Coser, *The Functions of Social Conflicts* (New York: the Free Press, 1956) p. 188.

v.   Federal Government of Nigeria. *Report of the Political Bureau* (Lagos: Printer, 1987)

vi.   *ibid*

vii.   I am indebted to Prof. Ali A. Mazrui, for this insight

Traditional rulers with mni include HRM Nnaemeka Alfred Achebe (Obi of Onitsha), HRM Alhaji Hassan Ahmed II (emir of Nasarawa), HRH Alhaji (Maj Gen) Muhammadu Iliyasu Bashar (Emir of Gwandu), late HRM Da Visitor Dung Pam (Gbong Gwom Jos), HRH (Maj Gen) M Sani Sami (Emir of Zuru), HRM Maj Gen MA Green (Wari Sembo of Dublin-Green War Canoe Ground Bonny Kingdom, HRM Eze Chief G. W. Iroanwusi (Paramount ruler of Agba-Ndele), HRM Maj Gen FA Mujakperu (Orhue I The Orodje of Okpe), HRH Rilwanu Akiolu (Oba of Lagos), HE (Brig Gen) M. Sa'ad Abubakar III (Sultan of Sokoto) and HRH (Lt Col) Waziri Abubakar Mahdi (Emir of Deba).

Index

www.ingramcontent.com/pod-product-compliance
Lightning Source LLC
Chambersburg PA
CBHW070356270326
41926CB00014B/2569